“No Offence, But . . .”

Also by Gina Martin

Be the Change: A Toolkit for the Activist in You

“No Offence, But . . .”

How to Have Difficult Conversations for Meaningful Change

Gina Martin

With contributions from
Daze Aghaji, Aja Barber, Koa Beck,
Charlie Craggs, Salma El-Wardany,
Ione Gamble, Ben Hurst,
Mariam Kemple Hardy and Azadeh Hosseini,
Cathy Reay and Nova Reid

bantam

TRANSWORLD PUBLISHERS
Penguin Random House, One Embassy Gardens,
8 Viaduct Gardens, London SW11 7BW
www.penguin.co.uk

Transworld is part of the Penguin Random House group of companies
whose addresses can be found at global.penguinrandomhouse.com

First published in Great Britain in 2023 by Bantam
an imprint of Transworld Publishers

A CIP catalogue record for this book
is available from the British Library.

ISBN 9781787636361

Typeset in 10.75/16pt FS Kim by Jouve (UK), Milton Keynes.
Text design by Couper Street Type Co.
Printed and bound in Great Britain by Clays Ltd, Elcograf S.p.A.

The authorized representative in the EEA is Penguin Random House Ireland,
Morrison Chambers, 32 Nassau Street, Dublin D02 YH68.

Penguin Random House is committed to a sustainable future
for our business, our readers and our planet. This book is made
from Forest Stewardship Council® certified paper.

Contents

Introduction

In my work as a gender equality activist and speaker, there's one question that comes up consistently and more than any other. At any given time, there'll be a bunch of different iterations of it sitting in my DMs. It's one that most of my friends have asked me and when I'm at speaking events, panels or workshops, it's *always* the first to be raised by the audience: 'how do you respond to ...?', followed by one of *those* sexist, harmful, defensive or well-meaning but bloody unhelpful comments.

I spend lots of time having conversations about gender, misogyny, sexual violence and power dynamics, so people assume that when faced with misogynistic microaggressions or gendered clichés, I can shut them down in a cool, calm and collected way. But that's not always the case. When I hear defensivisms that distract from the problems we so deeply need to solve and that deepen the chasms that divide us, I, too, feel exasperated. I, too, feel the internal conflict between trying to understand where the other person is coming from and allowing myself to feel righteous frustration. I, too, have yearned so deeply to be able to say exactly the right thing so they can just 'get it' and understand why what they're saying is problematic or harmful, putting myself under so much pressure in the process that, in the past, I've barely said anything. This entirely justifiable frustration has compromised my ability to communicate. It has made me feel less able to articulate my position, my message and my instincts, and instead has led to me laughing something off, snapping at someone, crying my way through a complex explanation of my feelings, or saying nothing and kicking myself later.

After doing this work for six years, I am better at navigating these conversations than I used to be, but it's taken this long to feel more confident doing so, and I still slip up and get frustrated. In fact, recently I did just this with a man I love very much when he challenged the idea that Britney Spears's life had been reported on through a misogynistic lens, to which I ended up responding 'Oh don't fucking worry, it's just my *literal* job to know this stuff.' Wow, Gina, so helpful! Good job!

Every time someone has asked me how I would respond to comments like 'not all men' or 'you can't say anything nowadays', or how I reply when someone diverts the blame of my own assault on to me, I have related so deeply to their frustration and their desperation, and this response is exactly why I decided to put together this book. I wanted to offer a starting point and a space to explore the problematic, distracting or lazy comments we so often encounter, to analyse them, and to find the confidence to respond to them. A book to come back to again and again, that can be passed to those with whom we've lost our cool, and that can be used to challenge our own understanding – and perhaps use – of these phrases. By digging a little into the perspectives and ideas behind these problematic or harmful comments, we can understand where they come from and better understand their impact. And in doing so, we can start to develop the necessary tools to respond and discuss them with more clarity, curiosity and ease.

For this project, I decided to tackle ten phrases; personally covering some that I'm most frequently asked about, some that are pervasive and recognized as such and some that are less commonly acknowledged, as well as a few that I just hoped to better understand and feel more confident in responding to myself. Phrases like 'The police are here to protect us' and 'The government are doing their best', for example, which at first may seem innocuous but which actually work to shield the institutions that are failing us miserably.

Alongside my own chapters, I have also asked a bunch of friends and people I admire to contribute essays that deconstruct phrases relating to intersecting issues. It didn't feel possible to support you in responding to gendered phrases without having other writers, educators, activists and advocates tackle certain phrases that uphold the hierarchies, systems, industries and events that so intimately intersect with gender inequality. Fatphobia, for instance, is a system of hate levied routinely and disproportionately at women. Climate breakdown acts as a threat multiplier to women and people marginalized for their gender. Anti-Blackness colludes with misogyny to oppress Black women. Women make up around 50 per cent of all refugees, displaced or stateless populations. The fast-fashion industry hires and exploits mostly female garment workers. These issues are all tied to the hierarchy of gender, and the writers tackling the problematic or harmful phrases that surround them are experts in their fields. When you read their essays, I hope you're inspired to buy their books, take their courses and support the heavy lifting they're doing – both to disrupt dominant narratives and ideas, and call in healthier, brighter, ultimately more human ways of thinking. You'll notice that contributors' chapters don't often have memoir elements; I didn't want them to write anything they didn't feel comfortable with – especially when these topics, themes and the phrases themselves can be so personal and linked to trauma. My chapters do have memoir pieces, which was a personal decision. I wrote them because the phrases I tackle are ones I feel comfortable discussing my history with. This will hopefully help you recognize how these phrases show up and how they exist in culture as well as demonstrate accountability and learning. Not everybody owes us that, and the contributors here have written their pieces how they wanted to write them.

Some of the phrases in this book are harmful ('I don't see colour', tackled by Nova Reid), some are distractions ('not *all* men') and some are particularly complex ('men aren't doing anything to help feminism', authored by Ben Hurst). They're all different and they are defined by different systems, power dynamics and assumptions, but almost all are typically said by dominant communities. The reason for this approach is because I belong to a dominant community, and see a big part of my work as exploring the things we do and say, and understanding how those things inform society and culture. If you're from a dominant group or community, you'll likely be exposed to the majority of these phrases and the ideas that underpin them (or you might use them). If so, you're therefore in a unique position to challenge, discuss or facilitate a conversation around them. Depending on your identity and where you sit in society, this may be more the case for some than for others. But gaining confidence in our understanding of these phrases and learning how to respond to them enables us to better advocate for equality and fairness. It is a small step, but an important one.

This book isn't about shutting down anyone and everyone with whom you disagree. It's about unravelling and understanding the things they – or we – say that are harmful, distracting or untrue, and feeling more confident in communicating *why* this is the case. The honest truth is that people won't immediately 'get it' and letting go of the idea that you must 'win' an argument is the first step. One conversation, one essay or one book isn't going to fundamentally change someone's mind. Bright and brilliant people have dedicated their entire lives to trying to offer alternative narratives and make people understand the issues at the heart of these phrases. It takes years of work, of internal reflection, reading and evaluation for someone to truly change their perspective. It can take years to even acknowledge that a problematic perspective has allowed them to remain comfortable in their ignorance, or to retain a level of power they've been reluctant or unwilling to evaluate. But none of this is a reason not to try because conversations are part of that growth. Just try to deliver your message and recognize that it might take time and multiple conversations to get someone to hear you.

I really, deeply believe that discussions about gender hierarchies and social justice issues should be available to absolutely everyone, and as someone who sits in a powerful social location, my lane is about making work that is accessible. The movement only gets bigger if someone like me can meet people where they are and then bring them along with us, and this book is an attempt to create that bridge. My hope is that if you aren't yet confident in your knowledge around these topics and if you don't already discuss them with others, you'll feel invited to get curious and ask questions about where these harmful ideas come from and why they persist. And if you are already well-versed in conversations about social justice, my hope is that you'll still find work in this book that challenges and sometimes confronts you, too.

I hope you recognize that this book is an *offering*, not a guide, that the title is a provocation and that the premise is simple: to question the things we say and give you a space to build confidence and literacy in doing the same in your life. Ultimately this book is about asking 'why are these hurtful, problematic phrases enduring?', 'how often do I challenge them?' and 'how can I best respond to them?'

"Boys Will Be Boys"

I don't remember how old I was when I first became aware of the concept of 'boys will be boys'. I could have soaked it up from the script of some nuclear-family US sitcom, from the playground at my village primary school, or from any one of the pre-teen mags I used to read on the sofa at home. It's likely I absorbed it from all three of these sources and more, and it wasn't necessarily delivered to me in those exact words; it might have been when I heard someone say something along the lines of 'you know what they're like . . .' in reference to a boy. It could even have been more subtle, like a shrug and an eye-roll in response to inappropriate behaviour. Rather than being made aware that 'boys will be boys' on one particular occasion, it was more of a slow, grinding realization that certain behaviour was to be expected and accepted from boys, and not from me and my female friends.

Now, as a 30-year-old gender-equality activist, I know that we cite these tired and damaging stereotypes of masculinity as justification for problematic behaviour from boys, which we've either accepted or don't feel prepared to hold to account. It wasn't until I was in my twenties that I had the language to articulate this, however, so younger me didn't stand a chance.

"No Offence, But . . ."

In the nineties I attended a small primary school in the north of England. I was skinny, looked young for my age, and was bullied for having a mole on my chin. It wasn't *that* big, but I guess it wasn't small either; bigger than a pea, smaller than a five-pence piece, and it raised sprouting little hairs, as all healthy moles do. On a little girl's face, though, it was very noticeable. Just as I would never see a seven-year-old kid with a mole now and think of her as anything but cute, I'm sure it was the same for most people looking at me then. However, kids don't really have the social filters or emotional intelligence of adults, so I was picked on by some of my classmates.

In my school, a cosy Church of England affair in a quiet village adjacent to my town, there was one boy who made bullying me his job. He pointed at my face whenever he saw me and, eventually, he managed to convince other boys to mock me. I remember he and his friend drew huge moles on their faces during one lesson, and sat across from me, staring, making themselves visible to me and trying to contain their laughter as a smattering of giggles broke out across the classroom. I sat frozen in my chair, head down, pretending to write, growing hotter and hotter by the second as tears pricked the back of my eyes. Then, on non-uniform day, bully and sidekick made a pact to 'dress up as my mole in poo-brown clothes' and proudly told me about their plan loud enough for everyone to hear. For two days, I was terrified that they were actually going to do it.

This constant ridiculing of a visible part of my body – one that felt impossible to change, along with the braces and glasses I wore – led me to become hyper-aware of how boys saw and responded to me. My bully happened to be a boy, and I felt scared of him in a way that I didn't feel scared of girls who didn't like me. I remember thinking boys were disgusted by me – all of them – and I was already somehow aware, at the tender age of nine, that my girlhood hinged on boys' perceptions of me.

It's wild how early this heteronormative script is established as the default dynamic when, actually, it should be the last thing any child is thinking about. At school discos, for example, the boys would stay on one side of the room and the girls on the other. The girls were already somehow aware of – but uncomfortable with – the idea that the boys might ask them to dance, and the boys felt pressured to 'take the lead', despite being literal children. In school we were also often organized and defined by our gender; ordered into girl and boy groups. (This was the late nineties, so there wasn't even a recognition that other genders might be catered to.) We were dressed differently, and separated when being taught a woeful, perfunctory sex-ed class.

All of this served to create invisible partitions between boys and girls. I had pals who were boys, but I couldn't play with them without being accused of fancying them, and a boy who hung out with mostly girls was instantly exposed to homophobic taunts from his male peers. At that age we were, in many ways, a mystery to each other, not necessarily because of our gender but because of these invisible partitions. I interacted with boys only as *boys*, rather than as *people*, and I'm certain that was the case the other way round. And as a girl, I felt that being fancied by boys was a key signifier of my worth; if they didn't, it was because there was something wrong with me. Confusingly, as the bullying continued over the course of the next two years, I was also told repeatedly that the reason the boys picked on me was actually because they 'liked' me.

On a couple of occasions the bullying became physical. The first time it happened, a bunch of us were playing a game in the playground when someone pushed me forcefully into the concrete. The boys laughed and walked off as if they were all in on it. The second time, I was jumping happily on a bouncy castle at a classmate's birthday. I wasn't at high school so I couldn't yet have been eleven. My bully pushed me into a corner, put his hand around my neck and started squeezing as his sidekick watched on. After a few scary seconds I managed to struggle free, slide off the edge of the castle and run to a grown-up.

'They just strangled me,' I whimpered, holding my neck and asking if it was red. The teacher in question – who was attending as his daughter was in our class – patted my head and let out a chuckle. 'Boys,' he sighed, as a disturbing mixture of amusement and boredom passed across his face. 'Run along and play,' he instructed, flicking me away with his hands. I didn't understand his response. It communicated to me, quite clearly, that boys were 'just like that'; that somehow, regardless of who they were as *people*, their gender was to blame for their behaviour. The way it was said seemed to imply something biological and beyond their control.

Not long after the bouncy-castle incident, I decided to address what I thought was the root of the problem, and got my mole removed. It was a painful procedure involving a number of injections and cutting away part of my chin, which left me with a wound that required stitches and a dressing. A couple of weeks into the healing process, as I wandered down a school hallway to the playground, a group of boys (including sidekick) tried to trip me over. Laughing, they called me 'Frankenstein'.

It was never really about my mole in the first place, of course. It was about my bully, whatever was going on with him, and his need to assert authority or dominance over someone to prove something to his peers. He was a child, so let's give him the benefit of the doubt; kids do misguided things. My teacher's response, and that of the adults who told me that he teased me because he liked me, however, are important to discuss because of the message they knowingly, or unknowingly, sent. The teacher I ran to on the day of the bouncy-castle incident had said only one word, but he'd actually told me *so much*. That word – 'boys' – accompanied by an eye-roll and a laugh had conveyed, in an instant, that he'd seen this behaviour many times before and had come to expect it. By choosing to do and say nothing else in the face of my complaint, he communicated that nothing could be done to solve it, and undermined its significance.

Although that frustrates me, I don't necessarily think the culpability for this kind of messaging lies *solely* with those who send it. It is embedded in the culture we've created and the limited, prescriptive way that we define masculinity and manhood. We reward men for being forward, assertive and dominating with each other and towards people of other genders. We expect and validate behaviour from boys and men that we don't tolerate from girls and women. When we perpetually and proudly recycle tired caricatures of masculinity we encourage boys and men to see it as a monolith: a self-serving performance of pursuing girls, numbing their emotions, expressing little to no feeling and attempting social dominance. In presenting boys with this singular narrative, we totally undermine masculinity's ability to be anything other than what the dominant narrative views it as.

Masculinity can be all types of things: sensitive, strong, empathetic, comforting, safe, patient. Think of different men in your life and you'll easily notice how one man's masculinity is different to another's – your dad might be more stoic and unemotional (traditionally masculine) while your partner, for whom that traditional kind of display and expectation of manhood is uncomfortable, presents as more sensitive. People are individual and so is their gender and gender expression – it's just that we're rarely encouraged to think about masculinity and its pluralities.

It wasn't until I discovered bell hooks' work and other feminist literature in my mid-twenties that I found the language to express the feelings and instincts I'd experienced to that point. I started to see myself as a full person and not simply defined by what it meant to be a 'woman' or a 'girl'. Only then, once I had this framework of theory and understanding, did I take more notice of how language is used, understand people's actions, and start to comprehend how gendered systems work. With this new lens, I witnessed the phrase 'boys will be boys', and its many iterations, *everywhere*. It was in the scripts of TV shows, implied by parents while trying to wrangle their sons at the local coffee shop, typed out plainly in the comment section under news stories on Instagram and used to excuse inappropriate or harmful behaviour in the mainstream media. It was even used to pre-empt behaviour that had yet to occur, such as in conversation about how a colleague's child would do at nursery: 'It's always hard to tell because you can prepare him as much as you can, but at the end of the day boys will be boys.'

When, in 2017, I began to try to change the law, to make upskirting a specific sexual offence, I found this same narrative being hurled at me left, right and centre in response to being sexually assaulted. On one occasion I sat opposite a well-known broadcaster on live TV when, in an attempt to clarify something another contributor had mentioned, she queried how the issue should be addressed, saying '. . . there could be a scenario, couldn't there, where a couple of lads [are] drunk, mucking about, and it's a prank – they take a picture. That's a little bit like in the olden days when kids would ping your bra strap in class. They do something like that and they get put on a sexual offenders' register for it and for the rest of their lives they're in a place where they perhaps shouldn't be compared with some of the other people on that register.'

The impulse to minimize and reduce assault to a 'prank' in order to lessen the perpetrators' accountability leans heavily on the 'boys will be boys' mantra – the idea that because of their gender, boys and men have less agency or choice over their actions. This news presenter may as well have said that she didn't think we should prosecute 'laddy' behaviour.

After that TV appearance, I received messages from men on the internet telling me that 'guys can't help themselves when they see a woman they like'. The idea that men can't regulate their own behaviour and that the resulting inappropriate actions and words towards women and those of marginalized genders weren't their responsibility, or were to be ignored, was even more pervasive than I'd thought. During the game of 'whose fault' we have been socialized to play when it comes to sexual assault, it is often the first card reached for and used to give perpetrators the benefit of the doubt. It is the easiest way to put the blame back on to the victim (in this case, me), so that we don't have to confront the idea that men might be *choosing* to assault people. A choice derived from socialization and misogyny, sure. But a choice nonetheless.

I began to unpick the 'boys will be boys' mindset because I needed to understand why this phrase had followed me all my life, and I became more confident in responding to it because I had to. If I hadn't, I would have felt as though I'd been publicly letting down victims and survivors by not challenging it. If I hadn't, I would have co-signed – in the context of sexual harassment – the ideas that both boys and men are a monolith, and that women are the regulators of their behaviour.

In Response to 'Boys Will Be Boys'

This frequently heard phrase is only ever used in response to questionable conduct, most commonly problematic behaviour from boys and young men engaging in something unacceptable, distracting or uncomfortably disruptive. For that reason, it becomes a sort of free pass out of accountability, or as speaker Ben Hurst says a 'get out of jail free card', simultaneously teaching boys that they are not responsible for their own behaviour and robbing them of agency because it suggests an inability to make good decisions. It's the kind of thing you might say if a bunch of high schoolers boarded your train carriage shouting football chants, roaring, laughing and chugging beer. A teacher might utter it in response to young boys fighting on the playground, or when teenage boys are caught 'hazing' their teammates in the football squad.

Being a child means not being fully aware of the consequences of your behaviour: you haven't yet developed an adequate social filter and aren't fully cognizant of social norms. This is why we work hard to guide and help children we're in contact with. We show them what's appropriate and what's not by explaining and modelling, rather than by writing off behaviour that feels difficult to deal with, as was the case for me on that day of the bouncy-castle incident. We try to allow children to grow as individuals but also ensure they understand the context that they exist within in any given situation.

The problem, whether we want to admit it or not, is that we guide kids to grow in different ways depending on their sex and gender. Whether we're a parent, teacher or mentor, after hundreds of years of social conditioning we've learned to treat people differently both consciously and subconsciously depending on a set of seemingly predetermined factors. It's the reason why, when someone explains that their gender is different to what you'd assumed – by sharing their pronouns, or correcting you on them – it might take you a moment to readjust. People can become uncomfortable because suddenly they are less sure how to interact with the person. In our very binary mindsets, it seems as though the rules have shifted, and we may feel the need to interact with this person differently because of this new information, even though we most likely don't need to. That gender-informed subconscious rulebook of how to interact also applies to how we treat kids; and we condition them, often unknowingly, to behave in certain ways according to the constructs of gender.

The characteristics and attributes of binary genders such as male and female have shifted from century to century. Many pre-colonial societies had an expansive understanding of gender, and as the historian, sexologist and writer Thomas Laqueur outlines in his book *Making Sex*, it was the West that first introduced a 'binary sex' model in the eighteenth century. Over time, the rules and norms of gender have evolved depending on the dominant culture and religion of the time, and as the philosopher María Lugones notes in her paper 'The Coloniality of Gender', it is critical to 'consider the changes that colonization brought to understand the scope of the organisation of sex and gender'.

Historically, enforcement of binary gender has only made sense to those in power; a hierarchy that works against the interest of people and in the interest of those in ruling-class positions. Nothing in nature works this way. Nothing in nature has a binary, it is fluid and full of multiplicity. In the words of storyteller and artist Amrou Al-Kadhi, 'It gives me a lot of comfort that if subatomic particles defy constructs all the time, why should we believe in fixed constructs of gender . . .?' It's too restrictive.

History shows us that millions of people can't fit into two boxes based on how they look, behave and act, and trans and non-binary communities have been imagining a world beyond these rigid gender stereotypes for centuries. From the Sumerian and Akkadian texts dating back 4,500 years that document the existence of transgender priests, to the Ancient Roman emperor Elagabalus who identified as a woman, trans and non-binary people are not new. Their history has been consistently erased on a global scale but they are, and have been, the blueprint for a less rigid and more freeing perspective on what 'masculinity' and 'femininity' look like; a blueprint from which cisgender men and boys can learn so much about how restrictive our current stereotypical perception of 'masculinity' really is, and how *masculinity* can become *masculinities.* Western colonial rulers created and exported models of gender across the world to organize people culturally and geographically in order to subjugate them, and white manhood was created as part of this. In *Mask Off*, JJ Bola notes that 'Cultures and ideologies have dominated over one another and imposed their beliefs and understandings on other natures and cultures, attempting to create a globalised singular view of manhood.'

Globally, gender isn't binary and never has been but the phrase 'boys will be boys' is a brilliant example of how we often perpetuate this false understanding. Author, educator and activist Tony Porter has spent his entire career exploring this fallacy. In his work he often talks about the concept of 'the man box': a prescriptive metaphorical box into which our society puts boys from an early age, and which assigns them traits and attributes that make up the gender of 'male'.

The 'man box' messaging is all around boys, from parents, carers, TV and film (see: James Bond), music, books, toys and their schooling system. Boys learn that to fit into the box, they must behave a certain way and demonstrate specific traits. These stereotypes shape boys' perception of themselves as they grow and therefore affect their self-actualization.

Some are not inherently dangerous or harmful, such as 'protector' (although even healthy traits can become corrupted when there's a gendered power imbalance). But some of them – in fact, too many of them – are unhealthy (especially due to the prescriptive way in which they are enforced), both for men themselves and for the women and people marginalized for their gender who encounter them as a result: 'dominant', 'aggressive', 'unemotional'.

Crucially, when we put boys into the 'man box', we are expecting them to exhibit behaviour that we typically associate with men, therefore adultifying them in the process. This is compounded when it comes to Black boys, who experience the 'adultification bias'; a form of racial prejudice that views and treats them as more mature than they are, therefore not affording them the same levels of innocence or vulnerability as their white peers.

In his TED talk 'A Call To Men', Tony Porter describes specific moments when he realized he was treating his kids differently because of their gender. 'When [my kids] were about five and six, four and five, Jay could come to me, come to me crying. It didn't matter what she was crying about, she could get on my knee, she could snot my sleeve up, just cry, cry it out. Daddy's got you. That's all that's important. Now Kendall on the other hand – and like I said, he's only fifteen months older than her – he'd come to me crying, it's like as soon as I would hear him cry, a clock would go off. I would give the boy probably about thirty seconds, which means by the time he got to me, I was already saying things like, "Why are you crying? Hold your head up. Look at me. Explain to me what's wrong. Tell me what's wrong. I can't understand you. Why are you crying?"' He pauses. 'He's five years old.'

This example demonstrates a moment of subconsciously enforcing 'gendered' traits and therefore behaviour. How many parents and carers do this without even realizing? We allow girls to feel their emotions more fully because we *expect* it from them (per the societal rulebook), and consequently we are less accepting of, or comfortable with, boys' emotions. This subconsciously communicates to boys that being 'emotional' and 'sensitive' are 'girl' traits – and 'girl' traits are not for them – which conditions boys not to show their emotions in front of other boys. We don't let boys express the same level of emotion as girls, but we get confused when a grown man punches a wall out of anger instead of crying.

We know there's a mental-health epidemic in men, yet we rarely consider it in the context of the pressures that come with 'traditional prescriptive masculinity'. Perhaps encouraging boys to cherry-pick the emotions they are 'allowed' to express makes it harder for them to talk about their fears, experiences and feelings when they are men? Maybe it has an impact on their ability to develop relationships and friendships that are built on vulnerability – something essential for receiving support from those around you? Perhaps it puts a limit on how deep they choose to go in conversations about their lives, fears, or life pressures with friends and family, and even affects their ability to build literacy around their emotions, which therefore denies them the tools to emotionally excavate their own feelings? These are all questions we should be asking.

In my work I have learned that we socialize boys into specific behaviours in *at least* two ways:

1. We encourage them not to feel or express the full spectrum of human emotion, specifically by numbing feelings of vulnerability, sensitivity and fear.
2. We validate specific qualities, such as bravery, strength and domination, and hold boys to a very low standard of behaviour because of this. By expecting minimum standards of emotional regulation and emotional maturity we remove their agency to develop healthier gender identities and hold them to lower standards of accountability than we would people of other genders.

If there was a tagline or slogan for the latter, it would be ‘boys will be boys’. This concept that boys and young men are predetermined to act out, misbehave or pursue girls in an inappropriate way is false. They are not. Although it might happen in enough circumstances to become a cultural problem, and to be discussed in the mainstream as a crisis, it is not in cisgender, heterosexual men’s biology to, say, turn a no into a yes, to resort to physical fighting over constructive discussion or to treat sexual encounters as a game. It’s not human nature, it’s not biology. It’s conditioning. It’s a result of damaging but often well-meaning clichés, such as ‘you’ll be a heartbreaker', which enforce the idea of sexual dominance as central to manhood, and tells boys from a young age that they are entitled to girls' space.

Often, in social-justice spaces, when we talk about how violent behaviours are mostly perpetrated by men, the feedback can be that men feel insulted; that they feel people think they are always doing 'something wrong', whether that's domestic violence, sexual violence or sexist comments. The Office for National Statistics reported that in the year ending March 2020, perpetrators of violent offences were most likely to be male – 82 per cent, in fact. I would therefore argue that recognizing the behaviours so many cisgender, heterosexual men continue to exhibit towards other men, women and people of marginalized genders isn't an insult. It's an observation; a fact.

For me, the real insult is our default expectation and acceptance of problematic behaviour in boys. We consign them to being a problem, which is a rejection of their full humanity. To see boys as naturally naughty or boisterous – something that occurs when dealing with boys from working-class or low-income families especially – reinforces the idea that they can't be more or do more – for themselves, for each other or for women and marginalized genders. It's giving up on them. This is dangerous because that sentiment grows and plays a huge part in their development. Boys will, after all, grow into men. Men who fulfil the expectations of the 'man box' only to become suffocated by it. Men who are less able to regulate their emotions and less willing to be thoughtful, sensitive and vulnerable; qualities that are all the more important given the high standards to which men are held when it comes to capitalistic, stressful endeavours such as 'success' and being able to provide.

When boys are taught that manhood entails viewing women and femininity as things to consume, dominate or control, that women and femininity exist for their benefit and therefore their ego, they become men who exhibit misogynistic behaviour. And when a grown man who is capable of making – and being held responsible for, and growing from – his decisions exhibits this behaviour, it's on the people around him to call him out. Even better, in the words of activist and scholar Loretta J. Ross, it's on those people to call him *in*. But prevention is the best form of harm reduction. We can help break those circuits way earlier than this if we learn to stop using such gendered phrases with our kids, and start holding our boys to higher, healthier, loving standards of masculinity.

When someone uses the phrase 'boys will be boys' – or any other sayings that brush off boys' behaviour and their ability to make better choices – it's important that we respond. Challenge the idea that these traits are a consequence of their gender. Draw attention to the fact that the behaviour in question isn't positive and that the boy will likely respond to being nudged in a healthier direction – and should be. Encourage them to ask the boy to use 'emotive' or 'feeling' words, and try to understand why he is acting the way he is. Help him to communicate his emotions so that he can develop his ability to understand his feelings and articulate them.

Remind anyone who brushes off 'bad' behaviour that a young boy who is acting out and being problematic isn't doing so *because* he's a boy, and that whatever is causing the behaviour may be harder to identify than it would be in a girl.

Remind them that his behaviour may be negatively affecting others. If the 'boy' in question is older, perhaps your brother or friend, and you feel comfortable talking to them directly, tell them that their behaviour isn't acceptable. Tell them how the behaviour makes you feel, that you think they're better than their behaviour, and that you want to see them work on it.

If you're made to feel uncomfortable by men in your life who are being misogynistic, remember that although they are a product of the culture in which they've grown up, their behaviour is still a conscious choice on their behalf. It isn't down to their biology. It's always important to voice how you're being made to feel and challenge misogyny, but it also isn't your problem to *solve*. The meaningful way to start making a change is to commit to challenging the idea that 'boys will be boys', and to remove binary gendered thinking from our minds and these kinds of phrases from our lexicon.

The way we, as a culture, develop and represent masculinity in this suffocatingly narrow ideal is a *choice*. The way we raise our boys differently to our girls is a choice. The way we hold on to stereotypes of masculinity because it's comfortable is a choice. The way a guy fails to pull his friend up on a sexist joke is a choice. The way men decide not to engage in this work is a choice. The way we roll our eyes and say 'boys!' instead of talking to men about their behaviour and helping them to explore other options is a choice. I'm not saying it's easy, but making better choices is possible. So, the next time you hear this phrase, use the name of Head Facilitator of Beyond Equality Ben Hurst's TEDx talk and respond coolly: 'Boys will not be boys. Boys will be what we teach them to be.'

Prompts for discussion

- What does it mean to 'be' your gender? Could we be encouraging behaviours that don't feel natural to kids when we say this?
- If the person you're talking to is a man who you are close to, ask if any types of behaviour were expected of them as a young boy – boisterous, naughty, silly, loud, and so on. Were they made to control their bodies and behaviour in the same way girls are, or not? Draw attention to the fact that we don't really have a similar phrase for girls that holds them to a low standard of behaviour.
- If you are talking to a parent of a boy who is struggling with their son's behaviour, remind them their son is capable of more than his current actions and words. Remind them that seeing past their child's gender is key because the stereotype imposed upon boys is narrow and may be stopping them from being their full self.

Information to remember

- New research from YouGov published in 2019 reveals that 67 per cent of 18 to 24-year-olds felt compelled to display 'hyper-masculine' behaviour in tough situations and 55 per cent said crying in front of others would make them feel less like a man, proving that we have gendered human emotions.

- More than half (61 per cent) of Britain's young men feel pressured to 'man up' as a result of damaging gender stereotypes.
- Most children between 18 and 24 months can recognize and label stereotypical gender groups, such as girl/woman and boy/man. Most can categorize their own gender by the age of three.

→ "I think boys/men are capable of more, I expect more"

lack of accountability

→ "I would argue that this behaviour is a consequence of their socialisation, not their gender identity/biological makeup"

↳ "Boys will be what we teach them to be"

Koa Beck is the author of the acclaimed non-fiction book *White Feminism: From the Suffragettes to Influencers and Who They Leave Behind*. She is a recipient of both the Joan Shorenstein Fellowship at the Harvard Kennedy School and the Alan Jutzi Fellowship at The Huntington. She lives in Los Angeles with her wife and foster children.

"Feminism Is About Women Having the Same Rights and Power as Men"

Koa Beck

Gender consciousness can begin not just with personal experiences, but with identifying what others do not experience at all.

It's the person who rides the subway without consideration of their race or their gender presentation suddenly rendering them unsafe; the colleague at a white-collar job who asks for more money and not only gets it, but doesn't need to generate an entire campaign to achieve it; the individual who doesn't have to worry if their children will be picked up from school on time and ferried home to childcare; the person who is the default authority, narrator and priority in every space they've ever occupied.

There's a deeply internal and personal contrast here: what some must very tactfully navigate versus what others do not even think about. The worry and anxiety that colonizes every thought some have ever had compared to the inability for others to even imagine such an impediment. This is the threshold you walk through and the matrix of gender is exposed.

A deconstruction of resources, opportunities and quality of life yields a distinct hierarchy determined by race, gender identity, class, sexual orientation, ability, size and immigration status. And once you see the shape of this hierarchy it becomes easier to locate who is consistently at the top. When you envision a better standard of living, a safer way to exist or more fairly compensated labour, you see the person at the top of that pyramid. And efforts to ascend take on the centrality of that main character: 'Feminism is about women having the same rights and power as men.'

What you don't see is the pyramid itself.

In the United States, where I am from, mainstream narratives on gender rights often present white cis men as the template for gender equality: you want and need what they have. Straight, able-bodied men are both a talking point and an institution, a long-winded way my country has told a story about merit, exceptionalism and power. They go to elite institutions, run successful companies, own homes and are constantly affirmed in their every execution. To be them is to have access and economic certainty; a conviction that everything, in fact, will be all right.

In response to this truth, some forms of feminism have

focused their organizational and strategic efforts on exporting that exact certitude to women through the pyramid: we need more women running Fortune 500 companies. More women need to be heads of departments. We need more female heads of state. Women need to accrue more capital. More women need to own property and control facets of our economic dimensions. More women need to exist in positions of power as cis men traditionally have. And these are not only the goals of 'feminism', but the metrics of its progress: women operating in channels of power; women existing as elite men historically have.

But if women and non-binary people are assuming these stations with these parameters, they are also inheriting a dark legacy. Because if you want the same structural power as cis men, you will ultimately be relying on the labour and the exploitation of marginalized people that got them there. What has perennially facilitated that coveted cis-male power is not just confidence, entitlement, assurance and money. It's also other women.

Low-income women of colour have historically maintained those palatial homes and estates. Junior employees within those successful companies have been worked into the ground (and then discarded) to produce those profits. Immigrant women have cared for the children of those men, usually for very low wages and without any days off to see their own.

Women and non-binary people have been recruited across centuries to make this type of dominion and influence possible – their bodies, health and quality of life casually sacrificed for the power-holder. And in this crucial context of power and mastery, they cease to be seen as women at all; they become resources. A well from which you pull the aid you need without ever giving anything back: cheap childcare, under-the-table domestic labour, fast eldercare, immediate special-needs support, inexpensive professional assistance. They become cogs that can be utilized to make a conglomerate run smoothly. They become conveyer belts that need to be optimized better, faster, cheaper. They become solely what they do: the cleanly stacked dishes and the prepared food and the folded laundry and the ever abundance of office supplies that nobody else bothered to order.

Cheap labour has always been intrinsic to power and profits in the Western world.

There is an enduring reason that a company such as Amazon, ranked the fourth most profitable company in the world, is challenged by its labour union for not letting warehouse workers take bathroom breaks. One has often been dependent on the other. Securing a both aggressive and rapid return has often meant you have not employed people fairly, respectfully and decently. Money that could have gone towards better working conditions, paid time off for illness, better healthcare options, paid parental leave and a more humane work process for everyone is siphoned into profits to appease board members. Cheap labour has often been the essential ingredient to make this fantastical ascent possible. And cheap labour has often been female.

Some forms of feminism have presented the answer as simply this: don't be cheap labour. This is what the practice and ideology of white feminism has advocated for in my country for a century. In the 1920s, it was middle- to upper-class suffragists asserting that white women having the right to vote would facilitate women having a presence beyond the domestic sphere. In the 1960s and 1970s, it was US feminists such as Betty Friedan advocating that middle-class women should work outside the home in order to secure their gender equality rather than assume traditional domestic labour as housewives. And in my lifetime, it has been the Lean In, #GIRLBOSS, corporate feminist mantra in which women quantify their businesses and capital as innately feminist.

What all these ripples through history have in common is that they see white cis-male rights and power as the goal for marginalized genders: they navigate gender oppression from the compass of 'feminism is about women having the same rights and power as men'. Each of these movements espouse and strategize a liberation that assumes men are the template for equality, and that the rest of us can and will assume that role too. But many marginalized people across gender have envisioned well beyond this benchmark when conceptualizing equality.

Around the 1920s, immigrant women from Europe and working-class women who worked in factories, laundries and industrial conglomerates were for the right to vote too. But they envisioned having the vote as a way to change power distribution rather than flatly assume it like their upper-class suffragist counterparts. While some second-wave feminists of the 1960s did find value in imagining their lives beyond domestic work, Black feminist groups made it known that they had been working outside the home for some time (in larger numbers than white women since the 1890s) and 'equality' was still elusive in their lives. And in the 2010s, as the number of female-identified business owners ascended and corporate figures became conflated with feminist ones, those same politics were not extended to the women and non-binary people who made those professional choices possible with their labour. Words such as 'outsource', 'delegate' and 'farm out' flooded the national discourse on 'feminism', erasing immigrant women, low-income women and many women of colour – childcare workers and cleaners – from national narratives on gender rights.

Assuming traditional male power and rights not only perpetuates disenfranchising marginalized people – it's also abysmally uninventive. The whole 'feminism is about women having the same rights and power as men' falls far too short. Feminism and gender rights for many have often been anchored in imagining and advocating a type of society and economic structure we have never seen. Many movements have aimed not to merely get ahead in this world as it currently is; they have envisioned another world entirely.

In the United States specifically, this has taken the form of many Native movements that advocate for clean water access but also have a rich history of gender variance that dates back well beyond colonial presences. Black feminism in my country has often been steadfastly socialist in its theories and approaches, considering labour frameworks that factor in domestic labour and childrearing as valuable work that should be supported. The disability rights movement has defied multi-decade able-bodied narratives about their capabilities and their needs, often by challenging a presumed state of wellness as the status quo. Fat activists have posed essential questions to the nation about a healthcare system that assumes they are 'unhealthy' before even taking their vitals, borrowing considerably from queer theories that challenge beauty, desirability and gender. And queer and transgender politics have disputed the Western conviction that there are only two genders and that they must exist within very specific relationships, roles and presentations to be deemed legitimate.

Feminisms and social-justice movements broadly are spaces where ideas can be freed from conventional limitations and well beyond the traditions of power. By definition, these concepts need to take flight beyond the pyramid: the urgency of performance metrics, the sanctions of gender, the immediacy of profits, the insistence of colonialism, the convenience of commercialism. It's the theories that have exceeded these confines that become the milestones of progress: birth-control access without the permission of your husband or father; the basic concept of a weekend; the obliteration of sex-segregated help-wanted ads; the ability to wear clothing of a different sex and not get arrested; interracial partnerships; casting a vote as a woman; and as I write this in June 2022 in the United States, the federally recognized constitutional right to an abortion.

All of these rights and abilities were initially deemed so far beyond the existing state of affairs, so lofty and outrageous, so outside the conventions of their time. And yet, this many years out, many of those victories and resources are now considered pedestrian; rights and ways of living that many don't even think about because, for some, they have always been there.

So many feminisms and approaches to gender rights have deeply varied origins, and for good reason. For the people who have been subjugated, their physical and metaphoric placement in the world often produces the framework through which they ask essential questions about gender: why don't we have access to clean water? Why can't we obtain affordable housing? Why are we paid less for the same labour? Why can't we have affordable healthcare access? Why does the criminal justice system see us as threats or not at all? Why are we food insecure?

But within the nuance and complexity of these enquiries, many movements from Indigenous to working-class to transgender to Black Power have simultaneously asked the essential question, what if we had a world that didn't rely on this framework to function?

And the answer across culture, country, time and space has never been 'feminism is about women having the same rights and power as men'.

Prompts for discussion

- Who is your feminism for? Be as specific as possible. Is it only for marginalized genders who are structurally challenged in the same way you are? Is it only for marginalized genders who are seeking the same rights you are?
- When a company, organization, brand, or public person uses a term like 'feminist' to describe their practices, what does this mean? How does this

'feminist' terminology interact with their workplace policies and protections for their employees? How does this 'feminist' body engage with the environment? The carceral state? What does this declaration of 'feminism' reveal about their queer literacy? Their relationship to making money?

- What is the difference between aspiring to whiteness and achieving equal rights?

Information to remember

- In 2020, school and preschool closures required 672 billion hours of additional unpaid childcare globally. Given the gender divide in care work, it's estimated that women assumed 512 billion of those hours.
- There are now more women and girls who are forcibly displaced due to war, climate change and human rights violations than ever before: about 44 million women and girls by the end of 2021.
- The lack of clean water claims the lives of more than 800,000 women and girls every year.

"To Play Devil's Advocate":

In Response to Discussions on Misogyny

There was a time when I assumed that introducing more complexity and nuance to a discussion could only *ever* be a good thing. I was in my early twenties, dipping my toes into feminism, and I had opened the floodgates to so much information and so many concepts that I didn't understand. Unsurprising, really, given that other than a few books and documentaries, my main source of information up to that point had been social media. I discovered ideas and perspectives that provided a lens through which I could view previous beliefs and opinions, making them seem rudimentary, flat and naive.

Overwhelmed and having not yet discovered the vocabulary to articulate my own instincts, experience and feelings,

I gravitated towards the grounding concept of complexity – anything that didn't *feel* simple must be putting me on the right track because it signified exploration and progress; the opposite of social inertia. My feed was full of Instagram posts promoting the idea of #NUANCE in punchy, bold typography. Whether or not these posts actually offered any insightful analysis, I would read, nod my head and remember to be open to any and all perspectives the next time I encountered them. This is the precise reason why, whenever I heard the phrase 'to play devil's advocate . . .' – most often from cisgender men in response to feminist discourse – I assumed I was being introduced to a new and valid perspective that I had been missing.

At school, I wasn't always an academic kid and struggled to understand 'big' topics, such as science and maths, that had right or wrong answers. I was better with subjects that centred on creative expression and for a long time I only recognized feminism as something academic rather than a set of ideas that had been built, explored and evolved over generations of experience. Seeing it as rooted in academia made it intimidating to me.

I had also been socialized to view white, cisgender heterosexual men who hold power socially or economically – especially those in white-collar business industries – as archetypes of intelligence and competence. I saw their characters enjoying social status on television and in movies, and I saw them dominate the halls of power in education, music, art, politics and medicine; I assumed they were who I should learn from and listen to.

Whenever men in pressed suits and ugly ties spoke on TV,

somewhere deep down I would assume they knew more than the women they were in conversation with. Although I couldn't understand or express it at the time, I now recognize this as sexism and misogyny. These men became my default image of competence, and anything that deviated from it I subconsciously perceived as somehow inferior.

I'm sure this played a part in why, when I began to debate concepts around sexism or misogyny with male friends, I found I couldn't articulate myself at all. I'd become frustrated or emotional while they remained totally calm and equally bemused as to why the conversation was such a big deal. While navigating my own internalized misogyny, I was trying to express why misogyny hurt me so much to someone I automatically assumed must be better informed than me, and who was socialized to believe the same. This wasn't great, given that such an inherently personal and complex discussion requires a level of mental clarity and eloquence just to be able to get through it.

I remember a particular debate vividly. It was around 2015, I was twenty-one and it was one of the first times I'd committed to a debate of this kind with a friend. I was sitting in one of my favourite London pubs with my partner, Jordy, and a couple we were close with. I don't know how it started, but about two pints of cider in, my friend Lee and I became locked in what can only be described as a fair, compassionate, but undeniably tense disagreement about whether it was acceptable to smack, tap or grab the bum of a woman you don't know.

'It's just a way to signal that you like them and want to chat!' said Lee with a sheepish smile.

I disagreed wholeheartedly. 'But . . . why would you not just *speak* to them *first* before *touching them?*' I replied.

'It's just something you . . . do. It's not even that sexual, it's just sort of like saying "ayup".' He seemed genuinely confused.

I pictured Lee doing this in a rowdy club. I saw him as more of a 'cheeky chappy' kind of guy than a sexually aggressive one, but I knew that that distinction didn't matter because, either way, the impact such behaviour would have on this hypothetical woman could be negative. It wasn't acceptable.

'Women don't want guys they don't know to touch them. It makes you feel weird . . . unsafe.'

'No woman has been scared of me doing it.'

I knew he didn't get the problem, and so I came up with a way to make him understand.

'OK . . .' I began. 'How would you feel if you were in a bar and a woman just grabbed your arse?'

I thought I had him. I'd put him in the position himself, and that would enable him to see my perspective.

'I'd find it funny and think they were confident!' he replied with a grin.

Confused, I felt myself lose the argument. Reversing the scenario had felt like a fool-proof way to prove how inappropriate his actions were but somehow his response had me stumped. I gave up and abandoned the discussion.

It was only on the way home, while I was going over and over what I should have said, that the penny dropped. 'Of course you would,' I said to Lee in my head, 'because you don't live in a world run by women where you are intimidated by and treated as inferior to them, and fear the ones you don't know.'

A couple of months later I was at a well-known Soho members' club, sitting with a bunch of people I didn't know. I was working at a small ad agency at the time and, somehow, would end up in one of these places at the end of an evening out. At first, these clubs were new, fun and mysterious, but more often than not, I'd find myself at a table with a bunch of unfamiliar – usually obnoxious – men, who were much older than me and who I didn't particularly like. They weren't the kind of people I'd ever choose to hang out with.

In these clubs, older men – especially powerful ones with money – often gravitate towards young women in their early twenties. It creates a power dynamic that I was uncomfortable with, and so I mostly sat and observed people. That particular evening, I noticed the only other woman at our table. She was clearly a bit older than me, a little tipsy, and was gesticulating to two guys who were listening with furrowed brows and negronis in hand. She was pointing towards the bar as she spoke, and I got the sense she was describing something that had just happened. The first guy sat quietly as the blond man next to him leaned across the table and seemed to be disagreeing with her. I heard her say, 'You don't get it.'

As she stood up to leave, the blond man raised his hands in confusion while the quiet man placed his hand on her forearm, as if to keep her seated. 'I'm just playing devil's advocate,' exclaimed the blond guy, leaning back in his seat. She stood up and turned to look back at them as if she expected them to follow. They didn't, and she exited via the wooden doors of the bar that joined the foyer.

With espresso-martini-fuelled confidence, I followed her

and we ended up in the bathroom. I hadn't yet spoken to her that evening, apart from to introduce myself, but I knew that if there was anywhere she was going to open up, it would be the ladies' toilets. An unwritten but totally understood cultural contract stipulates that this space is for four things: defecating, debriefing about dates, talking about dickheads, and bonding with women you'd never see again.

As we were both washing our hands, I asked her if she was OK. 'Yeah,' she sighed, 'my boyfriend's friend is being a dick. A random man at the bar was clinging to my waist and hips, and he doesn't understand why that's annoying.' I told her about the conversation I'd had with Lee and within a couple of minutes we were both shouting incredulously about how it feels to have your space invaded and, more importantly, have men – especially the ones in your life – see it as normal and acceptable.

'He thinks the guy did it "without realizing",' she continued, drawing air quotes with her fingers.

'Even if he did?' I remarked, leaving the question hanging next to her speech marks.

She waved it away. 'Oh, it's not like you can talk to him about it. He always just plays devil's advocate.' She laughed, before adding, 'But you can't fucking say that *after* the fact.' She straightened up and turned to the mirror.

'You were playing . . . you,' I offered.

We left the safety of the toilets, headed through the heavy wooden doors of the reception area and past our table to the bar where – before checking the handsy punter was no longer around – the woman ordered and paid for two espresso martinis. She passed one to me with a silent thank-you in the form of a smile. Our toilet chat had forged an instant bond between us and I could tell she felt lighter.

Back at the table, her boyfriend and his mate were deep in discussion. As my new pal sat back down, her boyfriend welcomed her with a hand on her waist. It was an affectionate gesture from him but a reflection of the kind of power the man who had touched her at the bar assumed he had, despite not knowing her. I took my spot opposite her and leaned into the conversation. They didn't ask why she'd left.

I never saw that woman again but I remembered – and meditated for a while – on what she'd said about her boyfriend's friend's response. I thought she was right. Specifically, what she'd said about *when* devil's advocate was used suddenly made sense to me. It's one thing to say it in the context of a purely speculative conversation about hypothetical events as a way to frame your opinion (although depending on the opinion, it can still be problematic). But to use it, as the boyfriend's mate had, as a get-out-of-jail-free card to retrospectively justify or distance yourself from something problematic you've just said is frustrating. Especially in her case, because she was sharing an experience, not an opinion.

After years of internalizing the belief that men in expensive bars such as the one we'd been in, wearing suits like *that*, must be the type of successful person who really knew what they were talking about, I'd always subconsciously assumed that using the phrase 'to play devil's advocate' and what followed was something I was not informed enough to understand. But that evening, I'd seen it for what it so often actually is: a way to vocalize a regressive, unbalanced or uninformed opinion on something while preserving some distance from it in order to avoid being challenged.

As always, it's not necessarily the words themselves, but how you use them. Context is everything, and there are certain circumstances when it could make sense to say 'to play devil's advocate'. Let's say you're in a corporate scenario during a board meeting. Company money is being allocated to something and everyone at the table is thinking only within the interests of the organization. Here, you – and the company – could stand to benefit from an outlier who offers a different perspective. You have the power over where that money or resource goes, and need to make a smart decision, but there are multiple contributing factors and options to consider, so thinking 'outside the box' helps. In this situation, it might pay off to have someone assume a role that allows the rest of the members to think outside of their own interests. When you're dealing with emotions and experiences, though, it's a whole different ball game; one where offering outlier ideas 'just because' isn't always helpful.

Since my early twenties, and in my work in gender equality especially, I've heard 'to play devil's advocate' used abundantly in day-to-day conversations – far from a boardroom setting – about everything from equal pay and refugee rights to domestic-abuse trials and discussions about the monarchy. However, the way I'm most intimately acquainted with this phrase is when it's used as a response to someone describing a misogynistic experience. Now that I know the reason it's most often employed in that context, it's becoming easier to respond to it.

Gina Martin

In Response to 'To Play Devil's Advocate'

There's a very specific way that this phrase is used to delegitimize the experience of a survivor of sexual abuse and/or protect the attitudes or behaviours that create those experiences of harm from being challenged. If you're a woman reading this, many of you will have been on the receiving end of it. If you're a man, you or someone you know may have pulled it out in discussions around sexual violence and not understood why it provokes such a strong reaction, or why it leads to someone abandoning the conversation, like I did with Lee. Either way, it's worth talking about this phrase, because it can circuit-break important discussions about misogyny, sexual violence and rape culture, and undermine the experience of the victims of these crimes.

Unlike some of the other phrases in this book, 'to play devil's advocate' has incredibly specific roots and, in its original sense, a clear intention. In the sixteenth century, being an advocate for the devil was a revered role given to a member of the Catholic Church during the canonization of a saint. A saint was, of course, a person the Church viewed as almost perfect in the eyes of the Lord; someone holy, who was known for their 'heroic sanctity'. They could be martyrs, missionaries, kings or queens, theologians, parents, nuns or priests, or an everyday person who lived their life patiently, purely and compassionately through service, dedicating their lives to the loving pursuit of God.

Canonization is the last stage of a complex process (yes, it still happens) whereby after a person has died, they are proved to be a miracle-maker residing in heaven and deserving of the title of saint. The advocate of the devil played an important part in the process because they were used to uncover or express opposing viewpoints on this individual, and allowed the church to assess them more objectively. In other words, the role of devil's advocate created a framework through which to uncover flawed realities of the person in question, and therefore make a better judgement call. It was eventually abolished by Pope John Paul II in 1983, as part of streamlining the whole canonization process, but for centuries it was used to justify holding someone to almost inhumane levels of perfection. It was used in the context of sainthood, not of everyday people doing their best to navigate complex systems, norms and expectations. And, although the use of this phrase is no longer confined to its institutional context, it is important to note that the Catholic Church, and in particular its missionaries, holds a long, dark history as a key player in colonialism and the transatlantic slave trade; a system that relied on sexual violence as a mechanism for control.

When we 'play devil's advocate' in conversation today, we choose to promote ourselves to a position of juror in order to cast doubt upon the validity of someone's statement or their experience, introducing an unwarranted power dynamic to the process. It also acts as a way to offer an opposing idea to the discussion without suggesting that we actually believe or therefore need to take accountability for it. It says, 'I'm going to try to win a debate by using a standpoint I don't believe in,' while also implying or unearthing the flaws we perceive in someone else's thinking. Often, it's used to challenge for the sake of challenging in conversations that make people feel uncomfortable and confronted.

In the context of a highly emotional conversation about sexism, sexual harassment, assault or suffering, playing devil's advocate results in delegitimizing or casting doubt upon the experiences or intentions of the person speaking. It positions those person's words as subjective or an opinion, and therefore open to interrogation. The voicing of one's experience of sexual violence should *not* be conflated with the voicing of an opinion. Often in these conversations, victims or survivors are sharing facts about and reflections on their lived experiences, neither of which should be seized on as subjects for debate.

Gentle questions, genuine curiosity and thoughtful advice from the men in your life in response to your experiences are understandable. Too often, however, topics such as gender double standards at work, subtle microaggressions you've had to deal with because of your gender, or being sexualized without your consent can be met with a level of interrogation from men. This partly comes, I believe, from a deep subconscious need to disprove – for their own sake – the fact that men as a group are overwhelmingly responsible for sexual harassment, assault and violence; destroy the evidence, deny the problem. They often feel implicated, and so, 'If it turns out she's wrong, I'm not complicit in the problem.'

While sharing a story of sexual violence might condemn the perpetrator, it is not an attack on the man you're talking to. In turn, a critique of toxic masculinity – an umbrella term used to describe learned behaviours or attitudes about manhood that cause harm – is not necessarily a slight on the individual, it's an attempt to identify the harm being caused by the culture that creates it, and to discuss it.

I recognize that selfish instinct to defend the dominant group to which you belong in order to exonerate yourself. As a white woman, I have experienced the racialized fragility, as Akala calls it, that leads to, as Nova Reid writes in *The Good Ally*, 'impulsive reactive responses present in anyone who is agitated by Blackness being centred'. When I'd hear or see women of colour women discussing or denouncing white women's historical and current role in white supremacy, I'd feel a defensiveness rise in me. Rather than listening, I'd feel the ego urge to reach for something that somehow disproved this reality.

Sometimes I still feel this urge, although by working on my racism and by going to therapy, I've learned to listen to my body, what my child-ego state is telling me. I breathe and remember to deprioritize myself in the interaction. The sensation of needing to rid yourself of the discomfort confronting *you*, rather than the problem that you contribute to, is the precursor to learning – if we allow it to be. Though it takes self-enquiry and work, men in conversations about misogyny could learn so much from this.

Deep down, I think many cis het men know that they are, in some way, complicit in the pyramid of sexual violence, even if they don't have an academic understanding of that framework. Even if they've never been violent towards a woman or someone marginalized for their gender, I think many men are aware that somewhere, somehow, they have engaged in, or still do engage in, behaviour, attitudes or language that strengthen the culture of gender inequity or help preserve it. Whether that be through sexist jokes or language, mentally applying stereotypes and archetypes to women, allowing the women in their lives to carry the burden of emotional labour, or treating sex as a conquest or game.

Without the framework of understanding, they may not be able to pull apart the more insidious, everyday acts of inequity and misogyny from the ones of overt violence. For the men who see themselves as the good guys – or, more specifically, the ones who haven't perpetrated acts of violence – this is where I believe those feelings of complicity come from. They have an instinct that their behaviour might contribute to conditions that eventually allow sexual violence to thrive, like so many of us do (even I have!), and the shame of that instinct leads to defence.

It can feel as though the less a man is actively working on what he has been socialized to believe about masculinity or manhood, and how he has been complicit when he's acted on those cultural ideas, the more likely he is to deny and defend himself when conversations around sexual violence crop up. One of the easiest methods of self-defence in this context is to put space between oneself and one's opinions by 'playing devil's advocate'. To do so is such an unhelpful choice, because when we're listening to someone talk about their experience, the experience of someone they know, or the culture they believe is responsible for these realities, most of the time they aren't expecting whoever is sat opposite them to apologize or take accountability for these harms. They are simply wanting to be heard as – in the context of gender – they so often aren't heard by society at large.

They aren't a saint to be proved wrong. They aren't a

perfect person who needs to be uncovered as flawed. But when someone – often a man – uses 'to play devil's advocate' to distance themselves from the lived reality of the person living under misogyny to whom they're speaking, they create a dynamic in which she feels interrogated or challenged. To me, the priority in this scenario is never – and will never be – to try to contest or disprove the impacts of misogyny or the pain and discomfort caused by sexual violence or harassment. All that does is add the burden of shame to someone who is already carrying so much.

Crucially, the uncomfortable power dynamic already at play in this scenario is made worse when men 'play the devil's advocate' in response to a woman talking about experiencing sexual harassment, intimidation and misogyny. To have a man attempt to disprove her becomes doubly exhausting because it gives voice to the kind of mindset that allows this behaviour to thrive in the first place; it's like dealing with the chicken, and looking at the egg. Navigating the biases and problematic attitudes of men who are misogynistic or ignorant of gender dynamics is hard enough, but doing so when men act as if they are immune to the discomfort they cause by using 'devil's advocate' is especially frustrating.

For example, I was once explaining (to someone who asked) the psychology around why catcalling or whistling can feel so intimidating, even if it's not sexually explicit. They then chose 'to play devil's advocate' to essentially voice that cis men can't help their sexual urges. They weren't calling into question my lived experience, but they were interrupting and undermining an important discussion about harm. They were non-combative in tone, and when I got frustrated with them using the phrase, they seemed totally unaware of the dynamic it had created.

They argued that if someone (although not them, obviously . . . which instantly devalued their argument) can't help their urges, they couldn't be 100 per cent to blame for catcalling. I didn't get into a discussion about how men 'not being able to control themselves' is a bio-essentialist myth, but I did say that the impact of what they were saying was more important than their intent. 'If I crashed into the back of your car and caused damage,' I noted, 'I could say it wasn't my intention to, but I did crash into your car, so I should just apologize and make it right – there'll be time later to explore how it happened.'

As I challenged this notion that men can't control themselves, the person I was talking to threw up their hands and reiterated that they were only playing devil's advocate. I struggled to discuss their opinion with them because they were *insistent* that they were 'playing a role'. How is it possible to have a constructive conversation with someone who isn't mentally acknowledging their emotional involvement in that very conversation?

During these discussions, instead of just listening and asking questions, if I've felt comfortable enough to do so, I've asked why introducing a counterpoint was a priority for this person when I'm confiding in them about something that affects me in negative ways every day. I believe, deeply, that as well as feeling complicit and needing to exonerate themselves, a lot of men don't fully comprehend how dangerous rape culture is, and so they find themselves challenging what is being said in search of the 'truth' (i.e., a comforting alternative explanation for a situation that paints their community's actions more favourably). This is because confronting the reality of the situation would mean taking a long, hard look in the mirror, conducting conversations with their friends and finding a new way of being, and, sadly, that's not something many cis het men have been given the emotional tools and space to do.

When you are the dominant group, parts of your identity are rendered invisible to you. For instance, when I say 'gender', cis men often think I mean women or trans people, as if they don't have a gender. When someone says 'race', white people often think the person is referring to Black people, as if they themselves aren't racialized and don't belong to a racial category.

The concept of the 'unmarked category', a term originating in linguistics, is used to explain how a dominant group in any context perceives itself to be the default and is also viewed as such by an unequal society – other groups must be 'described' because their identities are organized around the dominant group. Everyone else becomes othered, which creates a situation where the dominant group – in this context, let's say 'men' (by which we mean cis het men, but this is how society refers to them at large) – isn't encouraged to be introspective about its gender. That's partly why, even when men are well-meaning and engage compassionately, their starting line for navigating these conversations about gender, gendered power dynamics, manhood, masculinity and sexual violence is much further back from that of women, who have been made aware of their gender through discrimination and control of it.

Imagine you're talking with a white, middle-class male colleague, who is in a similar position of power to you in the workplace. He has a set of privileges that you don't, and unless he has interrogated those privileges and is trying to understand them, they will be invisible to him. In turn, they will inform his thinking and behaviour. This means that he's navigating a discussion about power (gender inequality) without having looked critically at the role he plays in this issue. That's the first big blocker.

Those who sit at multiple intersections of oppression or individuals who experience multiple forms of discrimination from dominant communities are more likely to have a better overview (or at least instincts if they don't yet have the language) of the intersecting power dynamics. Women, trans people, non-binary people, Black women, disabled women and Asian women have been exposed to the dominant culture of misogyny and the patriarchal systems that uphold it, all of which we have had to become accustomed to recognizing and navigating over the course of our lives, both interpersonally and institutionally. Now, as with all conversations around why people interact the way they do in society, it's incredibly complex and complicated, and there are many women who have internalized patriarchal rules and misogyny more than they have questioned them. But if you're a woman committed to educating herself on the topic, then you can probably communicate to some degree – with whatever language you have at the time – what examples of toxic behaviour look like, feel like and the impact they have had on you.

Part of the reason that women and those who are

marginalized because of their gender may be able to articulate their experiences – especially those of living under misogyny – more clearly than, say, a cisgender heterosexual man, is because to grow up female in our society is to be afforded more permission to feel and express vulnerability, shame and fear with other women. Even if these emotions aren't accepted in patriarchal arenas such as the workplace, or within a marriage, they still develop because femininity is encouraged to engage with femininity in feeling ways, and we often rely on friendships to develop our understanding of ourselves.

Historically, cis men haven't been afforded this freedom to the same degree, and as well as this being entirely unfair, I think it can often stunt their ability to understand and talk about themselves, their power and the issues it may perpetuate. As bell hooks writes in *The Will to Change: Men, Masculinity, and Love*, 'Learning to wear a mask (that word already embedded in the term "masculinity") is the first lesson in patriarchal masculinity that a boy learns. He learns that his core feelings cannot be expressed if they do not conform to the acceptable behaviours sexism defines as male.'

So, without excavating, evaluating and expressing the way in which they have been socialized, men cannot sufficiently examine their gender, their privilege and their power, and are less equipped to navigate conversations that are rooted in those topics. Add to that a sense of entitlement to knowledge – a pervasive but subtle trait instilled by the patriarchy and constantly rewarded in patriarchal spaces – and being in conversation with a woman who is exposing her feelings and experiences can lead a man to challenge her with logic and practical thinking instead of supporting her with softer, more empathetic responses.

Too often, I have found myself talking to a man who hasn't done enough self-work to navigate our conversation with compassionate and critical thinking. Defensiveness has become a priority for him, thanks to the years of societal repression of his emotions, as well as his complicity being invisible to him. That's when what may feel like a 'search for truth' to him becomes a search to remove discomfort by questioning and 'proving' me wrong. Playing devil's advocate remains an effective way to do this while distancing himself from the problem, retaining his 'good guy' status and not feeling a traitor to his gender.

There was a need for a character who tested the parameters of perfection in the process of canonizing a saint, but there is no need for one in informal conversations between messy, imperfect, feeling people in a messy, imperfect, painful world. Above all, there really is no place for role play in discussions with victims and survivors. The devil's-advocate approach reinforces the already prevalent, damaging and standard idea that victims must live up to perfect standards in order to be believed, or even listened to. The perfect victim is a myth, built on misogynistic and racist ideas, that aims to delegitimize survivors, especially trans and non-binary survivors, disabled survivors, Black survivors and other survivors of colour, refugee survivors and those in poverty, all of whom have the barriers stacked against them in terms of 'believability' because of '-isms' endemic in our society.

The perfect-victim fallacy is a direct precursor to victim-blaming, which shifts the focus from perpetrator to victim based on their perceived faults, reframing the perpetrator as a helpless individual unable to control themselves and the victim as the regulator of behaviour. It's a masterclass in removing agency from the former while demanding impossible standards of the latter, and allowing perpetrators to evade accountability in the process.

Showing up in conversations about human topics that have vulnerability built in requires the listener to show up as themselves; expressing their thoughts and feelings without a scapegoat, as well as accepting that they may be met with resistance if they challenge someone's experience. If not, we can't have a constructive discussion. Prioritizing challenging instead of supporting when discussing misogyny, sexual violence and more (do people in pain need to be challenged?) creates an environment where survivors and victims don't feel heard, and we already live in a culture mired in that.

When we have conversations with family and friends, we almost always expect people to come to them with humility, and to voice and own their opinions and thoughts. So what's the difference here? Without honesty and authenticity, we can't be constructive, especially when we're also wrestling with power dynamics. Those of us who do the work of talking about hard topics on a daily basis know that the (often subconscious) act of putting space between yourself and harmful 'views' or harmful 'behaviour' is a giant blocker to progressive thinking because it allows you to separate yourself from the problem at hand, and therefore never reflect on how you could be part of it.

That chasm permits us to see the topic as somewhat theoretical, which means we can't engage with it emotionally;

we can't *feel* it. So the next time someone says, 'I'm just playing devil's advocate' in response to actual facts from your life, take a breath and reply, 'OK, well, could you play yourself, because I'm being really vulnerable here? I don't need to be challenged, I need to be heard. And, as the saying goes, "The devil has enough advocates already."' That's precisely *why* we need to have these conversations.

Prompts for discussion

- Ask the person you're speaking to to consider where else in the conversation, or on what other topics, they would play a role to offer an opinion or viewpoint, and why.
- Ask them to try to articulate what exactly in this conversation needs to be challenged and why. What would be the outcome if it wasn't challenged?
- Offer that playing 'devil's advocate' is often for the sake of argument or to generate debate, and ask if they believe someone's experience should be debated or analysed, instead of being heard and supported.
- Be specific with your language and ask the person to whom you're talking to think about the culture being referenced in your discussion. Remind them that you are talking about something bigger than both of you, and even though you may be referencing a specific experience, this isn't about you versus them, it's us versus it. So, nobody needs to play a role.

Information to remember

- The devil's advocate was a position created by the Catholic Church to uncover flaws in a person who was to be canonized as a saint, not in regular people.
- An Ipsos global survey conducted in thirty countries in collaboration with the Global Institute for Women's Leadership at King's College London shows that a third of men who took part think feminism does more harm than good and believe that traditional masculinity is under threat. It shows that cultural attitudes about movements to deconstruct gender inequality differ across genders, and this could affect perceptions during discussions about sexual violence.
- Research published by the UK government in 2014 suggested that deep-rooted ideas about traditional masculinity, particularly those linked to controlling and aggressive behaviours, play a role in male violence against women. We have a serious cultural problem.

Charlie Craggs (she/her) is an award-winning activist media personality and author of *To My Trans Sisters*.

"Children Shouldn't Be Allowed to Transition Because What if They Change Their Minds?"

Charlie Craggs

In 2017 the *Mirror* – one of the biggest national newspapers in the UK – ran a front-page headline, '50 kids a week being sent to sex change clinics', accompanied by a picture of a (very) young pre-pubescent primary-school child with their head in their hands.

I don't need to break down the optics of this for you. Anyone with an ounce of common sense is able to see what the *Mirror* was trying to do by pairing this headline and its tactical use of the word 'kid' (a colloquial term for a pre-teen child) with an image of a young child looking distressed and overwhelmed.

What I *do* wanna break down, however, and what I'm hoping you'll in turn break down for people you meet who say 'children shouldn't be allowed to transition because what if they change their minds?', is that . . .

Kids. Aren't. Having. Sex. Changes.

I mean ... arguably, *nobody* is having 'sex changes', because this is an outdated term coined by those very same tabloids. But terminology aside, *children* DEFINITELY aren't having them. Logistically it would be pretty much impossible to perform a sEx ChAnGe on a child that has nothing to *change* (i.e., a penis the size of a baked bean). But never mind logistics, *legally* you have to be eighteen to have trans-related surgery here in the UK, and according to the UN, a child is a person under the age of eighteen. So I repeat, *children* are not having surgery, babe.

Unlike 'child', the word 'transition' is harder to clearly define because transitioning means something different to everyone. Some trans people take hormones, some have surgery, some don't feel the need to do either because being trans – kinda like being gay – is innate and not dependent on what you *do*, but rather who you *are*.

However, for the sake of making things as clear as possible as we unpack this phrase, why don't we agree that 'transitioning' in the context of this discussion refers to the most widely understood concept of transitioning, being both medical and surgical; because really, that's what people have a problem with. What if these young people transition and regret it? How can young people make such a LiFe-ChAnGiNg decision?

The notion of 'protecting children' is often used to justify thinly veiled transphobia as concern. When I say 'thin', I MEAN REAL THIN, because surely, if being caring was the

goal of the people who use this phrase, they'd be advocating to implement *more* support and intervention for gender-questioning young people to help catch the (tiny) minority that end up regretting transitioning. The veil is removed when you realize that their goal is actually often the opposite of caring, with many wanting to ban any support and intervention for these young people altogether.

Doing this won't help anyone, trans or not. It would only lead to an even higher attempted suicide rate among trans youth, a rate that is already disproportionately high at 45 per cent, according to Parliament's Women and Equalities Committee. Read that again. Not just suicidal, but *attempted* suicide. This illustrates perfectly just how little some people actually care about the children they're apparently so keen to protect.

People claim to want to protect children from making life-changing decisions, but those same individuals don't have any problem whatsoever with young cis people making equally (if not more) significant life-changing decisions; decisions such as having sex or having a baby, or joining (and potentially DYING in) the army. Legally, society considers young people to be capable of making these decisions at the age of sixteen, and it is deemed socially acceptable (if not encouraged) to smoke, drink and gamble well before the legal age of eighteen. Yet when it comes to gender-questioning, all of a sudden, it is crucial that we 'protect' young people from decision-making.

Do you smell that? Smells like transphobia.

To add salt to the wound, young people (trans included) can literally do any of the things on the list above without any supervision or assessment as to whether they're competent enough to understand what they're getting into. Trans healthcare, on the other hand, is gate-kept by medical practitioners who interrogate, analyse and make you jump through countless hoops before deciding whether or not they'll be kind enough to grant you access to the medication you require not to kill yourself. Even then, the decision-making process is deemed too risky and 'life-changing' for gender-questioning young people.

Given quite how much debate there is in the media about the subject, the irony is that *very* few trans people are even lucky enough to get on hormones or blockers by the age of eighteen, never mind have any surgery. On average, it's a four- to five-year wait for a *first appointment* to simply *talk* about transitioning with a specialist at a gender clinic. You won't be referred for surgery until *years* after that.

Even more ironic is that, for the very lucky few, the reality of what transitioning entails as a child is nothing irreversible. It is as simple as swapping things such as their hairstyle, their clothes or their name for ones that make them feel more comfortable. Life-changing changes that can be reversed in literal seconds if the child realizes that they're not trans. Hair can be cut, clothes can be taken off, names can be changed. But as easy as these choices are to reverse, they are none the less life-changing in the sense that they can be the difference between a child *having* a life or a child *taking* their life. What's better, a trans child or a dead child? *This* is where our concern should lie.

Despite these truths, the media is determined to push the narrative that young trans people are being 'rushed' through a process they're gonna regret. In fact, a week doesn't go by without a headline about my tiny community, despite the fact that trans people make up less than 1 per cent of the population. In her book *The Transgender Issue*, writer, editor and journalist Shon Faye reports that in 2020, '*The Times* and its sister paper *The Sunday Times* between them ran over 300 articles – almost one a day – on trans people.'

In my 2020 BBC documentary *Transitioning Teens*, I set out to debunk media misconceptions about the young trans community. Travelling around the country, I met the young people at the heart of this debate and saw the ways in which they're *really* being pushed – to the edge of suicide, into debt and into buying black-market hormones due to the disgracefully long wait times for first appointments at gender clinics. The doc also ended up offering a new perspective on the trans people versus detransitioners argument, which is so often cited by those who are 'concerned' with the wellbeing of young trans people.

People use detransitioners as a stick to beat trans people with, in a similar way to how 'ex-gays' (people who go through conversion therapy) are used as a stick to beat gay people with; their existence is supposedly proof that being gay is a choice and something that can be cured. In turn, detransitioners are used as proof that people – especially young people – shouldn't be allowed to transition in case they change their minds. In reality, the number of people who detransition is, according to Stonewall (Europe's biggest LGBT charity), less than 1 per cent, yet this is rarely acknowledged in the relentless media coverage of the 'trans debate'.

It's worth noting that most individuals who detransition

do so not because they realized that they aren't trans, but rather because they couldn't hack *being* trans. Being trans isn't very fun; you only have to go to my Instagram (@charlie_craggs *ding*) to see the viral video of a transphobe spitting in my face. So, it's unsurprising that GenderGP's survey of 27,715 people who had detransitioned found that only 5 per cent of them did so because it was the wrong decision for them, with 36 per cent saying they detransitioned due to 'pressure from parents', 33 per cent citing 'difficulty transitioning', and 31 per cent blaming the 'harassment and discrimination' they faced for being trans.

As validating (and sad) as these stats are, denying help and healthcare to trans people because 1 per cent of those individuals regret transitioning for *whatever* reason would be like banning abortion because 1 per cent of people regret having an abortion. When people use phrases like 'children shouldn't be allowed to transition in case they change their minds', they are tacitly supporting the withdrawal of help and healthcare for the trans community. This is not me being dramatic – in 2020, the High Court ruled that children under the age of sixteen were unlikely to be mature enough to consent to be prescribed puberty-blocking drugs, and that doctors treating anyone under the age of eighteen may have to consult the courts before they pursue medical intervention. This ruling was challenged and thankfully overturned, but people are *literally* trying to change the law in order to prevent trans youth from accessing medical care and treatment to which they are rightfully entitled.

Talking of abortion and bodily autonomy, you have to laugh that so many of the loudest anti-trans voices in the

UK – many of whom were pivotal in the (short-lived) (ha ha) success of this historic ban stripping us of our bodily autonomy – call themselves 'feminists'. The same middle-class white 'feminists' who churn out uneducated opinion pieces on trans people in their weekly columns for *The Times* and the *Telegraph* can go to their GP and ask for hormone therapy to ease the effects of the menopause, and will be given hormones on the spot. Meanwhile, a trans woman of the *same* age, with the *same* rights, paying the *same* taxes for the NHS will be put on a five-year waiting list to *discuss* hormone treatment, and will not see a hormone for at least another year *after* that five-year wait. Whether you like trans people or not, anyone with an understanding of fairness can see this is wrong.

While filming my doc I actually met a young person who *did* regret transitioning and detransitioned, but to both of our surprise, we came to the same conclusion that the solution to our respective problems was the same. For so long, we've been pitted against each other in this culture war but we agreed that the current trans healthcare system in this country is failing both trans people and people who think they're trans but aren't and just need some help in realizing that.

Banning support for young trans people is not only unfair to the 99 per cent who don't regret their decision, but also won't stop people transitioning. To draw a comparison with abortion again, banning abortion (out of fear that people may regret it) doesn't stop people *having* abortions; it just means they go about getting them in unsafe ways. It's the same with trans healthcare – stopping all support for young trans people out of concern that some may regret it won't stop young trans people transitioning. It will just mean they are forced to go about transitioning in a dangerous way, like Jess, a teenager I interviewed for the documentary who was forced to buy her hormones on the online black market without any guidance because she had no other choice. She had no one to support her.

Having read how trans people *and* people who detransition (aka the ONLY two groups who are affected by anything to do with this issue) both agree that the answer is not *stopping* support for young people who think they're trans, but rather *increasing* support for those who are and therefore catching the ones who aren't, I hope you can see that the people who veil their transphobia behind the guise of pRotEcTiNg ChiLdReN don't actually care about the children they're claiming to protect. Refusing to help them will lead to fewer trans young people, but only because those young people will be dead. They'd be able to reverse their transition (though chances are the majority won't want to) but they can't reverse their suicide.

Please have some compassion and just be glad you're not trans.

Prompts for discussion

- Ask them to explain their concerns about the wellbeing and safety of the trans youth. If they bring up detransitioners, remind them of the stat below but also of the disproportionately high attempted suicide rate amongst young transgender people. Ask them to consider where the real threat to their safety lies.

- Ask them why they are so concerned about this 'issue'. If it doesn't affect them personally in any way whatsoever, then ask why they are even talking about it.
- Ask them what they actually know about the transitioning process for young trans people. Remind them how life-changing (and life-saving) those choices can be for the lucky children and teenagers who are encouraged and supported in their journey.

Information to remember

- Children aren't having surgery. You have to be eighteen to have surgery. You're an adult at eighteen according to the UN.
- At eighteen you can make loads of other life-changing decisions, such as getting married, having sex, gambling, drinking, smoking or joining the army. How can you be competent enough to make these decisions but not competent enough to seek help if you're trans?
- Trans people make up less than 1 per cent of the population, detransitioners make up less than 1 per cent of that 1 per cent.

"If You Don't Want Attention, Cover Up"

I'm sitting in the green room at Television Centre in White City, London. I'm shaky, my chest feels fluttery and I can hear my heartbeat. I recognize these sensations from when I used to have to do presentations in school, but I haven't felt this nervous for a long time. It's about 6.30 a.m. and I'm roughly a month into doing media around my upskirting. I'm due to go on *Good Morning Britain* in just a few minutes to debate why it should be a sexual offence.

The producer for the show had called me a few days ago, while I was at my desk in Paddington, and asked me if I would come on to 'debate' the issue with Piers Morgan. I immediately felt pumped up about the idea and replied confidently that I would be happy to appear. Before I could think it through, I'd told him that 'Piers could do with being taken down a few pegs'.

The producer had laughed and moved on, telling me I'd also be appearing with an ex-police officer. 'She's a woman,' he noted, as if her gender automatically confirmed her position on the matter. I decided to ask, specifically, about her standpoint. 'She thinks that people who don't want to be upskirted should just wear trousers,' he replied. Then it was my turn to laugh.

Last night, I invited my closest friends around for a takeaway to belatedly mark my birthday. The day itself had passed in a blur as I grappled with going viral online for calling out the men who had upskirted me, and subsequently being thrust into the blinding light of the British media. I was full of fear about appearing on live TV for the first time, and I needed the people who knew me best to tell me whether they thought this was a positive opportunity to raise awareness, or whether I was just opening myself up to something way bigger than me and unforgiving – the opinions of the British public.

Rey, one of my closest friends, was supportive. I'd described what the ex-officer's position was and he immediately re-affirmed my decision, reminding me I had to go on the show to tell the truth about my experience and ensure the conversation was a balanced one.

While my friends and I huddled around my coffee table, feasting on takeaway curries, the producer had called to let me know Piers Morgan wouldn't be appearing after all and that Richard Madeley would be filling in for him. I was partly annoyed, but felt palpable relief. Piers was a steamroller of a presenter and I suspected he would have sided with the police officer's narrative, in order to whip up views. On the other hand, I was half hopeful that I could've shown him up with some common-sense comebacks that would have made his points look ignorant.

Now, sitting in the green room, I attempt to calm myself by remembering my only job is to tell the truth, just as Rey said. But even though my story is mine and there's no way I could tell it wrong, I am terrified by the pressures of live TV; I imagine the crew watching me while I sit there in silence, too nervous to speak, the lights bright and blinding, the presenters shouting. I have no media experience, yet I'm about to discuss how I was humiliatingly upskirted in public two months ago; a pretty exposing, vulnerable situation to be discussing in front of millions of people.

Right before I go on set, I am introduced to retired Detective Superintendent Sue Hill, who will be appearing alongside me. She is warm and polite, which I find odd for someone I'm sure is about to argue against me, a sexual-assault victim who is trying to change the law to make upskirting a specific offence. She takes my hand, tilts her head and sympathetically congratulates me on my campaign. I don't know how to respond.

It is in this moment I realize that not all shows I've grown up watching were created to broadcast impartial and balanced discussions. As a kid, I believed all current affairs programmes were a legitimate source of news and information because of their reach and power, but it seems that what is about to unfold will be debate for the purpose of entertainment rather than journalism. That this woman could privately praise me for fighting against sexual assault while publicly disagreeing with my proposal to make upskirting a criminal offence is to my mind proof, and by engaging in this debate, I am part of this farce.

Moments later we go live, and I am baffled by the conversation which ensues. Richard begins by introducing the concept of upskirting and clarifying with me that it is not currently a criminal offence before asking me to describe my experience at British Summer Time. I do so and explain that although the police were lovely, it became clear very quickly that my case wouldn't be followed up. In response to this, Sue suggests that as we're living against a backdrop of terrorism, the officers might have been more concerned with protecting the large crowds at the festival than dealing with my individual case. At this point, things take a strange turn when Sue draws a parallel with Ascot, specifically 'the photographs that are uploaded by the media [of] women in knickers'. Richard jumps in to point out that these are not comparable experiences. Then, the conversation takes yet another detour when he asks whether he would be prosecuted for punching 'some creep' who puts a camera on a stick between his wife's legs on the tube. Sue confirms that he likely would before mentioning her own daughter, who is in her early twenties and who uses the tube, and the fact that 'sadly, you have to look after yourself'; the suggestion being that it's the responsibility of women to safeguard themselves against sexual assault.

At this point, I feel I've completely lost any control over the conversation. Realizing that we are running out of time, I shut down Sue's first argument by asserting that I am not going to 'play the game of which is more important, terrorism or sexual offence' and that I understand there might be a resourcing issue but that she could 'take that up with the government, not the victims of sexual assault'. In response to this, Kate Garraway attempts to clarify another of Sue's points by comparing upskirting to when young boys would 'ping a bra strap' in the 'olden days', and suggests that perpetrators of upskirting 'shouldn't be compared with some of the other people on that register'.

When the interview comes to an end, I am left feeling like I've been in a washing machine. This ridiculous discussion was framed as a 'debate'; one that, for me, was about my *life* but in which I felt I was not really being listened to. I also felt the subject had been approached through a deliberately provocative lens, perhaps for the sake of a more 'lively' discussion.

Once we were clear and off-air, Sue turned to me. I thought I heard her say, 'I'd give you a slap . . .' but the rest was a jumbled mumble that I didn't quite catch because my heart was beating so loudly in my ears. 'Me?' I replied. She looked slightly shocked and then let out a small laugh. 'No! Them! The guys that did that to you! I'd slap them!' I went to reply that I did slap him, but I couldn't meet her eye, so I just stared straight ahead. 'Sorry, Sue,' I managed, 'I wasn't sure what you meant because there are just *so* many mixed messages.' I waved my hands to illustrate how baffling I found her, got up from my chair as the sound guy began to remove my microphone, and stood there in silence for a few moments before being shown out. I remember wondering if this bullshit was going to be my life now.

That interview was my first glimpse at what being a gender-equality activist in the public eye would be like. Since then, this kind of thing has become a depressingly normal part of my life. The bigger my profile grew as a result of my campaigning – and eventually changing the law – the more I was told to wear trousers if I didn't want people to look at me, to look after myself better if drinking, to dress more modestly if I wanted to be taken seriously, and to make 'smarter' decisions if I wanted to avoid being assaulted.

Unlike the abuse I encountered online, the victim-blaming

didn't just come from men, it also came thick and fast from older women. The men's response seemed rooted in anger at me wanting autonomy over who touches or takes photos and videos of my body. The likes of some guy called, let's say, Dan would tag his friends in the comments of a video of me on the news on Facebook and ask me to 'cover [my] dusty axe wound if [I] don't want people to see it', followed by five crying-laughing emojis to demonstrate how funny he was.

For the older women, however, the victim-blaming seemed to come from a different place: a sense that my decision to fight for this right was laughable because in their day (or during previous waves of feminism), women were fighting for 'fundamental' rights, such as the vote, access to birth control and, more recently, criminalizing marital rape – rather than what they saw as my 'trivial addition'.

Take the older woman I met on the street while filming content outside Westminster during the early stages of the campaign, who told me that 'young women get angry about a man touching their arm these days', and that 'they should just stay at home'. Like the men who contacted me, these women were uncomfortable with me challenging the status quo, but specifically because I wasn't doing it in the way they deemed acceptable. This gatekeeping of what was permissible within feminism was exactly why so many women hadn't got involved with, or felt part of, previous waves of feminism. And it was clear to me that, by disagreeing with these women, I was challenging something ingrained in so many of us and which we are hesitant to question: internalized misogyny.

Victim-blaming was a reaction I encountered from both men and women, regardless of their different experiences or motivations. They, on some level, believed that what had happened to me was my fault, and if I'd made different decisions, it could have been avoided. This affected me. As I continued speaking to crowds and working with journalists, I would feel the urge to over-explain details of the assault in order to exonerate myself or quell any suggestion of my involvement.

I'd describe the weather on the day of the assault so that the journalist and readers would connect the dots in their heads as to why I'd chosen to wear a mini skirt. I'd explain to a crowd that it was a 'family festival' so that they would see the violation of my space and body as even more unacceptable than if it had happened in front of adults only – in a bar or a club, for example; environments where sexual assault is often rife and we somehow expect and excuse it more easily. In supplying all this extra detail, I didn't even notice that I was victim-blaming myself, and that's because every single year of my life had prepared me for a guilty and shameful mindset to be my default.

As kids, I and all the girls I knew were victim-blamed in small ways for assaults that hadn't even happened yet; conditioned to anticipate coercion, invasion of space or violence being part of our life, and to regulate or control the threat of it through our clothing choices, actions and the decisions we made. I remember as my friends and I were beginning to learn about our own bodies, my friend's mother often insisted her daughter's bra strap, which had innocently shifted across the slope of her shoulder by an inch, be tucked into her shirt; the inference being that the sight of it was inappropriate and something to be ashamed of.

Consider how at thirteen, in an attempt to self-actualize,

we pushed the boundaries of our *enforced* feminine school uniforms by wearing short ties, tight trousers and short skirts – something society's perverse obsession with schoolgirl attire and the mainstream depiction of femininity through the male gaze had taught us was attractive. In response, the teachers would punish us or demand we control ourselves and restrict our self-expression, citing how 'inappropriate' our choices were and commenting that we were distracting male students (and even sometimes teachers). According to this logic, inappropriate behaviour could lead to men looking. For us, this could lead to danger, and for them, it could compromise their chances of success because they weren't able to concentrate on their education.

These rules and responses taught us that our bodies were not just bodies, they were inherently sexual. We also learned that if boys' behaviour became inappropriate – which it inevitably would through comments and harassment disguised as games such as 'kiss chase' – we and our bodies were to blame; not the boys who weren't taught to respect people's boundaries, and not the society that conditioned us to perceive our value solely according to our looks and our performance of femininity. As a result, we carried that knowledge with shame and guilt, and wouldn't tell our parents or teachers when something made us feel uncomfortable, because it was sort of our fault, right?

Add to this the fact that magazines in the noughties regularly printed non-consensually-taken upskirt and bikini shots of women for the public to scrutinize and mock, and it's not surprising that I struggled so much with the victim-blaming, both self-inflicted and from other people. I truly don't know what else I was meant to think. I don't know how I was meant not to feel some level of guilt for my own upskirting when society had always told me that rather than it being the responsibility of boys to regulate their own behaviour, it was my job to do so by virtue of the choices that I made, and that this kind of assault was normal.

Eventually, after months of TV interviews and receiving messages online that victim-blamed me in both overt and subtle ways, I got really sad. I got fed up. I stopped replying to the comments and I stopped expecting people to understand or learn. But now, six years later, I'm no longer only fed up, I'm also equipped and I expect people to do better. Because they fucking have to. Because when we excuse victim-blaming, we choose to re-organize our expectations *around* violent behaviour, as if this behaviour is natural and acceptable. In doing so, we give those perpetrators permission to continue their abuse without being held accountable, socially or legally. This total lack of accountability pushes the blame on to survivors and victims (and pre-blames women by extension), which forces them to feel shame for something they never wanted to happen in the first place. It's a never-ending cycle of distraction, blame and shame. And then we wonder why people don't report assault or harassment.

In Response to 'If You Don't Want Attention, Cover Up'

We live in a society where women's bodies are seen as something for masculinity to consume and restrict. Expectations of womanhood – the ideal traits, attributes, appearance and expression of femininity – are determined and imposed by what bell hooks called 'imperialist white supremacist capitalist patriarchy', a societal system originally created by powerful white men that values whiteness as power, capitalism and heterosexual patriarchy and leads to subjugation. Historical treatment of women shows us this, such as in the hyper-sexualization of Black women, from the 'Jezebel' stereotype of slavery, to the current adultification of young Black girls codifying perceptions of them as innately hypersexual, voracious and lascivious, endangering them and making them less likely to be believed than young white girls when reporting sexual harassment or abuse.

These interlocking systems create a patriarchy that dominates partly by imposing impossible rules and unattainable standards of womanhood (determined by Eurocentric ideals) on different women, who are then blamed or penalized for not obeying them. Look, for example, at the hair discrimination experienced today by the global majority – a collective term for non-white groups which constitute approximately 85 per cent of the world's population – often specifically the Black community. In reality, trying to obey standards of womanhood (as if there is ever one way to be a woman) is impossible because the goal posts are constantly moved, and because the rules were only about control in the first place; there was no way of 'winning' or securing freedom through obedience. The problem is, this strategy has created a widely held attitude when it comes to what is accepted and what is acceptable for women, and what isn't. It's an attitude that permeates society and our institutions, and you've probably heard or been on the receiving end of one of its hallmarks: victim-blaming.

> 'You're not wearing that out, are you?'
> *Parents when their teenage daughter dresses up to go out.*
>
> 'You know what you're getting into if you go to a hotel room alone.'
> *Pamela Anderson about those who went into hotel rooms with Harvey Weinstein.*
>
> 'She was open to meeting someone [because she was] wearing a thong with a laced front . . .'
> *A barrister during a 2018 Northern Irish rape trial.*

There are endless ways to blame the victim for their own harassment, assault or the violence inflicted on them, precisely because the parameters of womanhood are constructed and so they don't have to be logical or fair to be effective. However, the instruction to 'cover up' is the version I've experienced most frequently. Although not particularly sophisticated, it is one of the simplest ways that patriarchal systems seek to control women: through their expression of femininity, and more specifically, their clothing.

In the words of Laura Bates in *Fix the System, Not the Women*, 'normalisation breeds acceptance. We are so used to hearing it is our own fault that we start to believe it . . . we get so used to it that we stop fighting.' After years of exposure to the lie that victims are to blame for their sexual assaults, it's an easy connection for our minds to make in order to 'explain' the problem of sexualization without consent: if you don't want attention, cover up. But in reality, this phrase doesn't offer answers, it only perpetuates the problem and ensures the person who has dealt with that sexualization feels responsible and therefore more ashamed than they already did.

Half the time, someone using this phrase – or any other wording that attributes blame to the victim – might not realize how harmful it is. Its usage speaks to two ideas that we have been socialized to believe – that women's bodies are inherently sexual, and that men are therefore unable to control their behaviour towards them. These ideas have become normalized to the point that this phrase can even be seen as a 'caring', 'practical' or 'realistic' response, especially when it's coming from a parent or carer. For example, a mother telling her daughter to cover her body in order to stay safe and avoid attention might, when challenged, claim that she is just trying to take care of her daughter, and I don't doubt that's the case. But the problem is that it doesn't actually make her any safer.

Altering someone's clothing will not prevent them from being assaulted – the choice to behave in a coercive, intrusive or dehumanizing way is entirely the responsibility of the perpetrator. In her research into women's experiences of sexual violence, Avigail Moor, clinical psychologist and head of the Women Studies programme at Tel Hai College in Israel, found 'no relationship between wearing "sexy" dress and actual experiences of violence'. We also know that although women in the US military disproportionately experience sexual misconduct (as they only make up 15 per cent of the force), 53 per cent of incidents of unwanted sexual conduct were perpetrated by men against other men. Irrespective of gender, the military dress code is full-coverage three-piece uniforms and combat boots, and when discussing sexual assault against men, clothing is rarely offered as an explanation or justification.

The evidence suggests that a victim's clothing has little to do with what motivates a perpetrator of sexual violence. But even if, hypothetically, this was the case and clothing were a factor in a perpetrator's choice of victim, then a change of clothing would only shift that intent to harm on to another person. So, when we tell our daughters to dress differently, we may be looking out for them, but maybe we should be looking out for *everyone's* daughters.

The just-world hypothesis may answer some of our questions as to *why* we blame victims of sexual assault. First developed by Melvin J. Lerner in 1960, this theory states that we hold on to the fallacy that we live in a 'just world', where actions come with morally fair consequences, and where 'good' people get goodness in return for their behaviour and 'bad' people receive the opposite. This binary fallacy means we can also assume that when something happens to us, there *must be a reason for it*, and so when we hear that something awful has happened to someone – or when it has happened to us – we search for that reason.

Let's take the case of a woman stating that a man has sexually assaulted her. If we were to interrogate the scenario critically – trying to disrupt our biases or internalized misogyny while doing so – we'd be forced to think about the 'why' and potentially acknowledge the culture that creates perpetrators. In doing so, we recognize perpetrators not as the movie-worthy caricatures they are so often depicted as in pop culture, but as everyday people with jobs, family and friends, and people who love them – people we know. After all, researchers from Glasgow University found that more than 90 per cent of rape and sexual assault victims know their attacker. Recognizing this reality forces us to acknowledge how much closer we are to the risk of assault than we might originally have thought, and how we too could become a victim. It's something we don't want to face.

When it comes to sexual assault, I genuinely think every person who lives under the shadow of misogyny knows, on some level, that they are navigating this risk, and without the ability to think critically, victim-blaming becomes a comfortable way for people to distance themselves from the problem and seek to reassure themselves: 'It wouldn't happen to me because I would make different choices' is comforting, and allows us to retain the mindset that we live in a 'just' world where things happen for a 'reason'.

Throughout history, women and people marginalized for their gender have dressed in specific ways depending on who might see them, adhering to dress codes informed by class and how they were racialized. These expectations have been reinforced not only by societal expectation, but also by legislation, and it is essential to consider this social act of gendered voyeurism when discussing victim-blaming.

In *Ways of Seeing*, art critic John Berger explores the heteronormative conditioning of the male gaze and how a woman is 'forced to survey everything she is and everything she does because of how she appears to men'. We know that asserting dominance over women acts as an enforcement arm of patriarchy, and that the sexualization of the female form is a way to assert that dominance. So it makes sense that, in response, feminine gender expression throughout history has been informed by patriarchal standards that seek to both consume and control.

Take workplace dress codes, for example. For men, these are designed to communicate social power and competence. For women, depending on the 'needs' of their bosses or the institution, they either draw attention to their physicality (wear heels for the meeting!) or conceal their bodies to enforce modesty (low necklines are distracting!).

Black women's clothing and gender expression has been – and still is – painfully over-policed by white supremacist heteropatriarchy. We witnessed this when officials at the French Open – which has historically enjoyed a relatively relaxed dress code – banned full-body catsuits after Serena Williams wore one in 2018, stating that 'players have to respect the game and the place'.

Serena faced complications while giving birth to her daughter and needed the suit to prevent life-threatening blood clots. She was just trying to do her job, yet she was confronted with the same misogynoir she'd faced countless times throughout her career. In the words of writer Amira Rasool, 'the over-policing of black women's actions and physical appearance is much more serious and deep-seated than a banned catsuit. For centuries, black women have been exploited and criticized for their appearance, and subsequently placed in lesser positions socially, economically, and politically.'

This policing of women's bodies always had so little to do with who they were and everything to do with how a straight, white, patriarchal society saw them, and the decision to deliberately disobey or rebel against those standards has always led to the dominant group's attempt to control what they saw as theirs.

In 1919, Puerto Rican activist Luisa Capetillo argued publicly that women should have the same rights as men. After wearing a man's suit in public, she was imprisoned. Some one hundred years later, we are witnessing a revolution in Iran in response to the devastating murder of women who chose not to comply with the state's hijab regulations. Masc-presenting women have their appearance ridiculed by cis men and are treated as a punchline by misogynists. Conversely, we see women who live up to society's expectations of their gender 'too' keenly – expressing their femininity by dressing hyper-sensually or sexually (traits patriarchy demands from women but brands 'slutty' and 'sinful' when it comes from autonomy) – blamed for being assaulted.

To successfully challenge victim-blaming mentalities, it's crucial to remember that the long-held heteronormative idea that men *biologically* have little self-control over their sexual impulses is a pervasive, archaic myth. It relies on gender essentialism, a concept that supposes we have immutable traits due to our sex that determine our behaviour and urges. The theory completely omits decades of social and environmental conditioning, and is a rudimentary way to evaluate something as complex as gender, power dynamics and sexual violence. Various studies have debunked the idea that hormonal urges or 'high testosterone' make sexual urges impossible to overcome, as evident in highly controversial cases of voluntary chemical castration in convicted repeat violent sexual offenders. In the words of German sociologist

Andrej König, 'I have never met a patient who said they took the medicine and now have no sexual fantasies or urges of masturbation . . . It doesn't change their fantasies either.'

Not only does the idea that a cis het man is completely controlled by his 'innate' and 'animalistic' sexual desires dehumanize men, research proves that nurture (rather than nature) plays a big part in the development of sexually dominant behaviour: how we and our society define and raise boys to understand masculinity. A landmark 2015 study at the University of North Dakota found that nearly one in three male college students admitted that they might rape a woman if they knew no one would find out, and that they wouldn't face any consequences. But when the researchers actually used the word 'rape' in their question, those numbers dropped considerably.

What this suggests is that these students didn't truly understand the definition of rape and didn't associate the act of forcing sex on to someone with the crime of committing rape, because, as the researchers reported, 'sexual aggression becomes an appropriate and accepted expression of masculinity'. To me, this research shows that the 'right to sex' assumption held by so many men is much less to do with 'supposed uncontrollable sexual urges' and much more to do with their view of manhood, their masculinity and its inextricable link to socialized misogyny. It demonstrates that too many men see women as passive sexual objects to consume and control as a means of defining or asserting masculinity.

Committing to the bio-essentialist idea that a man's sex drive is uncontrollable (and something that can be coerced or incited by women) is useful in ensuring the patriarchy – which only retains power by putting cisgender heterosexual men's needs before everyone else's safety – remains intact. This is the system that makes us prioritize accommodating perpetrators' 'needs' (see: choices) by recommending someone cover up rather than denouncing those perpetrators and working to solve the culture that's creating them. The problem, as always, is that unless we are working to actively unlearn what society has taught us about femininity, bodily autonomy and gender, we will all have inherited and internalized these ideas without even realizing, and so victim-blaming becomes part of the landscape of our conversations.

If someone tells you that you should 'cover up if you don't want attention', ask them to define what they mean by 'attention'. Remind them that attention is welcome if it's a compliment that comes with respect and personal space, but that attention and harassment or assault are completely different things. Remind them that in any other scenario, a person who is harmed isn't blamed for that harm – if you're hit by a car, you're not blamed for crossing the road, or even stepping out without looking. If you're mugged, rarely would what you were wearing be used in court as evidence against you, and yet the specifics of a victim's underwear have been used by the defence in rape trials. Ask why that is.

Note that assault isn't about sexual attraction but about power. It's a *choice*, and those who have the capacity to assault someone will do so anyway. Men who don't, won't . . . regardless of what you're wearing. Send them a link to the *What Were You Wearing?* exhibition in Brussels and remind them that if everyone who blamed a victim spent that energy denouncing perpetrators, maybe there would be less reason to have this conversation.

Finally, ask them if they could handle spending every morning deciding what clothes to wear in order to avoid being assaulted. If they are a man who has never had to do this, ask them to consider what it must feel like. Explain that one may do this because they have internalized this understanding of what causes sexual violence, even though we know that it is men – not clothes – who are responsible for 90 per cent of sexual assaults against women. If they are a woman who replies that they have done this because they believe it's their responsibility to safeguard themselves, meet them with sympathy and say you wish they didn't have to, but that you refuse to live your life from a place of fear. Tell them that the more we uphold habits that enforce these ideas about victimhood, the less equipped we will be to handle assault in a healthy way that disrupts the response of shame. This safety and support is what we deserve.

The key to responding to victim-blaming constructively – if you have the patience – is to recognize that if it's coming from ignorance or fear rather than from malice (and especially from someone who's experienced and been hurt by it), it's probably underpinned by a need to retain a view of the world as fair, a desire to keep hoping that everyone has agency over what happens to them and a wish to create space between them and a very real risk. Managing to keep a dollop of compassion will allow you to evaluate the root of their perspective, and it will go a long way in being able to discuss exactly *why* this phrase is so unhelpful.

Remind the person you're talking to that the world isn't

fair for women, and although it might seem like a solution to 'cover up', if someone wants to hurt you, your clothing isn't going to make a difference. If this person is a family member or friend tell them that, in using this phrase, they're also suggesting that *you* should be mindful when choosing what to wear and that only makes you less likely to go to them if something were to happen to you, for fear that they'd see it partly as your fault. This might finally encourage them to understand how victim-blaming makes us feel less supported and more ashamed.

Prompts for discussion

- If the person you're talking to is victim-blaming by talking about clothing choices, tell them about the *What Were You Wearing?* exhibition in Brussels, which showcased hundreds of outfits, from police uniforms to children's clothing, to demonstrate people are assaulted when wearing all types of outfits and that clothing cannot protect you from someone who wants to harm you.
- Discuss with them how multiple studies show that adult women cite the combination of guilt and embarrassment as a primary reason for not reporting assault. Ask them where they think that guilt is coming from.
- Discuss the definition of keeping someone 'safe'. Given how sexual assault and violence affects victims' and survivors' mental health, relationships

and sexual wellness, safety can mean different things. Will different clothing realistically keep someone safer? Or is it more important that support, open communication and a nurturing response is available to women who are subject to any offence on the spectrum of sexual violence.

Information to remember

- In the UN Women UK data, 80 per cent of all women said they had been sexually harassed in public spaces in the UK. It is likely someone you know will have been harassed or assaulted and hears you when you victim-blame.
- Victims of abuse suffer secondary trauma from being blamed for the harm they endured. Placing blame on the victim also reduces the chance they will seek help in the future because they fear they will be shamed or judged.
- Amish, Mennonite and Muslim women who choose to dress modestly have fought against the idea that modest clothing keeps them safe from sexual violence. Recent research suggests that as much as 48 per cent of Amish, Mennonite and other Plain children may have experienced sexual assault.

Ben Hurst (he/him) is the Head Facilitator at Beyond Equality, a consultant, presenter, podcaster, model and speaker.

"Men Aren't Doing Anything to Help Feminism"

Ben Hurst

I like to consider myself a bit of a conversationalist, at least professionally. As a facilitator for Beyond Equality – a gender equality charity that works to engage men and boys in the gender equality conversation through workshops and talks in schools, universities and corporate spaces – my job consists mostly of having different conversations with different groups of people. Over the last ten years, I've facilitated discussions in youth centres, churches, banks, theatres, barbershops and parks. I've facilitated conversations about relationships and sex, race and class, faith and the climate crisis, but the majority of these exchanges have been about gender equality and feminism, and, more specifically, about masculinity with groups of men.

Unsurprisingly, one of the most common questions thrown my way is: 'Why aren't men doing anything to help feminism?' This is a difficult question to answer, and an awkward one. On one hand, the phrase feels true and reflective of the reality experienced by the majority of us most of the time. Even if you're someone who knows men who are doing something to help feminism, those men are usually the exception to the rule or have found themselves taking an active role by chance or by accident, right? Like, your boyfriend is a teacher in a girls' school, or your dad treats you equally to your brothers, or your grandad watches women's football after some convincing. On the other hand, the obvious elephant in the room here is that the statement 'men aren't doing anything to help feminism' is a *massive generalization*, especially when a core tenet of feminism is the idea that people do not fit neatly into homogenous groups who all think, feel and do the same thing according to their biological sex or gender. So, there's a risk that we jump the gun if we try to respond to the statement before we've done any real thinking about where it comes from.

At Beyond Equality, compassion is one of the cornerstones of our work, so at all times, we try to understand that there's causality for everything. One of our agreed rules for group sessions is that participants must suspend judgement. The idea here is that regardless of how hard a thought or an idea may be to understand, there's always a reason why someone might say what they choose to say.

Working off the assumption that you, the readers of this book, are engaged with or follow Gina and her work, I imagine that you will, to varying extents, identify as feminists. Usually when feminists say something like this to me after a talk or a panel event, it comes from a space of frustration; the men in their lives are underperforming. Whether that means the men they work with overlook women for promotions, the men they live with don't pull their weight around the house, or the men they engage with on social media are eerily quiet when it comes to women's reproductive rights in their Twitter feed, the common denominator is that the men in their lives aren't doing enough.

You can usually see the exhaustion on the face of the person sharing. That feeling of constantly having to fight or battle to be heard or be seen, the result of any significant period of time spent swimming upstream without any rest. I know that feeling and I feel their frustration. And again, I'm left not knowing how to respond. Also, as a man, the last thing I want to do is come across as one of those 'not all men' guys, even though this is one of those rare occasions when the words teeter uncomfortably on the tip of my tongue like a child hanging off the edge of a climbing frame.

As well as the men who aren't doing enough to support feminism, there are the men who actively hate feminists and feminism. You can see them on social media reposting Andrew Tate clips and memes about feminazis. In her book *Men Who Hate Women*, Laura Bates shares that if you are brave enough to venture on to popular online forum discussion sites, you'll find entire chat boards and communities of men numbering in the hundreds of thousands who really do believe that women and feminism are the most urgent problems men face in society today. However, it is important for us to remember that while these ideas are pervasive, the majority of men have not been radicalized into this worldview. In actuality, a survey by the research firm Ipsos and the Global Institute for Women's Leadership at King's College London found that only about 32 per cent of men think feminism does more harm than good and 33 per cent believe traditional masculinity is under threat, with about 23 per cent believing feminism has resulted in men losing out economically, politically or socially. Seventy-nine per cent of men surveyed believe that gender inequality is something that actually exists and 82 per cent of men (according to this survey) disagree that violence against women is women's fault or women's responsibility.

So if the survey is accurate and most of us believe the right things on paper, why do bad things still happen so much? This question always comes up for us in workshops because the numbers don't seem to add up. If a majority of men acknowledge that gender inequality does exist and that women don't deserve to experience that inequality, why don't we do more to stop it from happening? Why is it that in 2022, almost one in three women has been subjected to physical or sexual partner violence and why do most women experience violence perpetrated by current or former husbands or intimate partners? Why is it that women in the UK are still paid anywhere from 76p to 95p for every £1 earned by a man? Women are experiencing global health, economic and education inequality, and the stark reality is that when we look at women's representation in leadership in the halls of power and the spaces where policies are made, this is quite clearly a men's issue.

The good news for anyone reading this is that I can categorically say that the statement 'men aren't doing anything to help feminism' in and of itself is not true. Through my job, I've had the privilege of meeting men all over the world who are working to help feminism – and loads of men who do this by working to help men. At Beyond Equality we've trained over 600 men in basic intersectional feminist theory, exploring topics such as power, privilege and allyship, while equipping them to go into schools and universities to have these conversations about masculinities with young men and boys. I've led workshops with men in which we've ended up having really productive conversations about masculinity and sexism. Usually, there's a bit of default humour in the form of some jokes about who's been sexually harassing who in the room, or some casual emasculation via the questioning of another participant's sexuality, followed by some defensiveness when challenged, which usually takes the shape of finger-pointing in someone else's direction or informing our facilitation team that the men in the space do, in fact, know and love their mums, sisters, daughters, aunties or wives. But then you see some deep reflection followed by a lot of questioning.

Most of the men I work with start from a position of not understanding that feminism is about them as well. Men almost automatically link the word feminism to the idea of being feminine (which is something they are socialized not to want to be) and so they equate feminism with issues pertaining to women, without understanding that gender equality actually includes men; that *man* is also a gender, and that gender equality is about the things that they've been denied as well.

In fact, if we want men to be involved in the movement, we may actually be starting with the wrong question. I often find that rather than asking what men are doing to help feminism, the question of what feminism has done to help men leads to really interesting conversations. Most men don't realize that feminist activists at the Feminist Majority Foundation created the Rape Is Rape campaign, which pressured the FBI to change its outdated definition of rape in the US from 'carnal knowledge of a female forcibly and against her will' to a definition that now includes all forms of penetration and no longer excludes men. Lots of men don't realize that there are feminists fighting for male survivors of domestic violence who feel that they can't speak about the harm they've experienced, or that feminists succeeded in getting laws overturned that discriminated against men being entitled to an equal amount of paternity leave, which in many cases equates to men's legal rights to access and perform caring roles within the family. And most men don't realize that better policies and practices for people of marginalized genders means better policies and practices for all of us.

Once men can acknowledge this, we can change from the statement 'men aren't doing anything to help feminism', to a new question: What does it actually look like in practice for men to help feminism? This is an important question because, historically, the bar for men has been super low in this respect – so low, in fact, that the criteria for joining the club seems to comprise a willingness to drop the F-bomb on a social-media or dating-app bio, or wearing a T-shirt that tells onlookers *you* are what a feminist looks like. The reality is that feminism is and has to be more than well-wishing for equal rights for women and girls. Feminism is and has always been a movement dedicated to the active work of challenging and dismantling the patriarchy wherever we find it, whether that is in ourselves, or in our communities or institutions. So where do we start?

Gender consultant Nikki Van Der Gaag suggests starting small – as a start, a good idea is for men to take up 50 per cent of unpaid domestic tasks. A study by the International Labour Organization in 2018 reported that, globally, women take up over 75 per cent of unpaid care work and researchers at King's College London and the Global Institute for Women's Leadership found that girls spend 40 per cent more time (that's 160 million more hours per day) on unpaid work compared to boys. These statistics have only been exacerbated by the Covid-19 pandemic. All of this only goes to show that the home is one of the easiest places feminism can start from and have an impact on, and that there's a lot men can do.

At Beyond Equality we encourage men to start by talking to other men. Another one of the most effective actions men can take is to address the harm that masculinity can cause with the other men in their lives. This might mean building emotional literacy about the subject or tackling the entitlement and sexist attitudes that underlie sexual harassment and sexual violence: calling out our friends or colleagues when they 'offer compliments' non-consensually to strangers in the streets, or picking up on the sexist jokes that often go unchallenged in our WhatsApp group chats.

When talking to the men in our lives about gender equality, it's also important to consider whether phrases like 'men aren't doing anything to help feminism' achieve what they set out to do. Most women I've met who say or have said phrases such as this do so in order to motivate men to take action. The problem with this approach is that almost nobody is motivated to action by shame. Shame and guilt actually often have the opposite effect – they paralyse people. In her work on Shame Resilience Theory, Brené Brown speaks about shame as '. . . the intensely painful feeling or experience of believing we are flawed and therefore unworthy of acceptance and belonging'. So, if our end goal here is to spur men to action, maybe instead of telling the men in your life that they're useless, or trash, or doing nothing to help, we can offer a solution or at least point them in the right direction.

The next time you hear someone use the phrase 'men aren't doing anything to help feminism', start by acknowledging their feelings with an 'I know what you mean . . .' Then ask them what they'd like men to be doing in an ideal situation. Point them in the direction of some men who *are* doing something to help feminism. Remind them that most men would consider themselves to be in agreement with the principles of gender equality, and therefore aligned with the ideals of feminism. They might just have trouble understanding the words we're using.

If you know men who are looking for ways to help, they can come and volunteer with us at Beyond Equality or find another organization that equips men to work towards gender equality. They can read books or watch videos and have conversations with other men in barbershops, at bars and pubs, or wherever it is that they hang out. They can pick up the slack for the women in their own lives – doing their fair share of the washing-up or the ironing or whatever unpaid domestic tasks are relevant. It's not really important what they do. They just need to feel like they can do something. And once they're doing something, they can think about doing something else, too. Not everybody has to be a campaigner or an activist to effect change in the world, but all of us need to do something, men included.

Prompts for discussion

- Do you have any examples of men who are actively supporting feminism and gender equality? Are there men in your personal or professional life who are doing this work in some capacity? It's useful to identify this before starting a conversation!
- Try a conversation starter with a man you know and explore their response with them, for example: 'When did you first become aware of your gender (not your sex)?' or 'What did you learn from your dad about masculinity?'
- Can you think of any concrete ways that a more gender-equal society might benefit men, in addition to women, trans and non-binary people?

Information to remember

- Currently, Beyond Equality has 111 active facilitators working across schools, universities and corporate spaces to engage men and boys in gender equality and masculinities conversations. Beyond Equality has trained over 600 men in total to facilitate these conversations in a range of spaces.

- Men Engage Europe is an international network for social transformation which has over 100 member individuals and organizations working towards ending patriarchal power and supporting women's rights, LGBTQIA rights and human rights.
- There are many organizations working to engage men and boys in gender equality around the UK, through campaigning, conversation and education, including White Ribbon UK, Future Men, Mentivity and the Smiling Boys Project.

“Not *All* Men”

I began to walk off stage as the thousand-person audience started to clap; a pattering of palms quickly turning into rapturous applause filled with whoops and whistles. I was having to take short steps because this talk had been about upskirting and, ironically, I had ripped a hole in my leather trousers as I’d entered the building. Generally, I avoid looking at an audience when I finish a talk because I can’t accept the applause without feeling slightly uncomfortable, but this time, in my peripheral vision, I noticed that some people were even standing, so I snatched a glance and was so touched.

As I tottered down the steps of the stage and snaked along the front row to my seat, I clocked two grey-haired ladies on their feet, nodding their heads as they clapped. Their expressions told me that something in my talk had resonated with them, and I hoped that I’d have the opportunity to speak to them after the event. Nothing makes me feel fuller than discussing shared experiences with women across different generations and from different backgrounds. I love the feeling that comes with it. It affirms my faith that the ‘solidarity’ we speak about does live between us in *some* way, even if we’ve never met.

I sat down next to Reyhaan, one of my closest mates, who was grinning and looking proud of me. Grace Dent was next to speak. She took to the stage and, within minutes, had the entire audience in stitches. I was laughing harder than I usually might and I know it was because of adrenaline or relief. I was so pleased the talk had gone well because Rey was here with me. Only a few friends have ever made the effort to come to my talks, and I can't believe how much comfort it brings, given how these years of campaigning have been the hardest of my life.

After the event, Rey made his way to an old English pub across the road to grab drinks and I hung back to thank the organizers and meet people after the talk. Eventually, I made my way out of the venue and, as I crossed the street, a middle-aged man stopped me. 'That talk was really hard-hitting and amazing,' he offered. He was genuine and seemed full of energy – or beer – and was excited to chat to me, which isn't something I take for granted. When part of your job is sharing stories and having discussions that critique the behaviour of a dominant group, members of that community can sometimes become defensive, often because they don't recognize themselves in what you've talked about. It's something I've experienced in my work when cisgender, heterosexual men sometimes approach me after talks to challenge me on my experience or opinions.

So, I had initially braced myself when the man had approached, but felt relieved that it didn't seem to be one of those occasions. I thanked him for the compliment and we began to exchange small talk before he gently revealed his guilt about having let slide some 'shady' behaviour from other guys in the past. Then came the response that I've noticed almost all guys will offer if they're yet to pick up a book on gender inequality: disbelief.

For about five minutes, I listened and nodded intently. I could tell this guy clearly didn't get to talk about this stuff with other people much – namely other men. It's something I know to be true from talking to the men in my own life, which is why I felt compelled to give him the space to express what he was feeling. As he talked, he seemed to become aware of the time he was asking of me, and tried to cram in as many observations and questions as possible.

'I just don't understand it. Like, how could you do that?' he exclaimed, pushing his hand down and then up to illustrate the act of upskirting someone with a phone. 'It's so clearly a minority ruining it for everyone. It's not *all* men. Would you say so? That it's not all men?'

I scrunched up my nose, tilted my head and nodded. I didn't ask, 'Not all men do what, specifically? Upskirt?' I didn't offer him the opportunity to define 'the problem' he was referencing, which would have given me the chance to explain that sexual assault wasn't the extent of what I was discussing. I didn't really say anything, to be honest. Because although he was well-meaning, and although he only wanted fifteen minutes of my time, I was exhausted. I was overworked.

Every time I deliver a talk – one that's taken me three days to prepare and forty-five minutes to deliver – I'm immediately met with the same responses, as if I haven't just offered a more nuanced way of thinking about said issue ten minutes beforehand. I smiled at this guy and asked if he was coming over to the pub. He nodded and put his hands up to gesture that he was creating space between us, as if he'd overstepped a boundary that I hadn't established.

'Oh! Yeah. Sorry, I'm chewing your ear off here!' he apologized. I reassured him and we took a few steps over the narrow road together.

'It's just so interesting to me . . .' He trailed off.

As we walked, I thought about how these oppressions can – at least in part – only ever be theoretical to people who don't experience them. I also considered whether that is part of the reason we are making such slow progress when it comes to building coalitions between cis men and women with a view to solving issues such as gendered violence, and what it would take for those theoretical problems to become cis het men's responsibility to help solve, too.

'Yeah. Me too.'

The pub's entrance was obscured by clusters of people holding pints and smoking cigarettes. I noticed an unusual number of them clock me as I brushed past. 'Your talk was great!' someone shouted enthusiastically. I laughed and thanked them. The guy I'd been talking to peeled off without saying a word and joined two other men who were crouched over a tiny wooden table covered in empty pint glasses.

In my overwhelmed state, I felt slightly miffed by this. It can feel as if I give my time to those who want it, but they check in and check out so easily. I brushed off the feeling as I saw Rey standing at the bar, grinning. He offered to buy me a drink and I smiled back, feeling the adrenaline start to wear off. I settled back in the warm comfort of my friend's company and asked for a large glass of red.

I come across 'not all men' consistently in my work, and always have done. Not just in post-event conversations, but in the comments sections under YouTube clips of interviews

I've given and articles about me on news sites. When audiences have been prompted to ask questions at my events, men have raised their hands to exclaim it in front of the audience – often framed in a hypothetical way as if it's something their friend has said, not them – and it's a card that's been drawn during drinks with friends.

'Not all men' is a reflexive, knee-jerk reaction from men in response to stories they don't want to hear, or ones they can't quite believe because those tales don't reflect their own experience or behaviour. It's the pub-chat version of Shaggy's 'It Wasn't Me', and although it is flawed thinking – because the bad behaviour of one individual doesn't necessarily implicate a group of people – it works in shutting down discussion brilliantly. It flummoxes you because of its factual accuracy. It's the kind of irrefutable statement that makes you more frustrated than you were to begin with – one that causes all your knowledge and arguments to fly out the window, leaving you able to offer only an exhausted, 'Well . . . no, but that's not the *point*, is it?'

Our society was built by and for white, upper-class, heterosexual, cisgender, non-disabled men and the ideologies that preserve their power. That's a fact of history. A specific demographic of people monopolized the development of systems both in the West, and globally through colonization (the brutal seizing of land and resources), establishing structures and ideologies, and planting the seeds for the society that we live in today. Many men today still inherit this power, both financially and socially, and the majority of our political, state, financial and media institutions are populated and run by this same demographic.

Systems and institutions being created by and for these men has resulted in a patriarchal society that is set on retaining power and upholding a gender hierarchy, and as a result, a society that seeks to control the feminine. That control of femininity, coupled with a cultural acceptance of masculine power as the status quo, means that if cis het men live within the gendered parameters set for them, they are widely accepted by society and retain power (though this isn't to say this restrictive archetype of masculinity doesn't come at a cost to both themselves and others). The behaviours and attitudes that were seen as 'masculine' (dominance, strength, and so on), and were historically enforced and traditionally encouraged, are now seen as the default. They go on relatively unchecked, because those dealing with their effects – especially the most destructive of them – lack the power to do so.

As a result, cis het men enjoy and expect certain liberties – the freedom to place their needs first, the freedom to engage with women and people of marginalized genders in a way that makes them feel powerful, the freedom to use violence or dominance to protect or to punish, and so on. These freedoms can feel under threat when they see a powerful man being held to account, and the bro code – which has taught cis het men that they must stick together or have their freedoms limited – is activated.

This power imbalance allows too many men to feel entitled to sexually abuse others without being held accountable, socially or legally. It's an imbalance that all cis het men benefit from and, when they allow it to go unchallenged, uphold. If you were to bring up a perpetrator in conversation, too many men's responses demonstrate that they see the recognition of others' acts of sexual violence as being too close to an admission of personal guilt.

This is especially true if the man in question has any misogynistic tendencies, because the expectation of accountability being levelled at the perpetrator demonstrates what could also happen to them if they were ever exposed. They know, on some level, that they have benefited from this power imbalance or leveraged it in certain ways, and so comes a defence that aims to extricate themselves from that commonality.

I believe this is one reason why 'not all men' is so often used reflexively. Sadly, it is at best unhelpful and at worst even harmful. In an instant, it can derail a conversation about a very real and terrifying problem, and instead prioritizes absolving the community responsible for perpetrating the issue. If uttered in response to someone talking about their experiences of sexual violence, as it was to me, it also implies one thing: 'You're exaggerating the problem.'

In Response to 'Not *All* Men'

The phrase comes up so often in discussions about misogyny, male violence, gendered violence and sexual assault, and historical data shows that the overwhelming majority of sexual assault and harassment offences against all genders are perpetrated by cis men. In the years ending March 2017 and March 2020 combined, 98 per cent of victims who had experienced rape or assault by penetration reported that the perpetrators were male.

The data suggests that men deal with sexual violence at the hands of men at a lower rate than other genders, and non-sexual violence at the hands of other men at a higher rate than other genders. Sexual violence is an epidemic perpetrated almost entirely by cis men against majority cis women, trans women and other people who are marginalized for their gender. In the UK, the year ending March 2020 saw the Office for National Statistics estimate that 4.9 million women had been victims of sexual assault at some point during their lives. But in the following year, Rape Crisis reported that only 1 in 100 rapes were recorded by the police. Given that the same report stated 5 in 6 women who are raped don't report it, the real number is expected to be much higher. Disabled women, who – according to ONS data for the two years preceding March 2020 – are almost twice as likely to have experienced sexual assault as women without a disability, face compounding barriers to reporting. Dr Hannah Morgan, a senior lecturer at Lancaster University's Centre for Disability Research, says there is 'strong evidence that disabled women have been less likely to be believed or seen as credible witnesses'.

Reporting numbers are even lower when sexual violence happens at the intersection of misogyny and anti-Blackness, and Black women are even less likely to report assault to the police. This is not surprising given the history of violence towards Black communities by the police, and the stereotyping and racism to which Black women are subjected in our legal system. In a 2020 joint report by multiple leading charities, Black and minoritized practitioners spoke of the daily challenge of supporting and preparing victims and survivors for the institutional racism and intersectional discrimination they are likely to encounter within the criminal 'justice' system.

South Asian women experiencing intimate partner violence also face unique barriers to reporting. Between 2013 and 2015 the British Academy conducted a study of police responses to women in South Asian communities who had experienced intimate partner violence. Amongst the reasons women cited for not reporting their assault included the belief that the police were all men who did not understand their specific cultural needs, the fear that their stories would not be believed, and the assumption that police would side with patriarchal figures in the victims' families.

For the year ending March 2020, an estimated 773,000 adults aged 16 to 74 years were victims of sexual assault (including attempts), with an estimated 618,000 female victims and 155,000 male victims. This reality that men are also victims of sexual assault is often brought up to deflect from the scourge of sexual violence against women, instead of having its own dedicated discourse, but who are the perpetrators of these assaults against men? Ninety-eight point five per cent of the rapists identified as men.

It's clear that male violence, and specifically sexual violence committed by men, is a terrifying problem, not just in our society, but globally. Every 10 minutes, somewhere in the world, an adolescent girl dies as a result of violence. Although its impact and extent differ across the world, the problem as a whole transcends class, race, culture, faith and geography; every single country is united in the common challenge of misogyny and sexual violence.

When you belong to the demographic that is responsible for creating gender inequality and that continues to perpetuate and benefit from it, conversations about the subject can be uncomfortable and confronting. In turn, discussions about male violence against women can make men feel implicated and complicit in some way, and compelled to remove any suggestion of their personal involvement. And look, given the scale and urgency of the problem, an immediate gut reaction of discomfort is understandable, particularly since men are socialized to reject feelings of vulnerability. However, rather than responding to this discomfort by using the phrase 'not all men' to shut down the conversation, more men have to take a breath, recognize the emotion, sit with it, pop it in their back pocket and work on it later. Remember, conversations about pain and trauma don't exist to make *anyone* feel comfortable. They exist to remove shame, create solutions and build emotional literacy about a shared human experience.

When we talk about sexual violence, even if we are specifically addressing a certain type of assault, the context of that discussion includes more than just the men who commit specific acts. Be it coercion, groping, upskirting, verbal objectification or anything else that results from the sense of entitlement that many men feel towards women, we are referencing a *spectrum* of behaviour that is born from a culture of misogyny in which these acts are normalized and expected; a culture where harmful iterations of masculinity can be left unchecked; and where the protection of toxic, harmful traits is prioritized over the safety and liberty of others. And it impacts everyone negatively.

Whether by action or inaction, consciously or subconsciously, most cis, straight men perpetuate a *culture* of entitlement and non-consensual sexualization (or objectification). Even if a man wouldn't commit assault himself, if he fails to question gender double standards, he is refusing to disrupt a culture of inequality that breeds violence. If he tells sexist jokes, he is complicit in that culture. When all of this is taken into account, the phrase 'not all men' starts to look quite different. Sure, if we're talking about rape and domestic abuse, then of course it's not all men, but if we're talking about the whole spectrum of misogyny – a cultural norm resulting from power imbalance and bred through social conditioning – then it becomes a majority of cis men. Almost all men are complicit, and although we can see things punitively ('he should be punished!'), when we offer men the reality of their actions with compassion, we also give them the opportunity to recognize their place in the problem and start to grow from that knowledge.

So, in response to 'not all men', if we're talking about the sharp end of sexual violence then no, of course it's not all men. But it's still too many. And if we're talking about sexual violence in general, then it's far, far too many. Too many men feel entitled to the bodies of others. Too many cis men believe that people of other genders exist in proximity to – or socially organized around – them, or for their own gratification.

Structural systems of oppression and restrictive Western ideals of masculinity have caused crises of masculinity that result in a spectrum of violence. During intimacy, too many men are *assuming* consent, having learned from a male-made, male-lensed society that their pleasure is the priority.

In the same category, too many men in bars are trying to turn a 'no' into a 'yes'. Too many men are letting their shady friend's actions slide, therefore green-lighting their behaviour. All of this behaviour contributes to and reinforces the spectrum of sexual violence. So no, not all men, but enough, and it's their job to help us solve this problem.

When the phrase comes up, how do we see it for what it is? Imagine, for example, you are mugged, and the first response, as you sit with your friends at the pub a week later, detailing the event, is: 'But not all people mug!' You'd be confused about the relevance of that statement to your story. Equally, imagine if your house is robbed by a group of teenagers. Precious items are stolen and the comforting familiarity and safety of your space is compromised by some unknown individuals. If your friends' or family's response is 'not all teenagers burgle', you'd question what would make them say that, because it would derail the very sensitive and immediate issue you're sharing with them.

What we require is for people to prioritize comforting you in that moment, not the reputations of people who have no relevance to the situation. That wouldn't make sense. Referencing the men who 'don't [insert action here]' is the same. It's not relevant. When someone is discussing any part of the spectrum of misogyny and 'not all men' is said or the innocence of other men is offered, whether they mean to or not, that person is prioritizing defending men they don't know. They're prioritizing distracting from their behaviour over listening to someone who is right in front of them – often someone they care about who is sharing a painful truth. That person is trying to open up about a traumatic experience that is happening, has happened, or they feel *could* happen to them and the people they love.

If we really want to shine a light on what men's role is in this space, then we should be responding to 'not all men' by discussing exactly what positive steps they aren't taking but *could* be taking in this fight:

- Not all men are calling out their friends when they say something sexist, degrading, mocking or harmful, and which they would never say about a cis, straight man.
- Not all men are self-educating, learning what 'rape culture' *really* means (past the buzzword) and how misogyny operates, which they could do if they picked up books by writers such as Jackson Katz, bell hooks and Clementine Ford.
- Not all men are courageous enough to recognize and admit that they might not understand the complexity of gender and what the gender binary is responsible for.
- Not all men are recognizing that they would rather engage in preventative measures that are traditionally masculine, such as walking a female friend home, than those that appear less 'heroic', such as having hard conversations with their friends.
- Not all men are listening instead of questioning and searching for evidence to soothe their own discomfort.

If someone employs the phrase 'not all men', tell them that of course not *all* men are perpetrators of sexual violence. However, all men are part of a system that encourages it or looks the other way, therefore encouraging it by inaction. Tell them that we are supporting a construction of masculinity that is born from the absence – or forceful rejection – of intimacy, vulnerability and softer traits, traditionally associated with femininity, and that this culture breeds dominance. Tell them that to start to solve this, we must challenge the unequal division of social, political and economic power among genders and disrupt the hierarchy, both in interpersonal situations (such as conversations like this) and in our institutions, because this system is hurting everyone, including the cis, straight men that are complicit in it. Our struggles may be different, but they come from the same roots.

Tell them that, most importantly, we know the majority of men are not making this conversation a part of their lives. Tell them that instead of pointing to who *isn't* perpetrating violence, there is a real opportunity to look at who *is*. And then remind them of the opportunities present in these types of conversation, because existing within the community that perpetuates a problem means being in a position to play a role in addressing it. Tell them that not all men join in this fight, but if they did, we may be having fewer conversations about sexual violence.

Men are in the room with the community that makes gendered hiring decisions, uses sexist language, hypersexualizes women because of how they're racialized, and perpetuates and encourages a type of masculinity that rewards dominance, entitlement and the manipulation of others, all of which leads to dehumanization, misogyny and the enforcement of harmful hierarchies. Tell them that if they are *in* the room, ultimately they have the power to *change* the room, instead of looking around and saying, 'Well, it can't be all of us!'

Prompts for discussion

- Although the phrase might not seem harmful, it is, because it distracts and derails a conversation by prioritizing the feelings of imaginary men who aren't relevant to the discussion over the safety of the person telling their story of sexism/violence. Try using the mugging/burgling analogy. Tell them it feels like they're prioritizing mending a perceived perception of themselves over comforting you or learning about the problem.
- Saying that the majority of violence is perpetrated by men is different to suggesting that all men perpetrate violence. Explain the difference. Sexual violence is only one part of the puzzle, and not all men perpetrate it, but enough do that we have an epidemic. If we can't accept that, we can't talk about it. And if we can't talk about it, we can't make it better.
- Show them the pyramid of sexual violence. Rape culture is everything from sexist jokes and language to violence, and all men are – whether participatory or passively – part of that culture because of an imbalance of power. It's not just about rapists, it's about all the stepping stones that get us there.

- Give the person you're talking to an opportunity by saying, 'The best way to prove "not all men" is to exclude yourself from being complicit in the harm caused by traditional masculinity. The only way to do that is to question it in your daily life and demonstrate a better, safer one that benefits all of us. Including men.' Less prescriptive masculinity means better relationships, less pressure to 'man up', parental rights and more.

Information to remember

- The Crime Survey for England and Wales (CSEW) reported that, in the year ending March 2020, perpetrators of violent crime were most likely to be male, being reported as so in over three-quarters of violent incidents (82 per cent).
- 6.5 million women in England and Wales have been raped or sexually assaulted since the age of sixteen, but RAAIN reported that only around 310 out of every 1,000 sexual assaults are reported to police, so the number is expected to be much higher.
- Worldwide, 1 in 3 women have experienced physical or sexual violence – most at the hands of an intimate partner.

Aja Barber (she/her/they) is a writer, editor and author of *Consumed: The Need for Collective Change: Colonialism, Climate Change & Consumerism.*

"We Need Fast Fashion for Poor People"

Aja Barber

I remember a period when I shopped all the time. And I don't mean once a month, I mean once a week, sometimes twice a week. I shopped for any reason and all reasons. Because I needed to cheer myself up, because I had a demoralizing and draining job. Because I felt like my self-worth was tied to my appearance and I am a Black person in a very white world. Because it was totally normalized in our society to shop that way.

I also returned a great deal of things. So many things it stresses me out to remember. I always had a weird feeling about what I was doing and my motivations for shopping the way I was. It certainly wasn't because of any great need, and as I began to dive into understanding the system that I sometimes felt trapped in, my mind was opened to many facts, some of which I definitely tried to avoid acknowledging. But there just came a point when I realized I no longer wanted any part of the system because I knew, at its core, it was rotten. Thus was born my platform.

Thanks to that period of endless shopping, I now own enough clothing that if I were to wear everything consistently, I probably would not need to buy another item for at least five years. Maybe underwear, but besides that, I'm good. My clothing is stylish, comfortable and fits me well. And if you're someone who shops pretty regularly, that's probably the case for you as well.

You ever feel poor? I bet you have. I have. Life is supposed to get better with every generation, but in recent decades, things just seem to be getting worse. I'm a millennial but I think Gen Z can get behind me when I say, 'How much more do we have to tolerate before things get better?' I graduated straight into a recession. And then there was another recession. I keep hearing that we're overdue another one. Today, more of us are graduating with enormous student loans, which feel hard to pay off. Credit-card debt is also rising in many countries. Want to buy a home? Well, good luck with that – according to the *Guardian*, adults in their mid-thirties to mid-forties are three times more likely to rent than 20 years ago. Oh, and on top of that, we're facing a little something called the climate crisis, which looks like (checks notes) mass extinction and a possible end to the human race and life on earth.

I mean, with all that to look forward to, literally no one can say we've been given an easy ride. It feels like the cards are really stacked against us and, at times, it doesn't even feel like we can look to our world leaders for answers. So, what do we do instead? We go shopping. We shop a lot. We buy five times the amount of clothing than we did in 1990. We can't solve the world's problems, but we sure know how to find a quick dopamine kick.

In a nutshell, it really doesn't feel like things are getting better. So, we buy things to pacify ourselves. But also because consumerism is everywhere in our society. As a matter of fact, those very same politicians who may not seem to be working together to solve the climate crisis sure do come together on one message, which is that we can shop ourselves to happier moments. I remember during the height of the Covid-19 pandemic, around Christmas 2020, when the then chancellor, Rishi Sunak, urged UK citizens to part with their money post-lockdown: 'I think people have been sitting at home, building up some savings hopefully and we would like to go and spend them when we get back.' Sunak is very, very wealthy. I . . . am not. It was reminiscent of when, post-9/11, George W. Bush encouraged Americans to get back out there and . . . shop.

Our increasingly consumerist society has significantly changed the way that we buy clothes. With 150 billion garments being pumped out annually, we have access to a constant stream of new items at increasingly low price points. For those of us with a certain level of wealth, our buying habits are often no longer need-based. Despite this, the language surrounding the purchase of clothing – particularly in the media – is still very much consistent with 'need'-based decision-making. It's not uncommon, for example, to see lists in fashion magazines itemizing the things that we 'Need! Want! Must Have!', particularly in September issues.

Thanks to the pervasiveness of this need-based messaging,

very few of us in the global North and wealthier countries have managed to avoid the pitfalls of fast fashion. You'd really have to have avoided most high streets and shopping centres in order to say you've never bought into it. And if you have ever felt the desire to buy things you don't actually need, then unconsciously you're a part of it, too. Even brands we grew up loving, like the Gap, who originally moved at a slower pace, began to speed up their own production around the year 2000 to keep up with the H&Ms, Topshops and Zaras of the world. Today, nearly every large brand has sped up its production to keep up with the pace of trends and microtrends, which move faster and faster as the race to the bottom has become the norm.

There is much to criticize about the world of fast fashion, yet somehow, to do so is often met with defensive retorts that you are being classist and simply don't like the 'poor' people who would supposedly be disadvantaged if we were to eradicate fast fashion entirely. Whenever I've heard this take come up in conversation with someone who buys fast fashion, it has always smelled a little bit off to me, not least because the people who are most impoverished aren't included in that narrative at all. To move the conversation to the class of the buyer without acknowledging the class of the garment worker is no doubt a half-baked argument, and it also obscures the already murky conversation about the supply chain. This approach reflects a problem I see again and again when people use rhetoric in the wrong way in order to make an invalid point . . . or to win an internet conversation. But if someone accuses you of classism in order to guilt you into being quiet so that they feel no guilt while consuming fast fashion, then, well ... nothing ever changes.

When we talk about fast fashion and its presence being to alleviate the needs of the 'poor', who exactly are we talking about and who are we including in the conversation? Unfortunately, I have really bad news. Fast fashion creates and keeps more people in poverty than it lifts out. And when I talk about those being kept in poverty, I'm speaking about the millions upon millions of garment workers who are most definitely not being lifted out of this system by the industry. When we talk about fast fashion and we don't include *everyone* in the conversation, including the garment workers, then we are engaging in something called 'protecting our own' and internalized colonialism; we're only deciding that fast fashion is a good thing because it looks like it's good for some of us. To talk only about the consumer in these conversations is to overlook the people who make these clothes, many of whom are some of the world's most poverty-stricken. But we do so because systems of colonialism and oppression have allowed us to 'protect our own' for many years.

Fast fashion isn't bought by every human on this planet. It's good to remember that half the world's population live on less than $5.50 (£4.60) a day. Those people can't afford to buy fast fashion and therefore aren't contributing to the problem. If you think fast fashion exists *because* it is consumed by poor people, I have really bad news for you. Take the United States as an example. The US is one of the largest consumers of fast fashion in the world, but guess how much wealth poor, working-poor and working-class people control as far as the United States net wealth goes? According to the

Resource Generation, it's 2 per cent. So, within that 2 per cent of the United States' wealth, do you think there's enough money to build as many billionaires as the fashion industry currently has? Look up any company in your local shopping centre. Look up the owners. Look at their wealth. Do you really think working-poor and working-class people did that with their spending power? Because I think we both know they didn't . . .

So, who is buying all these clothes? You and I. People with privilege and disposable income keep this system afloat and rolling. People who are shopping often. If you're buying only what you need, then you're not a huge contributor to the demand because those profit margins require customers who often shop multiple times a month. It's high time we understand our place in it all.

In conversations about fast fashion, we need to hold a mirror up to what is being said between the lines. Ever hear a friend or an acquaintance remark, 'Well, that's a good job in that country,' when talking about exploitative jobs in the manufacturing sector? Do you ever challenge their words? Would you ask the person if they would like to do that job? Because that's my response and the truth is . . . no one ever bounces back from it. What's between the lines is that none of us would want to have that job because it's an awful job. And the very idea that we believe someone from a country that has less economic advantage than our own should be so happy to work in such a dangerous or exploitative environment is riddled in the dehumanizing of others.

Take the example of the Rana Plaza factory in Dhaka, Bangladesh, which, in 2013, collapsed on top of workers and killed 1,134 people. The worst part is that workers had noticed cracks in the building but were threatened with job loss if they didn't continue to work. No one should have to work in those conditions and, often, it's even dangerous for workers to advocate for their own safety. Jeyasre Kathiravel, for example, was a victim of this. Kathiravel was a garment worker and union organizer who specifically spoke out about gender-based violence in the workplace. She was murdered by her supervisor. Dangerous.

Ever hear a friend say that they're too poor to shop anywhere other than fast-fashion stores? Hold your hand up if you have been poor. No safety nets. No idea how you were going to pay that bill with the red ink. No one to help. No couches to surf. Zero resources. Risking actual homelessness. No parents who you can eventually move back in with. Be honest about this. Now imagine that you live in Bangladesh, where the only job available for you is in a factory, which sometimes pays you, and when you and others ask for fairer wages you're threatened with dismissal (or worse). You dropped out of school at a young age to help support your family. You endure fourteen-hour working days and you could never afford to purchase the clothing you make because most days you can barely afford to feed your family.

Now, ask yourself – sure, different levels of poverty exist in the world, but do you fit any of those descriptions? For real. Because I truly don't believe the majority of us who regularly buy fast fashion (weekly or monthly) are poor at all. I've never been poor in my life. And when I say this, I mean no safety nets whatsoever. At the peak of my fast-fashion consumption, I would tell myself constantly that it was because

I was 'poor'. At the time my income didn't support me very well, and I'd be willing to take a stab in the dark and say that's the case for those of us who don't have any generational wealth. In the years that I made more than $20,000, I was doing well by my own standards, but those were poverty wages in the Washington, D.C. metropolitan area where I resided for much of my life. So yes, by those standards, I was definitely not considered one of the prosperous ones. But while understanding that my socioeconomic status didn't put me in the category of 'rich', I still found the cash to purchase fast fashion, sometimes more than once a month.

We might be broke. We might feel the squeeze of an economy that doesn't seem to be lifting many of us to the places we want to be. But remember, it takes a lot of money from the pockets of every class to create a billionaire. And if you look at who owns the majority of the world's companies that make cheap clothing, it's all billionaires at the top. Sometimes multiple billionaires. But you swear you do actually want to help those who struggle with financial insecurity?

Now that we know that fast fashion isn't going to lift anyone out of poverty, let's talk about the solutions that actually will. Jobs. Raising wages. Everywhere. For you and for the person making the dress. The truth of the matter is, we shouldn't live in a world where anyone has to make a decision whether or not to buy a sweatshop garment. And we certainly shouldn't live in a world where someone has to make the sweatshop garment. If you're the person who truly doesn't have to buy a garment made in a sweatshop, maybe you should be the first person to stop.

That was me. I know it sounds shocking but buying nothing or buying less is one of the best things you can do to improve this system. Taking your money and putting it elsewhere when you have a choice has enormous impact because, as I noted in my book, *Consumed: The Need for Collective Change: Colonialism, Climate Change & Consumerism*, the consumer voice does have a lot of power. We're not going to have a better, fairer world if we participate in the same systems that have built and maintained themselves off the exploitation of others. Never going to happen, and many of these corporations have had plenty of time to fix their faces. The global lockdown of 2020 was one such example when, given an opportunity to do the right thing, many big brands decided to walk away from clothing orders and refused to pay for clothing from factories. And they did it because they could. No one who's making billions of dollars is that interested in changing the system from which they continue to profit.

Consumerism encourages us to approach shopping from the perspective of what we want rather than what we need. So, it's crucial that we all learn to separate needs from wants. A need for me would be something like 'I don't have enough underpants to last me two weeks, so I need to buy new underpants.' A need isn't 'The trends have shifted again and none of my summer dresses from last year are on trend, so I need five new ones.' Participation in trends is very much a luxury but the trend cycle isn't something I miss at all. This system is not good for any of us and, ultimately, at the end of the day what I want most is for us to get free . . . together. All of us.

Prompts for discussion

- Feeling a real need to shop and don't like it? Unsubscribe from every marketing newsletter you're signed up to and uninstall all your retail apps. They exist for a reason and that's to tempt you. It'll feel weird and maybe make you sad at first. But by the second week you'll feel an enormous peace of mind. Trust me – I went through the same thing.
- Clean up your social media. Who are you following? Do they inspire you to buy things you may not need? Unfollow. I promise they won't even notice!
- Change how you spend time with your friends. Do you and your friends get together and shop a lot? Try redirecting those hang-outs. Movies. Museum visits. Hikes. Or, even better – volunteering! When I stopped buying fast fashion, my best friend did too, and our friendship grew enormously because of it.

Information to remember

- The fashion industry produces 100 billion items a year and the average shopper buys 68 items of clothing per year – that's a lot of clothes that we don't need. Challenge yourself to buy fewer new items. Track every purchase, including how much you spend, and see if you can reduce to perhaps 30 new items, and the rest being second-hand. See how long you can go without buying a single new thing.

- The fashion industry is a large contributor to the climate crisis – yup, we're cooking the planet for our clothes. According to the Fashion on Climate report, 'the fashion industry contributes approximately **2.1 billion tons of greenhouse gas emissions** in a single year, equivalent to 4 per cent of all global emissions'.
- This is a feminist issue. Approximately 80 per cent of garment workers are women and the fast-fashion industry disproportionately disempowers women.

"I Don't Do Politics"

In the spring of 2015, I was in the heady first year of my first paid job in advertising. If you worked as a creative – an 'ideas person' – in adland, it was an all-consuming job. I was a junior art director and Jenn, my best friend at the time, was my copywriter. We'd met at university in Leeds, where we'd both studied Creative Advertising. We made a good pair. Getting our first ad jobs meant we threw ourselves headfirst into London life, and we could finally afford to buy a glass or two of wine at the pub instead of sharing a five-pound bottle at work before we headed out in Soho.

It was an exciting time. I was young, new to city living and thought about nothing else other than my career, my family and friends, and fun. I was twenty-three and although I had a rudimentary understanding of feminism (not that I was prepared to call myself a feminist out loud), I hadn't made critical thinking and conscious learning part of my everyday life. I responded to news stories about social inequality and the suffering of others with anger or despair. I'd read a story on my phone on the way to work and it would ruin my day. If I talked to someone about it, I became easily riled. In my work, I often looked for ways to help; I worked with a collective of women who created marketing campaigns pro bono for a wonderful cancer charity. When briefs came in that were for social-impact initiatives or charities, I was desperate to work on them over other brands.

Despite these inclinations, I'd be lying if I said I cared deeply about politics back then. Keeping up with the news, for me, meant reading the *Metro* every morning on the Northern Line and skimming through the *Evening Standard* on the way home. I spent more time poring over the 'Rush-hour Crush' section than I ever did current affairs. I only really picked up a newspaper with any interest when my insulation from the world's problems seemed to grow thinner and I started to feel more exposed to the issues dominating the headlines. When the 2011 riots happened, I didn't make enough effort to understand them until they broke out in Leeds – where I was living at the time – and I felt involved. In 2013, when the UK's terror threat level was raised to 'severe' and the media began constantly covering the rise of ISIS as well as reporting on what thwarted terror attacks meant for London – a city I'd just moved to and was already intimidated by – I'd spend hours at work scrolling through news reports on the subject, the images burned into my mind.

In 2014, when the Ebola outbreak in West Africa was at its height, I had a similarly obsessive reaction, filling my head with information about the outbreak and washing my hands at every opportunity – even though the virus hadn't been detected in the UK. The way I reacted to news stories and current events – and the ones I chose to react to – was driven by fear for my personal safety. I didn't consider the collective, the context or where the problems I read about in the news were coming from. I never connected the dots.

I somehow saw catastrophic weather events happening but often didn't link them to climate change. I was too wrapped up in my own world, and any interest I had was always around the 'what' and never the 'why'. The news was something somewhat removed from my life, given it rarely touched me personally. I was a privileged person living in an individualistic way because society allowed me to do so.

If, over an espresso martini on a night out, you'd asked me if I was political, I would have most likely replied that I hated politics. And I did. I'd grown up in a working-class family – although my father's job as a session drummer allowed us access to some middle-class experiences – and we weren't a 'political' family, in that my parents didn't have a vested interest in politics. They were very much of the mentality that politicians don't represent or understand regular people. In that sense, as a family, we still feel that way. Like so many others, our evaluation is that politics is about power, profit and status, not about people.

My familial heritage for generations stretches back through Liverpool; a city on the fringes of Britain geographically and politically. It's a world away from London, and it would be disingenuous to act as if that hasn't had an impact on my political leanings. Liverpool's history is heavily rooted in industrial labour and its socialist heart is due, in part, to the fact that 80,000 of its inhabitants lost their jobs between 1972 and 1982 when the labour economy collapsed. The city was forced to rebuild itself in the shadow of Thatcherism and there's no doubt in my mind that a Scouse, working-class mentality is part of the reason my family rejected politics.

Over the years, my dad – who is knowledgeable about history – is the person from whom I've learned the most about world events. We still don't discuss politics in the 'traditional' sense, though, and I'm certain this is because he sees it as a grossly corrupt, elite and disheartening system over which he has no influence. This became my mindset, too, which crystallized as I grew up and continued to see politics as something both geographically separate from me (London and the North feel like wildly disparate places) and at odds with our experience in the world.

I also felt some sense of misguided pride in not engaging because it meant I wasn't then engaging with the corruption, greed and elitism that defines politics. It wasn't that I didn't have any interest at all, but when I read about Westminster, or the different political parties, it made me angry, depressed and confused, and so I just . . . didn't. Political science calls this political apathy, and it's characterized by a distinct lack of interest. It causes you to totally avoid all mention of politics, and lack curiosity not only about what's happening in the Houses of Parliament but also in anything associated with it: elections, political events, public meetings, voting. So many people I know feel like this. So many of us see politics as a cynical contest of egos that's best avoided.

By 2016, I'd left my ad job and moved to Greece to work on boats. It had taken less than two years for the stressful long hours and partying of London adland to get to me. I was done with slugging away on a pitch until 3 a.m., falling asleep on the way home in an Uber I couldn't afford and making my way back into the office for 8 a.m., all while trying to survive on a living wage. I couldn't save a penny and I couldn't see a day when I'd be able to rent a place of my own, so I decided to jump before I outstayed my welcome, and took a year away to join my boyfriend and work on the ocean.

Four months into our season, one scorching hot day during the height of summer, I was picking up groceries when I saw an English newspaper with Theresa May's face plastered across the front of it. I wandered over and flicked through the pages; May had just been elected prime minister. I'd been so isolated out on the sea that I hadn't even heard updates on the leadership race. I gleaned, by reading only a few lines, that the narrative around Theresa May's election focused on her gender, and the more I read, the more this was confirmed – 'First Female Leader Since Thatcher' was to be the default messaging.

The point of such a narrative was to suggest that by virtue of being a woman, May's policies, decisions and priorities must automatically benefit all British women. Even as a fairly ignorant young, white feminist living on a boat in Greece, I knew this not to be true. Her priorities and politics were regressive and didn't reflect mine, and she wasn't advocating for working-class people. If, as a cis, straight white woman like her, I felt this way, then there would be many more who felt that difference much more keenly. She absolutely didn't represent all women by dint of being one.

I've since learned the details of Theresa May's political career, and how right my instincts were. She spearheaded Britain's racist and inhumane immigration policy, gloating that the aim was to 'create . . . a really hostile environment for illegal immigrants'. I learned through my job in marketing when I returned to the UK that she ran an advertising campaign that featured an image of a person in handcuffs, which told illegal immigrants to 'go home or face arrest' and was emblazoned with green text in the style of an official stamp stating '106 arrests last week in your area'. These racist intimidation posters were placed in six London boroughs with substantial populations of Black and Asian communities and directly fed into the ethno-nationalism and inhumane treatment of immigrants in Britain.

In 2018, she oversaw the Windrush scandal, in which members of the Windrush generation of Caribbean British citizens were threatened with deportation by the Home Office and, in at least 83 cases, were illegally deported from the UK. The scandal also caused thousands of people who were in the country legally to be sacked from employment and denied access to health care. The Home Office demanded money from them illegally, exiled them and prevented their return to the UK, leaving so many destitute.

I discovered that May's austerity policies made working women's lives harder. In their report 'The Impact of Austerity on Women in the UK', the Women's Budget Group found that women use more public services and are the majority of welfare benefit recipients, and that during May's tenure central government funding for local government, which is responsible for a range of local services, fell by 30.6 per cent in 2017 and 2018. They also found that since 2010, 17 per cent of specialist gender-based violence refuges in England have closed and that a third of all referrals to refuges are turned away due to lack of available space. May's policies negatively impacted disabled people, including disabled women. She oversaw the abolishment of the Disability Living Allowance, replacing it with Personal Independence Payments, which resulted in disabled people across the country losing access to benefits. There is no world in which Theresa May's leadership was better for women simply because she was a woman.

Although I didn't have the words to articulate this back in 2016, I felt that this media over-simplification was damaging. I didn't 'do' politics, and I didn't have faith in Theresa May, so for the rest of 2016 I took no interest at all in her leadership, or British politics, as I sailed the Ionian Sea. Little did I know that by the same time the following year, I'd be working with her.

It wasn't until I was in my mid-twenties that I started to be more of a critical thinker; someone who recognizes cultural, social and geographical contexts and applies theories, such as the framework of intersectionality[1] established by Kimberlé Crenshaw – pioneering scholar and writer on civil rights, critical race theory and co-founder of the African American Policy Forum – to analyse and evaluate social realities and the system that creates them in order to draw a more contextualized and informed conclusion. (By comparison, the analysis of someone who doesn't engage in critical thinking will be determined mostly by their automatic emotional response, their personal context and existing opinions.) So, even when I reached the point where I would happily call myself a feminist out loud, without critical thinking I wasn't able to leave the comfortable confines of white feminism – which was built around self-optimization and individualism and encouraged me to view everything through the lens of my whiteness and my view of the world.

Without learning about and trying to implement critical thinking, I wasn't able to analyse things intersectionally and in a way that reflected the diverse, complex realities and systems that make up our collective experience. Rather, I thought about things individualistically and in an interpersonal way – racism was walking down the street and calling someone a slur; misogyny was your boss not paying you the same salary as your male counterpart, a man not taking you seriously or – God forbid – assaulting you.

Viewing everything through this interpersonal lens meant that I lacked the necessary context to see the bigger picture. I hadn't yet zoomed out and figured out frameworks to understand things *structurally*; that society is a constellation *built* and developed on complex contexts, and that the levers and pulleys of its construction work every day in ways that benefit specific ideologies, people and outcomes. To use an analogy, if my car brakes failed, I never stopped to consider the mechanics of the car to understand why this had happened and what had caused it.

When I started to learn about frameworks and apply them to my thinking, I began to understand that the patriarchy is a system and social order – an ecosystem of sorts – built by men that impacts everyone, including men. I understood that racism is hard-baked into our institutions and organizations, and is reinforced by rules and policies that prevent equal opportunities and representation. I also came to understand that inadequate wealth distribution exists today because it was, and remains, one of the tools of white supremacy to construct and maintain social hierarchies.

In the past, my inability to prioritize structural thinking

meant I had no real idea of what created the environment that *allowed* me to reject politics. I just couldn't picture something that big and complex. I had no sense that so many people *couldn't* 'opt out' of it in the ways I had, and I didn't understand what my choosing to do so meant for everyone else. Back then, I saw politics as an institution confined to Westminster, rather than a holistic system that affects every aspect of our lives. I saw myself as an individual, separate from it. I certainly didn't see myself as part of that very system that prioritized or de-prioritized people depending on who they were and how much value they brought to its agenda. In my eyes, my political action – or inaction – was something that affected only *me*, and because of the life I lived – who I was and the privileges I enjoyed – I subconsciously knew that it wouldn't affect me that much.

Life-changing events such as living in unsafe housing, being denied healthcare or living in constant fear of immigration forces weren't challenges I faced, and they still aren't. However, maybe if those kinds of fundamental struggles had been part of my experience, I would've been more politically motivated, because fighting would have been critical to my quality of life, my survival and, potentially, my way out of struggle.

In my everyday life, because of my whiteness, I don't deal with constant racist microaggressions and dehumanization. I don't have to defend myself and my rights against both people and institutions. How society racializes me doesn't create barriers that jeopardize my chances of getting a job or buying a house, or even just being safe when I give birth in a hospital. Because of my status, I don't have to fight against being forcibly removed from the country or being excluded from certain aspects of civil life.

Although historical erasure of women, their bodies and their biological experiences in medicine puts me at a disadvantage when seeking healthcare compared to men, my gender is recognized and accepted both socially and legally by health services. Therefore I face fewer barriers to traditional healthcare services than trans and non-binary people, and I am not subject to the experience of dehumanization, or a lack of options when it comes to treatment within the system. As a woman without a physical disability, society is built for me to navigate.

When I started to apply critical thinking, I understood the absence of these barriers as social advantages, and not engaging in politics meant that I wasn't using these privileges for the common good. I was leveraging them for myself, and nothing else. 'Not being political' was an easy option for me that required no effort or self-reflection. To subscribe to apathy meant my life would stay relatively the same. However, for others that wasn't the case; they couldn't choose to opt out. Their very existence was *made* political.

It wasn't until I'd returned from Greece in 2017 and attended a day festival that politics became personal to me, and I was jolted out of my ignorance. That was when I was upskirted, and was told there was nothing that could be done. That was when I looked into the law to find upskirting wasn't a sexual offence in England and Wales, even though it had been in Scotland for ten years. That was when I decided to take politics into my own hands. I decided to 'do' politics. Quite honestly, it shouldn't have taken something that traumatic or that drastic for me to properly engage. And therein lies our problem.

In Response to 'I Don't Do Politics'

This phrase is one I'm sure is uttered in households across the country every single day. It is grumbled to end a particularly terse conversation around the dinner table, shouted at the television before switching off the news, or muttered at the pub in an attempt to get back to more light-hearted conversation. Honestly, I empathize somewhat with the people who use it, because rarely is a conversation about politics a positive one. And crucially, there are a number of reasons why someone might not want to engage with politics in the first place.

I refused to do so because I didn't recognize my part in it and benefited from not engaging with it. For others, the inherent imperialism and academic nature of politics might feel intimidating or infuriating, or they might be uncomfortable facing the reality that the system is corrupt and morally bankrupt to the highest level. There's a chance they might come from a fortunate background and be insulated from the struggles that politics fails to address, so therefore see no reason to engage. On the flip side, it might not have occurred to them to engage in politics, having never seen anyone who looks or sounds like them represented in the halls of power. It's also true that the systems that operate within British politics have caused so much pain and struggle in some people's lives that not listening is simply an act of self-preservation. The greater the impact political engagement has on a person's mental and physical health, the more understandable it becomes for them to have tapped out of engaging with the political system.

Our motivations for not engaging in politics might differ, but when we do engage, there's one thing we all have in common – we are worn down by it, and I don't think that's an unintentional consequence. There's nothing as divisive, complex, elitist or exclusionary as traditional politics, and UK politics is no exception. It's not only the leadership battles, the slanging matches in the press or the lack of empathy shown by our representatives; Westminster itself is just *exhausting*.

Everything about it feels ostentatious and drawn out by design. Even the language used to describe basic aspects of the system is inaccessible and archaic. For example, the individuals in charge of maintaining order within their parties are called 'whips', but if MPs act inappropriately, they might also have their 'whip' removed. To confuse us even further, whips send out a document to party members each week called 'The Whip'. Doorkeepers – who let MPs in and out of the Commons – shout things like 'Who goes home?' when the House rises. No one answers.

All of this turns politics into a sort of unrelatable spectacle instead of a working representation of modern British life. Our system of governance clings to its long imperial history – its legacy – and, in doing so, alienates most of us. Westminster is something to be *deciphered*, and that's not to say the average person doesn't have the ability to understand it, but the number of traditions, customs and rules within the institution simply make it harder to put in the time, energy and effort to do so.

I felt like that. For example, I used to see engaging with British politics as a potential solution to assault. My work since has afforded me a new perspective on this, but at the time I started campaigning for the law on upskirting to change, I had no understanding of the process of how a law comes to be, what a bill is, who can table one (and who can't), or even how the first-past-the-post system and elections actually work. These are important footings of the current system under which we exist and they change how we live, so we should understand them, right? Sure. But it's hard to engage with something that's, well, not at all engaging.

Take the voting system, for instance. It's an outdated relic from a previous way of life and it's intentionally kept that way, rather than developed into something that reflects the post-digital age in which we now live. The system doesn't support automatic registration, and even our voting card looks like a piece of boring junk mail. Call me a conspiracy theorist but I think much of this is deliberate. If Parliament really wanted to make its processes more digestible, accessible or transparent, it could, but it doesn't serve its interests. It actually works out perfectly for Westminster that so many people – especially young people – feel confused and frustrated by the process and tap out.

Successive recent cabinets, the majority of whom are privately educated, wouldn't have been able to retain power in such an effective way if they weren't protected and cocooned by a system so complex, exclusive and intimidating that infiltrating or potentially having a positive effect on it feels absurd to the average person. It's understandable, when you look at the British political system, that so many Britons see voting as the most they can do, and not the least.

Despite this, for decades, groups have organized and coalitions have been built across identity lines to fight, vote, petition and strike for their rights. In many instances they may have felt they had no choice, because to sink into apathy would be to allow things to get worse, affecting the material conditions of these individuals' livelihoods, infringing on their rights or potentially putting their lives in danger. It's unquestionable that class struggle arising from the organizing of diverse working-class communities has allowed for material improvements. In 1842 the Early Closing Association fought for retail workers' rights and lobbied the government to keep Saturday afternoons free for worker leisure in return for a full day's work on Monday. This laid foundations for healthier working conditions, which, along with union lobbying and Jewish workers advocating for the Sabbath day of rest, led to the modern phenomenon of the weekend. Without labour movements, gender-equality movements, community-action groups, campaigners for safe housing and those fighting to change discriminatory policies, who knows how much more challenging our day-to-day lives would be? It's difficult to recognize a reality you *didn't* have to endure, but that's what some campaigning and advocacy does. It prevents as well as progresses.

Most often, it's the people who are enduring discrimination and inequality who are driving change, but those efforts to move the dial have to fit in around everyday life; a life that, especially in the absence of financial and social status or privilege, is punctuated with challenges created by the glaring systemic failings you want to be solved in the first place. Caring for your children when childcare is extortionate makes the fight for parental rights harder. Dealing with poor mental wellness and advocating for increased awareness of mental-health issues is harder when mental health is insufficiently accommodated by an increasingly privatized NHS. The people fighting to make change are 'doing politics' even though our political system continues to hurt them.

This is why it's so disheartening when those who are insulated from these struggles and have economic and social privileges – disposable income, time and resources – proudly proclaim they 'don't do politics'. For example, a single mother on a low income may already be fighting to keep her job and care for her kids, so to advocate for the change she needs is outside of her emotional and practical bandwidth. However, a more highly paid man she works with, who is also a parent but isn't impacted by the motherhood penalty, could more easily use his time, position of power and experience to advocate for better parenting rights in their workplace. For him to throw his hands up, write off parenting discrimination in the workplace as office politics and not get involved is incredibly frustrating, because women such as his co-worker have been doing that heavy lifting on advocating for parental rights.

When you take this example and apply it to society as a whole, you see that the only reason those with social advantages and privileges *can* kick back in the first place is because other people are continuously doing the work *for* us. To be a person of multiple, usable privileges and disengage from 'politics' is to apply more pressure and responsibility to marginalized communities and miss an opportunity to apply pressure to powerful and corrupt individuals who run the country. It is a waste of power rooted in the fact that so many of us don't (or aren't forced to) see the personal as political. But it is. Politics is omnipresent. It is to be found wherever humans negotiate and decision-make. Every single government policy will have a social and economic impact on every one of us, in every area of life – be it the flow of traffic in our town, the cost of our heating bill, or how readily and quickly we're able to seek treatment if we break an ankle.

To engage in society is to engage in politics, and helping people shift their idea and definition of 'politics' from the macro (Defence spending! Foreign policy! Leadership battles!) to the micro (The language in your employment contract! Redistributing money! Not backing down to your landlord on your rights!) makes engaging with it feel more emotionally manageable; less a specialist, academic subject to opt in to and more a normal part of your life. When you ask, 'Why hasn't the local council filled in that pothole?', 'How could this dress from Shein possibly cost £3?' or 'Can I take a lunch break even if my boss wants me to work through it?', you are engaging in politics.

This re-framing can be a vehicle for viewing traditional politics in a new way. Instead of talking to your uncle who doesn't 'do politics' about the prime minister misleading Parliament from the dispatch box or by-election outcomes, start with something relevant to him, like how his pint costs more because of inflation. Instead of political conversations being about what 'trickle-down economics' is (although can we agree we reject that theory?!), when your family member brings up the price of gas, maybe mention that energy firms have recorded record profits while in April 2022, the largest increase in gas and electricity prices ever pushed a further 2.7 million UK households into fuel poverty (and that there's a petition you want them to sign if they have a second). Linking everyday experiences to the bigger picture demonstrates that these things are the result of policy decisions and aren't just abstract, or 'the way things are'.

Responding to 'I don't do politics' with examples that demonstrate how politics affects us *every single day* is useful because connecting it to the mundane and everyday makes it feel more digestible, relatable and *real*. Instead of picturing multi-millionaire Rishi Sunak when your uncle thinks of politics, he might begin to think of everyday people doing everyday things; people he relates to. Because that's what politics is actually about – people. Us. It refers to how we are organized, the hierarchies that were designed to manage us and the power at play; it exists in our workplaces and relationships. Our lives are inherently political – some are made more political than others by our government – but no matter who we are, we engage with politics every single day. We can believe we are outside the system, but that doesn't make it true. We need people to acknowledge that even when they say they don't 'do politics', they do it without even knowing it. Then, step by step, we need them to start engaging with it in a way that's empowering to them.

This is exactly why it's so important that we make conversations about politics more accessible for everyone, and knowing how to respond when someone says 'I don't do politics' is a bloody easy place to start. In the first instance, ask them why they feel this way, then really listen to their answer.

Try to put yourself in their shoes. If they say that it's depressing, then agree with them and acknowledge the validity of their response – *agreeing* that politics is depressing instead of shutting someone down can give you an opportunity for a chat to go further on another occasion.

If the person you're talking to rejects politics because they think political discussions are only for highly intellectual or academically minded people, tell them an elitist system makes it seem this way but there's no need to know it all when it comes to having honest conversations. Tell your friend or relative that being political doesn't have to mean learning the vocabulary of Parliament, mastering a set of complex ideas, or analysing the ins and outs of the political processes. It does not mean having a hot take on the latest by-election, or knowing what a 'whip' is. It means talking, in *our* words, about the things that matter to us, being open to honest discussion about how those opinions impact others and grounding our actions in a compassionate understanding of what makes a fair and decent society for *everyone*.

If they reject politics because they think being political requires grand ambitions or committing to specific kinds of action, tell them that it isn't defined by organizing marches and doesn't have to mean becoming a member of a political party, especially if those parties have been part of your community's ongoing subjugation and disenfranchisement. It can mean reading, listening, starting small and, going at your own pace.

If you're talking to someone who is living at multiple intersections of oppression and 'doesn't do politics' because the candidates and policies on offer at best don't represent them, and at worst have historically caused them harm and continue to do so, be compassionate. Recognize that in the same way as engaging when you have power and privilege is important, disengaging when you are being consistently hurt by the system is an act of self-preservation and courage. We might disengage in traditional politics for different reasons, so, during discussions, it's all about trying to park your political affinity and judgement at the door and understanding their 'why'.

Being involved in politics simply looks like understanding where you sit in society, knowing where you hold power and privilege, and using that where and when you can – to make life a little easier for people who need it. It means seeing us as connected in a society that encourages us to prioritize only ourselves and those who look and sound like us. And sure, at the absolute least it means voting, but doing so unselfishly, and in the interests of the majority.

It all starts with a conversation. So, the next time someone says 'I don't do politics', respond warmly with a question and listen to them. Hear them. Are they flippant or are they angry? Are they mocking? Are they fearful? Are they beaten down? Is there positive political stuff you can chat about? 'It's so cool that the Lionesses are trying to make it so that every girl in the UK can play football,' will inevitably be followed with 'What, they can't already?' and, technically, you have yourself a political conversation.

Find a way in that interests them and encourage them to find out more on their own time. In the words of Steven Horwitz, author and director of the Institute for the Study of Political Economy at Ball State University: 'Every time we engage in the conversation about what is wrong with the world we live in and how we might make it better, wealthier, more just, or more peaceful, we are being political.' Remember that discussions about politics don't have to be centred around politicians, that it isn't always about the people in the ornate halls of Westminster, it's about you and me, and looking after each other.

Prompts for discussion

- Consider the things you care about most and think about a law that governs them. Instantly you'll see how much politics affects you. Reflect on how much more time you'd give to it if it affected you in a significantly more negative way than it does now.
- Do you think your apathy about politics as a whole is because you dislike traditional politics, hate how complex it is, or disagree with how it operates? Use this 'why' as a starting point for compassionate discussion.
- Try to think of examples of politics that aren't 'Westminster' per se, but more 'everyday' and are relevant to that person, and offer, 'you do politics when you _____'. Examples might be: dealing with payroll at work, buying a house, choosing where to send your kids to school, and so on.

Information to remember

- Of the 27,000+ people surveyed for the UN Youth Envoy X Body Shop campaign 'Be Seen Be Heard', eight out of ten respondents thought current political systems need drastic reforms to be fit for the future. It is normal to want to reject politics.

- 'Big-P politics' is traditional politics, including democratic systems, parties, policies and law.
- 'Small-P politics' is groups of people working, delegating, workforces, 'office politics', and the daily organizing of life and roles.

Mariam Kemple Hardy was Head of Campaigns at Refugee Action from 2016 to 2022, campaigning for a just and compassionate refugee protection system in the UK. Prior to this she worked on international refugee issues as Head of Humanitarian Campaigning at Oxfam International.

Azadeh Hosseini is the Communication and Engagement Officer at Refugee Action and a refugee from Iran, where she was a journalist. In the UK she has worked for Persian-speaking media, political parties and human rights organizations, including Amnesty International and the International Bar Association's Human Rights Institute.

"They're Really Just Illegal Migrants"

Mariam Kemple Hardy and Azadeh Hosseini

Azadeh: I have tasted the bitterness of being in the asylum system, and I have decided to wear my experience proudly, as armour, to fight against injustice. In that fight, I've lost count of the number of times I've heard 'they're really just illegal migrants' to justify hostility towards refugees and people seeking asylum. This language is degrading and a direct insult to anyone who has experienced living as an asylum seeker at some point in their life. It sparks several emotions – anger, confusion and fear – and one question: what makes them illegal? Google 'illegal migrants in the UK' and among the top results is a site on 'how to report illegal immigrants anonymously'. It advises you to report migrants to the police and the anti-terrorist hotline. Is being an asylum seeker really a crime equivalent to terrorism?

To better understand quite how damaging the phrase 'they're really just illegal migrants' is, let's first delve into and dismantle its wording:

- 'They're' suggests a faceless lump of people. It strips them of their individual experience, their story, their humanity.
- 'Really' emphasizes truthfulness, the only credible source to the exclusion of all others, particularly the other devious party.
- 'Just' is a simple word that in this context degrades a group of people and establishes them as undeserving of human rights.
- 'Illegal' assumes a crime has been committed and, in turn, criminalizes the whole person for who they are, not what they've done.
- 'Migrants', in this context, suggests that there is something wrong with being a migrant, but people move, and they have done so since the start of human existence. In this phrase, 'migrant' might as frequently be 'refugee'. These terms are distinct but using them interchangeably creates problems for migrants and refugees alike, and devalues people's claim to seek safety. It erases the need for protection

for refugees and it sets up a false test for non-refugee migrants to meet.

Mariam: Every part of this phrase is harmful. I heard it all the time while working as a campaigner on refugee rights at Refugee Action. Sometimes it would come from well-meaning friends genuinely confused about the issue, who were then shocked when I explained the reality of the situation faced by those seeking asylum. But mostly I heard it from politicians and their supporters, particularly in the media, who were using it with cynical malintent.

One of the most damaging consequences of the phrase is that it creates a false narrative that there is a 'pure' refugee experience, an experience to which people seeking asylum are unfairly compared. In this 'pure' scenario, a refugee is forced out of their country and miraculously gets on a plane direct to the UK. This journey is the only 'official' route sanctioned by the UK government. Any other route is suspicious and criminal.

The inconvenient truth is that it's almost impossible for refugees to reach the UK this way. The phrase therefore creates an inaccurate understanding of how refugees travel to reach safety and, when used by politicians, it allows the government to describe most refugees as unworthy of protection.

Azadeh: Perhaps the phrase is a not-so-subtle excuse to ignore reality. Maybe, in the words of the writer and civil-rights activist James Baldwin, people who use it 'cling to hate because they know that once the hate is gone, they will be forced to deal with pain'.

Baldwin's words remind me that we can't continue this conversation without talking about racism. The fact is institutional racism underpins our immigration system. It enables policymakers to other us and repeat phrases such as 'they're just illegal migrants' without feeling discomfort. When the government introduced its Hostile Environment Policy in 2012 – aimed at making life hell for undocumented migrants and asylum seekers – its effects rippled out to anyone who 'looked' or 'sounded' foreign. A Home Office report into the Windrush Scandal of 2014 revealed that UK immigration policy was driven by deep-rooted racism against black and brown migrants, yet eight years later, nothing has changed. Racism still shapes public perception of those seeking asylum – you only have to look at the response to Ukrainian refugees compared with those from Afghanistan and Syria. I will never forget the racist statements aired on TV during coverage of the war in Ukraine, when pundits revealed sympathy with 'blond-haired and blue-eyed' Ukrainians but not with 'some Syrians'.

Mariam: We can now see how deliberately misleading and discriminatory the phrase is. In order to help change perspectives, it's important to have a clear understanding of the terminology that is so often co-opted and misused. With that in mind, let's explore who the 'they' in the phrase actually are.

The 1951 Refugee Convention defines a refugee as someone who 'owing to a well-founded fear of being persecuted for reasons of race, religion, nationality, membership of a particular social group, or political opinion, is outside the country of his* nationality, and is unable to or, owing to such fear, is unwilling to avail himself of the protection of that country'.†

However, even if they meet the above criteria, refugees aren't legally recognized as such until they have had their claim for protection checked and approved by the government of the country where they have asked for protection. From the moment they arrive in the country to the moment their claim is approved, they are a person seeking asylum.

In contrast to 'refugee' or 'person seeking asylum', there is no formal legal definition of the term 'migrant'. It is generally understood to refer to anyone who changes their country of residence, but the term doesn't specify the reason for that change. Often people distinguish between short-term migration and long-term migration, with those who fall into the latter category often called 'immigrants'. Refugees are therefore a type of migrant, but the reason for their change of residence is very legally specific.

Azadeh: As well as understanding the difference between these terms, it's crucial to understand that 'refugee' is not only used to describe people who flee war and conflict, but

* Ignore the use of the male pronoun here. UN documents such as this often reference the male as the default human. As ever, smash the patriarchy!

† For a tiny minority of refugees this happens out of the country before they are brought to the UK as part of a resettlement programme. This small number of people, around 1,200 a year as of May 2022, will not have the status of 'person seeking asylum' in the UK.

also those who are persecuted for their political views, religion, race and social status. Sexual orientation and gender identity officially became grounds for eligibility for refugee status in 2012. Climate change will soon drive millions of people from their homelands and has already played a part in causing or exacerbating conflict. Hunger and drought in conflict-affected countries such as Yemen and South Sudan forced people to leave in search of food.

People from all walks of life claim asylum for different reasons. When they flee their home country, they risk everything. And on top of this, when travelling to the UK, they risk their lives to cross the Channel in search of safety. The merits of their claims must be determined by their need for protection, not public perception of what a refugee 'should' look like or where they 'should' come from.

Mariam: Similarly, it's important to understand quite how chaotic it can be to escape from crisis. Let's look at an example. In August 2021, the Taliban retook control of Afghanistan. The world witnessed the horror as desperate people clung to planes or handed children over airport fences. Evacuation flights saved thousands, but it was painfully clear these measures were not enough. So, people who want to come to the UK – and many do because of the UK's decades-long engagement in Afghanistan – must cross many countries and seas to claim asylum here, possibly stepping into a small boat on the French coast for the last leg of their journey. Each of these journeys fails to meet the myth of the 'pure' refugee, despite those taking such journeys having an overwhelming claim for protection.

Azadeh: Many of the same people who share in the horror of this chaos will also be the first to ask why refugees want to come to the UK. Why don't they stay in – or go to – other countries? Many people in the UK are first- and second-generation migrants from countries once part of the British Empire – Sudan, Sri Lanka, Afghanistan, Sierra Leone and more. This has created a familiar and often familial environment where refugees can find solace and opportunities to settle and integrate. An ability to speak English also plays a major role.

At the same time, it's important to understand that for many refugees the decision about their destination isn't straightforward or necessarily in their control. A refugee may initially reach another country that they thought was safe only to experience abuse by the authorities, which pushes them to take one more treacherous journey to another destination. In fact, it may not be their choice to end up in the UK at all. A lack of routes means that it's actually people smugglers who often make the final decision on refugees' destinations.

Mariam: 'Why don't they claim asylum in France?' is another phrase that comes up a lot. We are an island, making it nearly impossible to arrive here without passing through another country, and the government often uses the stretch of water that separates us from France as justification for turning its back on refugees. What would happen if every country took the same approach? The international refugee protection system would crumble.

People make journeys to the country where they want to rebuild their lives by whatever means they can. The journey can take months, even years. The 1951 UN Refugee Convention acknowledged that people are forced to take irregular journeys. That is why it's clear that no one should be penalized for taking an indirect route to the country in which they wish to claim asylum.

When people ask 'Why don't they claim asylum in France?', remind them that refugees are trying to claim asylum in the UK, and that they may be doing so for any number of reasons.

Azadeh: Arriving at their destination is not the end of the hardship for refugees, not least because of the hostility surrounding how they are perceived. *They are going to take our jobs! They are here just for the benefits!* Which one is it? Hostility rarely makes sense.

As well as this discrimination, those arriving in the UK are faced with the whirlwind that is the asylum system. Until the 2000s, if you arrived in the UK, you could:

- Claim asylum when you arrived or felt able to do so. Some people are trafficked and enter modern-day slavery and will not be able to claim asylum immediately.
- Expect your claim to be processed relatively quickly. In fact, there used to be a target of six months.
- Live in the community, with support for housing and essentials that worked out at about 70 per cent of mainstream benefit levels.
- Work if you had waited more than a year for a decision on your claim.

- Stay in the UK and eventually apply for citizenship once you'd secured refugee status.

The system did not always work. There were significant delays and people could be left hungry and homeless because they did not receive what they were entitled to. But it wasn't an entirely broken system. However, as a direct result of underfunding and government hostility, that is now the case.

The Home Office dropped its pledge to decide on claims of asylum within six months when waiting times grew to the point that it could regularly take years. While awaiting this decision, you have no permission to work, to open a bank account, or to rent a home. You live in temporary accommodation, often pokey hotels or disused army barracks. You get three poor-quality meals a day and an £8 weekly allowance, if you're lucky.

If you are moved to longer-term asylum accommodation, conditions can be shabby, even dangerous. You will be at risk of collapsing ceilings, rat infestations and toxic levels of mould. You receive almost £6 per day to cover all essentials. If the Home Office refuses your claim, you can appeal. But government legal-aid cuts make it tough to obtain the advice needed to fight your case.

Mariam: The system is brutal and, thanks to recent changes to the law, it has become so much worse. The UK refugee system is no longer about keeping people safe, it's about keeping people out; something that this phrase – and others like it – reiterates.

In 2022 the UK government passed the Nationality and

Borders Act (also known as the Anti-Refugee Act), which criminalized the process of arriving in the UK 'irregularly' (i.e., arriving in the UK outside one of the 'official' routes, such as refugee resettlement), regardless of whether people are seeking asylum. Ostensibly, this Act responds to the gangs that smuggle refugees across the Channel in small boats; something the government has relentlessly repeated its desire to address since 2020. But these gangs do not create the problem, they respond to it. They see that there are no safe routes for people to reach the UK, so they fulfil that need. This is their business model. Rather than creating routes for people to travel here to claim asylum, the government's solution is to deter people from reaching the UK. Predictably, their 'solutions' have not stopped people risking their lives in small boats. What they have done is undermine the spirit of the UK's obligations to the Refugee Convention, which clearly states that no one should be penalized for how they enter a country if they are claiming asylum. Under the Nationality and Borders Act, if a person is found to have arrived 'irregularly' – which, remember, is the case for most refugees because of the limited 'official' routes – they will have fewer rights should their claim be successful (such as access to family reunion), and could be sent overseas for offshore processing, or deported to third countries, such as Rwanda.

To see the implications of the government's increasingly hostile refugee system, just look at the recent changes to the UK Resettlement Scheme. Previously, this committed the government to resettle 5,000 of the most vulnerable refugees from across the world in its first year. In reality, this was reduced to just 1,445 refugees in the twelve months to March 2022.*

Azadeh: The Anti-Refugee Act is the final nail in the coffin of our refugee protection system, and it is underpinned by the myth that 'they're just illegal migrants'. The Act dehumanizes people seeking asylum to the point where it legitimizes government policies that traumatize and punish people who have already suffered so much. In doing so, it diverts attention from the government's real failure: to build an asylum system that is effective, just and compassionate.

Mariam: So, that's what we need to do. We cannot reform the current system – a system that is founded on a racist philosophy that seeks to keep people out, not keep people safe. We must build a new system based on protection, not punishment. We must stand up for asylum.

Prompts for discussion

- What would you do if the UK suddenly became a place that was no longer safe to stay? What country would you aim to seek safety in and why? And how would you get there?

* This scheme followed the successful Vulnerable Syrian Resettlement Scheme set up by David Cameron's government that saw over 20,000 Syrian refugees resettled in the UK between 2016 and 2021.

- Why do you think the UK government's response to supporting Ukrainian refugees has been so different to other crises where the UK is also deeply involved, such as Iraq and Afghanistan?
- Do you think you could live for years on £5.84 a day while waiting for a decision on your asylum claim? How do you think it would affect you and your family?
- If you were in a foreign country where you didn't speak the language and weren't allowed to work until you received refugee status, how would you go about rebuilding your life and become part of your new community?
- How do you think the UK should treat people seeking asylum?

Information to remember

- 61 per cent of people crossing the Channel are likely to get refugee status.
- 85 per cent of people who crossed the Channel in 2021 and who had their claims decided by October 2022 were given refugee status.
- 73 per cent of people are waiting longer than six months for a decision on their claim.
- People seeking asylum receive £5.84 per day in support.
- 69 per cent of refugees stay in a neighbouring country, while 0.6 per cent of the UK's resident population came to the country as an asylum seeker.

"Innocent Until Proven Guilty":

In Response to Sexual Assault Allegations

I spent much of 2017 in Portcullis House, the Ministry of Justice and the Palace of Westminster, trying to add the act of upskirting to the Sexual Offences Act. My 'real job' was based in Paddington, where I spent my days tapping away at my laptop writing copy for social posts, websites, or voiceovers for TV ads. I worked with a great group of people – creative types who were kind and fun – and I enjoyed my work, but my mind was in Westminster.

My nine-hour days were punctuated by WhatsApps from my lawyer, Ryan: *Have you seen the news? What did [redacted politician's name] say? Make sure you read through the private members' bill before tomorrow, G!* I'd huddle in private call booths trying to fit in media interviews between work tasks. At lunchtime, I'd spend an hour scanning the Twitter trending tab and reading the news, on the lookout for any stories, discussions or viral threads that I could support or leverage in some meaningful way, or through which I might connect with like-minded people. I was new to this work and knew I had to play the PR game, just like politicians would play it with me, but I hadn't yet figured out how best to do it.

One morning shortly before Hallowe'en, I was once again on the bird app, scrolling through the noise, when I clocked a tweet by US actor Alyssa Milano: 'If all the women who have been sexually harassed or assaulted wrote "Me too" as a status, we might give people a sense of the magnitude of the problem.' I clicked through to read the comments. Tens of thousands of women were posting 'Me too' back. My eyes shifted to the sidebar where the same words were trending, globally. As I read on, I gleaned that women were showing solidarity in response to allegations against movie-making powerhouse Harvey Weinstein, who had been outed by *New York Times* journalists Jodi Kantor and Megan Twohey earlier that month.

Witnessing this mass admission in real time felt incredibly powerful; like an outpouring that could shift into a movement. In fact, it *had* been a movement. Tarana Burke – who in 2003 also developed the non-profit programme Just Be, for Black girls aged twelve to eighteen – had launched Me Too in 2006 on the early social-networking site Myspace to illustrate the prevalence of sexual violence. As Alyssa – a well-known famous white actor – used the phrase to create a Twitter dialogue, Tarana's work was being erased, but her legacy was growing, and once it took off, she would return to the helm of one of the most influential online movements in history.

Like many people, I first encountered the phrase 'Me too'

when I read Alyssa's tweet and, in response, I tapped out those two words myself. Once I'd clicked 'send', a hum of fear came over me, as if someone would soon force me to prove my experiences. I recognized this as the ingrained expectation of not being believed; a default response that women and people of marginalized genders must navigate in the pursuit of validation or justice. 'Believe women' – a phrase of solidarity designed to pre-empt biases – would later become a catch-all term born from this zeitgeist-shifting moment.

As I tweeted that day, I had no idea that #MeToo would have an impact on my ability to change the law. You see, you can't predict or measure how current events will shape people's attitudes or understanding, but in the months that followed October 2017, people in positions of power needed to be *seen* to be taking sexual harassment, assault and rape culture more seriously. God forbid they look out of touch or, worse, complicit.

Whether politicians genuinely cared about how misogyny ruins lives, or whether they were just leaning in for the optics (usually the latter) was up for debate. But for a moment, this global movement forced a majority white, older male political institution, sculpted entirely from power, imperialism and binary gender roles, to either take part or risk looking like a moral outlier. Think pieces were written, allegations were levelled, and this red-hot period of female anger and honesty made many institutions – and the men that ran them – really uncomfortable. A hard truth was being spoken in Hollywood meetings, across university classrooms, in booths at bars and across social media. Women of all kinds, all over the world, were telling their stories and sharing their experiences at the hands of men. But this time – spurred on by each other's courage and honesty – they weren't telling them quietly or with shame.

The scale, variety and particular detail of the testimonies meant men and boys across the country were suddenly forced into awareness about their complicity in a cultural problem, whether they considered themselves to be at the sharp end of that problem or not. Not all men were committing atrocities like Weinstein, but they were all complicit in allowing a culture of sexual violence to continue unchecked. Unable to escape the discourse completely, many men were prompted to look inwards and question their past use of language, their behaviour and their beliefs; to consider moments when they had witnessed something inappropriate and chosen not to intervene, or done something inappropriate themselves, and ask themselves 'why?'

British politics – an institution with its own serious history of misogyny, racism, sexual harassment, assault and violence, and reputation for inaction when it comes to recognizing or working to solve these realities – suddenly became incredibly aware of itself. I was taking meetings throughout this period, and I believe politicians became nervous. One question must have been on their minds: 'After Hollywood, will politics have its own reckoning, too?'

Towards the end of 2017, after months of #MeToo, I noticed that something had shifted ever so slightly in the corridors of Westminster. MPs didn't avoid the questions as much as they might have in the past. They opened the door a little wider and they listened – or pretended to – more intently. They were more open to discussing issues of sexual assault publicly; to be seen to be advocating for victims and survivors would be to mark themselves as the proverbial 'good guy'.

I've since learned that Conservative MP Andrew Griffiths, who took it upon himself to advocate staunchly for our campaign, our work and our legislation change (though I never worked with him personally), had been operating as a sexual predator himself while doing so. Andrew sent over 2,000 sexually explicit messages to female constituents, sending women £700 for X-rated pictures and videos, and asking them to tie each other up. He'd also received complaints of inappropriate touching and later was found, during a civil trial, to have physically abused his wife, Kate Kniveton, and raped her while she slept. (She later stood for election and took his seat as the MP for Burton.)

As the #MeToo movement took hold, men in power who had perpetrated these types of violent offences or problematic misogynistic behaviours were suddenly aware that they might soon be held accountable for their actions, so they leaned in to anything that would shield the truth. For Griffiths, that was my campaign. I was always wary of anyone who would publicly support me but wouldn't contact me or work with me personally. I still am.

Other male MPs used proximity to women, or feminists, as a distraction, and so they took meetings with me, which helped my and Ryan's political strategy gain momentum, but it felt uncomfortable and I retained a healthy sense of suspicion throughout. Their interest seemed inauthentic because I knew it would die down once the movement left the focus of the mainstream media. I had this unsettling realization that I and my work are only valuable when female pain and trauma is at its most visible, and when engaging with me is a way for people to be seen looking like they care. It's the same feeling I get now when I see a surge in my number of followers right after the news cycle is filled with the story of another innocent woman dying at the hands of a man.

For many women, including me, the online response to #MeToo was exposing, in that our painful realities were laid bare for the world to see and discuss, but it was also a source of support because we formed this vast digital unity – a space to find validation. Traditional media coverage defined the movement in the eyes of the public. It focused on allegations against powerful white men in Hollywood and the experience of victims, who were mostly white women with social capital, which made it anything but inclusive. Social media, however, gave a more nuanced and comprehensive indication of the scale of the problem. Online spaces were awash with reports about men in other industries. I was interested in the Hollywood exposé, but to scroll through all these real women's stories online was a more cathartic experience for me. Seeing both the upper-class scandal unravelling on TV and the outpouring from regular women online was a duality of exposure I hadn't witnessed before. I began to realize that it had indeed become, in Tarana Burke's words, not just a moment, but a movement.

Offline and online, discourse collided to create top-line public knowledge of an issue that transcended feminist or even mildly progressive spaces. It was a declaration of acknowledgement that something on the pyramid of sexual violence was happening in every workplace, home and public space. However, mainstream reporting wasn't intersectional enough to invite the kind of nuanced debate required to deconstruct the roots of the problem, and the truth is that many women were forgotten by the #MeToo movement.

Black women, Indigenous women, South Asian women, disabled women and trans women were markedly missing from the discourse. Anne Wafula Strike noted in her *Guardian* piece 'Disabled women see #MeToo and think: what about us?' that 'most things about disabled women's lives remain shrouded in taboo – our sexuality above all', and that 'women with disabilities all over the world are trying to push forward, as I did, but it's hard when campaigning is still so focused on rights and opportunities for able-bodied women'.

Tarana Burke herself drew attention to the difference in the timelines between bringing Weinstein and R&B artist R. Kelly to justice in the courts. For decades, Kelly had been plagued by allegations of child sex abuse, grooming and trafficking young Black girls, and in 2008, he was acquitted of child pornography charges. Yet allegations against Kelly continued to fall on deaf ears in the majority of white-owned media until the Netflix documentary *Surviving R. Kelly* was released in 2019, sparking celebrities to condemn the singer and birthing the social media movement #MuteRKelly.

'We are socialized to respond to the vulnerability of white women, and it's a truth that is hard for some people to look in the face, and they feel uncomfortable when I say things like that,' commented Burke to *The New York Times* in 2021. 'But it is true . . . [There's a] stark difference in what it takes to get attention around Black women and girls.' In 2022 Kelly was eventually found guilty of multiple counts of sexual abuse.

In the long run, critiques about the lack of inclusivity within the movement must be heeded as they are rooted in the ultimate objective of naming, disrupting and deconstructing systems that oppress and subjugate women. All women. They pose valid and important questions from which dominant communities of women – those who are prioritized in these movements – have the opportunity to learn as we continue to build awareness of sexual violence and create work around the issue.

As the discourse about #MeToo rose to a crescendo, we also saw a different type of critique emerge. From the safety of their computers or smart phones, it became commonplace for men to angrily discredit the movement and the survivors whose experiences it aimed to uplift. The idea that you could be outed for your behaviour – especially online – became a real fear for men, but so too did the assumption that you could be implicated without having committed any acts of sexual violence yourself. Some became concerned that women would issue false accusations in order to gain social status or sympathy, rather than to tell the truth and make their voices heard.

When it came to online discussion about this, facts didn't really matter. Keyboard warriors came out of the woodwork, tweeting that men were more likely than ever to be falsely accused of rape. Fear-mongering memes advised, 'Mothers of sons should be scared. It is terrifying that at any time, any girl can make up any story about any boy that can neither be proved or disproved, and ruin any boy's life.'

When I came across these comments, I would reply that false claims are extremely rare, making up roughly 3 per cent of all rape reports in the UK. It's a level similar to that of false reporting of any other serious crime, and double the current prosecution rate for rape, which stands at an abysmal 1.3 per cent and it would be much more helpful to discuss that. They would ignore or mock me. I found it interesting that these people were more focused on the potential harm caused to men by false rape accusations than the actual harm being done; in reality, men are more likely to be raped than to be accused of rape themselves.

Twitter soon became somewhere I could barely spend time because of the mass of guys reinforcing exactly why women and others marginalized for their gender feel, or are, unsafe. #HimToo and #MenToo became trending hashtags; the digital embodiment of how, when discussing abuses of power, rather than just *listening*, too many men divert attention away from allegations against others in order to centre their own lived experiences, or worse, hypothetical outcomes. The supporters of these hashtags failed to acknowledge that men are nearly twice as likely as women to be victims of violent crime and experience that violence mostly at the hands of other men. Neither did they acknowledge how toxic masculine ideals hurt people of all genders – including men – and that the #MeToo movement could form the basis for coalitions that could help liberate men from those very ideals.

The possibility that people across genders could unite in combating male violence just didn't come up. What *did* come up, of course, were comments about 'ruining men's careers' (as if a career were more valuable than a woman's life or well-being), and time and time again, the 'good guys' would pipe up to helpfully point out the oldest platitude in the book when it comes to accountability and justice: 'innocent until proven guilty'.

In the wake of #MeToo, 'innocent until proven guilty' became a catch-all phrase to quash any type of discussion about male sexual violence. It sounds so logical and irrefutable that it can feel impossible to argue with. Often I'd see women, angry and hurting, replying to this phrase online as if their credibility hinged on being able to legally prove a perpetrator's guilt in a series of 180-character tweets. And despite being active in the world of gender equality and deep in the throes of learning at the time, when faced with this phrase, I would roll my eyes and feel completely unable to articulate exactly *why* it frustrated me so much. In fact, it wasn't until a year after the inception of #MeToo that I finally began to unpick this response.

By September 2018 my campaign had become one of the country's most-talked-about news stories after a backbench Conservative MP rejected our private members' bill, and around that time I became deeply invested in the Ford–Kavanaugh hearing. Professor of Psychology Christine Blasey Ford reported that Brett Kavanaugh, who was due to become a Supreme Court justice following President Trump's nomination, had sexually assaulted her when she was fifteen and he was seventeen. Ford had taken a polygraph test, administered by an FBI agent, that corroborated her claims, and historical therapy-session notes detail her discussing a 'rape attempt' and being attacked by students 'from an elitist boys' school' who went on to become 'highly respected and high-ranking members of society in Washington'.

Watching the hearing on YouTube, I was entranced by how Ford – who had clearly wrestled with whether to come out publicly and name her abuser – held space so calmly and powerfully as she spoke about her assault in front of the entire world. I also watched footage of the US lawyer, educator and author Anita Hill testifying against US Supreme Court nominee Clarence Thomas with the same grace – not just in the face of misogyny, but racism too.

My small taste of media pressure was enough to make me want to crawl into a hole every now and again, yet Christine and Anita had told their stories to the world with clarity and ease, describing how trauma had affected them. In contrast, Kavanaugh, to me, was the epitome of fragile masculinity – shouting, spitting and arguing, totally unable to control his emotions in the face of questioning. His demeanour was wild compared to Ford's, which was worrying given he would soon be taking on the most important and difficult judicial role in one of the most powerful countries in the world. Kavanaugh's fellow Republicans and Democrat supporters boldly fought in his defence, often citing 'innocent until proven guilty' in the process.

It dawned on me that although I'd heard this phrase in the halls of power, in pubs and bars across the country, and countless times on social media, only here was it being used in a legitimate context: a hearing. Regardless of Kavanaugh's lack of emotional regulation and the evidence that seemed so clearly to support Dr Ford, 'innocent until proven guilty' was relevant here. The hearing had to follow this process, and so Republicans citing this principle in the press to defend Kavanaugh weren't wrong; in this context, he was innocent until proven guilty. But this didn't mean that victims and survivors watching the hearing weren't entitled to recognize their own experiences in what was unfolding, and to vent about, question and commentate online. It also didn't legitimize the silencing of those voices, online or in person, often by the use of that very same phrase.

Pulling out 'innocent until proven guilty' during a conversation to silence others and suppress debate gives the phrase a totally different meaning and impact, and that was the root of my frustration at seeing it used so much online during October 2017. This phrase was a *legal principle*, not a stick with which to beat survivors and plant doubt about their experiences. The presumption of innocence is a tool used to ethically establish guilt in the eyes of a very specific system. To be viewed innocent by the law until proven guilty is essential, but for society as a whole to have to assume this innocence is not. Innocent until proven guilty does not exist to tell us what to believe. It exists to support legal procedures. Those are two *very* different things, and it's worth remembering this when you hear the phrase being used to halt discussions about sexual violence.

In Response to 'Innocent Until Proven Guilty'

'Innocent until proven guilty' feels hard-baked into our lexicon. It's a conversation-stopper because we all agree, in principle, with the logic; how (and why) would you criticize the idea that someone is innocent until it's proven that they are not? But like with so many of the phrases being explored in this book, the literal definition isn't necessarily the problem. Rather, it's the use of the phrase in a particular context.

Although the phrase has become a colloquialism, it is in fact a legal maxim. Though it's not considered evidence of a defendant's innocence in a trial, the presumption of innocence is a legal right. It's an enshrined concept that ensures, in court, that the guilt of an accused person can't be presumed – they must be assumed innocent in the eyes of the law until proven otherwise. In *The Right to Sex*, philosopher Amia Srinivasan offers that 'the presumption of innocence . . . answers to our sense that it is worse, all else being equal, for the law to wrongly punish than to wrongly exonerate'. It aims to ensure the good-faith expectation of innocence to be retained in order to keep court proceedings fair until contrary evidence has been introduced and the burden of proof delivered by the prosecution, who must prove – beyond reasonable doubt – that someone is guilty as charged.

The phrase 'innocent until proven guilty' sprang from ancient legal process but its conception is hard to pinpoint. English jurist Sir William Blackstone published his seminal work *Commentaries on the Laws of England* in 1760, which stated 'all presumptive evidence of felony should be admitted cautiously, for the law holds that it is better that ten guilty persons escape than that one innocent suffer'. The Roman legal document titled *Constitutio Antoniniana* detailed rules around presumption of innocence all the way back in the third century. Regardless of who coined the concept, it has been a maxim in law around the world for centuries, is enshrined in the Universal Declaration of Human Rights, and has steadily leaked into the public consciousness as a fundamental principle, which is why, in the wake of #MeToo, it was unsurprising that it became a device to shut down conversations about sexual violence.

We must remember there are fundamental differences between legal systems and complex and nuanced social situations. We see this in rape and sexual-violence trials where legislation is woefully unequipped to effectively tackle questions around consent, such as non-verbal consent, the concept of ongoing consent and the withdrawal of it. Legal systems don't adequately reflect or mirror social realities – they flatten them.

In 'Colonialism, Crime and Social Control', Professor of Crime and Justice Studies at UMass Viviane Saleh-Hanna describes crime as 'a distinctly European concept that was institutionalized into the criminal justice system through the penal code, created in the 1700s', and explains how the penal code, which was written during the height of 'Europe's genocidal colonial wars and chattel slavery . . . excluded, and continues to exclude mass atrocities and violations committed through these institutions'. The systems that define the parameters of criminal activity are rooted in institutionalized racism and misogyny. Occasionally, they deliver accountability but they primarily exist to maintain a social order, and the truth is that our legal system has some deep and fundamental problems – just look at the neglect experienced by sexual-assault survivors.

Using the legal system as the only framework to evaluate human morality is therefore grossly inadequate. As the Secret Barrister writes in their book *The Secret Barrister: Stories of the Law and How It's Broken*, 'For me, the lesson of history is that the state alone cannot be trusted to find the truth.' The legal arm of the state does little to recognize people's complex emotional experiences, which is why it can be so harmful to enforce a legal standard intended to control court proceedings during complex discussions about traumatic experiences. Especially if it is used to silence the person who's been on the receiving end of said experience, which was so often the case during the Me Too movement.

Since #MeToo, scores of famous men have been accused of behaviour that sits somewhere in the pyramid of sexual violence. Whether indecent exposure, groping, digital sexual harassment, coercion or rape, each story precipitates an explosion of debate both online and offline about how we discuss allegations, what the process should be afterwards, and what the act (and the reaction to it) means in the wider context of sexism and misogyny in society. Conversations about these allegations with male friends, boyfriends or with men online can be challenging because those conversations can reproduce the perspectives and ideas that underpin the culture that causes harm. And during #MeToo, it became even more tricky because this open dialogue and evaluation of the problem was brand-new territory for them.

How many times, throughout their lives, have men who don't live under intersecting systems of oppression been forced – or even encouraged – to look at society through the lens of gender or power dynamics? Even when it's something urgent, how often do we – when we have never, or will never experience something – take the time to meaningfully explore and understand it? So many of us don't do this, even if that inaction could be causing harm or adding to a culture that is damaging.

It's partly for this reason that cisgender, heterosexual men are often ill-equipped to evaluate stories of sexual harassment or assault in a nuanced way that allows them to zoom out further than 'person A did this to person B', and view the constellation of structures, systems, influences and cultural norms that bred and therefore shaped and informed the situation. On top of this, when discussing alleged high-profile perpetrators, there can be a sense of affinity and emotional allegiance that distorts their ability to view the allegations objectively – 'Woody Allen's films made me who I am!'

Many of the accused stars embodied traits that endeared them to your average Joe. They'd become famous for portraying an aspirational masculine ideal on screen or were seen as geniuses behind the camera; writers or directors with creativity, power and influence. Maybe they were beloved music artists or comedians who gave voice to the kind of thoughts your boyfriend or friend had, which made him feel legitimized and powerful. Because of this, men in our lives could become defensive and protective when discussing allegations against these high-profile offenders because they saw themselves in them.

This potent combination of lack of structural understanding and defensiveness is what I believe makes conversations about sexual-assault allegations with cisgender heterosexual men so infuriating for so many women; it's precisely what leads men to reach for the seemingly irrefutable shutdown of 'innocent until proven guilty'. Sometimes, you'll hear it even if there are tens of corroborating accounts and allegations about the individual in question. I've personally had a friend use it in response to the reports of Louis C.K. masturbating at women and exposing himself to them in 2017, even though C.K. *himself* had admitted they were true.

Using this phrase to shut someone up is laughable because it only applies to legal proceedings, not to discussions in the pub. It ensures that a person can't legally be sentenced if reasonable doubt can be established, not that you can't have emotional reactions to allegations of abuse in the company of your friends, or that you can't believe the victim based on your assessment of the circumstances and available evidence. Using it to stop conversation says, I am uncomfortable with this discussion because it is making me . . .

a) question my perception of someone I revered/loved
b) question the behaviour of me or someone I know
c) engage with the reality that I am part of a culture responsible for hurting women, non-binary people and trans people in unique and wide-ranging ways
d) feel frustrated that I don't have the scope of knowledge to contribute in the way I am able to contribute to most conversations as someone who benefits from the patriarchy.

Although all of the above are valid emotional responses, they aren't reasons to stop a discussion, especially when expressing feelings about these cases isn't just normal chat. For most women and people of marginalized genders existing under patriarchy, these discussions are *tools* that enable them to understand the systems that have hurt them. Discussions help us draw the roadmap to liberation by recognizing feelings, evaluating a situation and talking about its impact. So, someone suppressing a conversation because *it makes them* feel uncomfortable is detrimental, especially if the person doing the suppressing happens to belong to the community reinforcing that culture and perpetrating most of that harm. Trying to shut down any conversation on sexual violence is a weird move, but throwing 'innocent until proven guilty' out there is particularly frustrating because it sees a member of a dominant community sideline the discussion in order to protect the supposed innocence of a hypothetical man. It is a distraction technique and it also puts the onus on the person recounting the allegation to prove the perpetrator's guilt before they can continue talking. The reason you suddenly feel like you have to assume the role of a prosecutor? Because this phrase is directly lifted from law and doesn't belong in regular conversation.

I used to see criminalization as the primary solution to sexual assault, but I've since educated myself on what little effect these institutions have on stopping the problem of sexual violence. I now come at this work from a much more preventative angle. Even if you do see criminalization as the solution, using legal process as a framework to discuss sexual violence is laughable because the legal system so often doesn't deliver justice for victims.

In England and Wales, court backlogs have left victims of

sexual offences waiting an average of eight to nine months for a trial. Analysis by the Criminal Bar Association reveals that a record 179 trials were ditched in 2021 because no judge was available to preside over them. Even if your case gets to trial, the whole process is managed by individuals who themselves cannot be free from misogynistic or racist biases and ideas about rape culture or sexual violence. Survivors and victims tell the press time and again that they felt as if *they* were 'on trial' during court proceedings, and that the system retraumatized them. In the words of Andrea Simon, director of End Violence Against Women (EVAW), 'For too long, survivors have faced appalling treatment when reporting rape – not being believed, being retraumatized throughout the justice process, and ultimately not seeing a conviction.'

The misogyny that pollutes our institutions goes all the way to the top. Live on LBC radio, ex-prime minister Boris Johnson said he believed that the government's investigation into 'historic [child abuse] offences and all this malarkey' was 'spaffing money up the wall'. Our 'justice' system is quite honestly a mess and, to top it off, almost 99 per cent of rapes reported to police do not end in a conviction and only one in a hundred rapes are reported to the police. This means that almost all rapists aren't 'proven guilty', so by the logic of 'innocent until proven guilty', must we assume almost all of them innocent? And should we quell discussion about those 99 per cent of cases because guilt hasn't been 'proven' in the eyes of the law? Of course not.

To purposely shut down discussion – which remains one of the only tools survivors and victims have against a system hurting them – with a maxim used by the very institution that fails to bring them justice is a double sting. And in a world where we have a 1 per cent to 2 per cent conviction rate, the 'innocent until proven guilty' narrative only serves to compound the issue by allowing perpetrators to swerve critique in society just as they evade accountability in the courts. If you want to discuss an actor against whom multiple victims have filed reports, a man you know who has allegations against him, or how you or someone you love has been through some sexual harassment or violence, you have every right to.

This isn't to say that we shouldn't think carefully about 'trial by media' and critique it as a workable or ethical solution to sexual-assault allegations. Unchecked, unabated online debate by thousands of people who have little access to the information of a case can be toxic and sets a dangerous precedent, as shown during the infamous Johnny Depp–Amber Heard proceedings. Thoughtful discussions online and with friends are different to a social-media feeding frenzy, however, and conversations about these topics should always be protected.

It's particularly interesting how, by using 'innocent until proven guilty', someone protects the perpetrator by demanding evidence of their guilt while undermining the victim and anyone who believes what they see as a 'baseless' allegation. It reveals that the speaker doesn't have evidence either – something they're claiming is critical for allegations of sexual violence and essential for the conversation to continue. They're effectively saying, 'You've sided with the victim and are assuming the perpetrator's guilt baselessly,' whilst they side with the perpetrator and assume their innocence baselessly.

While I would argue that nuanced knowledge and understanding of patriarchy, white supremacy, misogyny and gendered power dynamics as well as rape culture and how it operates isn't 'evidence' of anything – especially not guilt – it does allow a 'lens' through which to evaluate situations with more context. As a result, you might notice patterns of behaviour and red flags that others might not. It could be the case that women and people of marginalized genders who have navigated experiences of misogyny, transphobia and sexual harassment are entering these conversations with a breadth of understanding that so many cisgender, heterosexual men just don't have, and so their evaluation of an allegation may be rooted in something other than just an emotional response to either defend or condemn (especially if they are adept at critical thinking). No, it's not evidence, but even if we're just having a conversation at the pub, I'm engaging with the topic using far more resources, knowledge and experience than Cameron who has never picked up a book on gender and who just pulled out 'innocent until proven guilty' because the conversation makes him uncomfortable.

In order to respond constructively to the phrase, calmly question why it's being used in *your particular* conversation. Explain that it's a legal maxim linked to the presumption of innocence and that it doesn't mean conversations about allegations shouldn't be had, or that we should automatically doubt reports of sexual violence. Voice your belief that discussions about allegations are a useful tool for those who live under patriarchy to understand what is happening to them and why.

Offer that even if a sexual assault case gets to court, it's not guaranteed to end in a conviction, and that in many cases, depending on the act, it's unlikely to do so. Supply some information on this and use it to remind the person you're talking to that 'innocent until proven guilty' doesn't even necessarily hold weight in court, because perpetrators rarely are proven guilty. Note that, online, too many men can be worryingly quick to defend perpetrators against allegations but rarely defend the person making them, and ask them why they think that is.

Finally, note that when discussing allegations of sexual violence, you, personally, tend to start by giving the victim the benefit of the doubt, because coming forward is such a traumatizing experience, proves costly, and because even if you get it wrong – which is unlikely because false allegations of sexual violence across the board are under 5 per cent – you would rather be the type of person to prioritize extending grace and support to a potential victim than to a potential perpetrator of sexual violence.

Prompts for discussion

- If you can, assume a position of curiosity over accusation. For example, 'I wonder why it's so hard for us to condemn the behaviour of someone we don't know, because we like their work . . .' Ask the person you're talking to if they feel uncomfortable when these discussions come up.
- Remind them that hypotheticals can really derail important conversations like this one, and there

aren't many opportunities to talk about this because there's a lot of shame around it. Encourage them to ask questions instead, or if they are someone without experience of what's being discussed, ask them if they could just listen.

- Offer a response that explains the reality of how the legal system is failing victims and note that we don't want to uphold a similar culture of suspicion around survivors in society. Courts use the presumption of innocence to be able to uphold a fair process when trying someone, but this case isn't in court, and even if it was, discussion about a potential assault is an essential part of trying to figure out why this stuff happens. Plus, conviction rates for sexual offenders are very low anyway, so acting as if the legal system is the solution to these guys – and using it to silence people – is misguided.

Information to remember

- 'Innocent until proven guilty' is a legal maxim designed to ensure fair legal proceedings, not to stop healthy debate and discussion.
- A 2018 survey covering thirteen countries showed how cis men vastly underestimate the level of sexual harassment women experience in their lifetime. Men estimated that 36 per cent of women have experienced sexual harassment, whereas the figures show it's closer to 60 per cent (likely still an underestimate).

- Sexual offence victims face the longest-ever waits in courts, and from 2018 to 2019 only between 3 and 5 per cent of sexual offences ended up in a charge or court summons. Only 1.3 per cent of rape cases result in a charge, which shows perpetrators of the most violent acts of sexual violence are benefiting from one of the lowest charging rates across all crime.

Salma El-Wardany (she/her) is a writer, speaker, poet, spoken-word artist, broadcaster and author of *These Impossible Things.*

"Islam Is an Oppressive Religion to Women"

Salma El-Wardany

I'm sixteen years old when the waitress I work with leans in towards me, rests a gentle hand on my arm and, with a mixture of pity and compassion laced across her face, asks softly, 'Do you have to have an arranged marriage?'

I'm nineteen years old when my seminar partner at university looks at me curiously and, chewing on the end of his pen, asks, 'What happens if your dad catches you without it on?' He's referring to the hijab I'm wearing and the look on his face tells me he thinks his question is thoughtful and considered.

I'm twenty-four years old when my colleague leans across his desk, nudges his packet of crips towards me, and whispers, 'Don't worry, you can eat. I won't tell anyone.' It's the middle of Ramadan and I'm fasting, and the look on his face tells me he thinks he's helping me out.

My life is, and has been, a revolving conveyor belt of comments and questions like this, all which labour under the same misconception: as a Muslim woman I am oppressed, trapped and devoid of agency; that I am somehow in desperate need of saving, which is curious, because we don't employ the same narrative when it comes to other religions. No one is frantically trying to save Catholic or Jewish women, yet when it comes to Islam, some people can only see a damsel in distress and a horde of evil Muslim men keeping her under lock and key.

Of course, I don't need saving, but the story the media, politics and entertainment has told about Muslim women has informed the public consciousness. It's what leads people to wonder if I know the Taliban or if I'm going to be whipped for marrying against my family's desires – all questions that have been posed to me. People will often roll their eyes when I tell them this and dismiss the minority as 'stupid'; however, it's not the minority and people aren't that stupid. They've been fed a single story about Muslim women so consistently and with such conviction, they have done the inevitable and believed it.

That story starts decades ago with colonization and the idea that the Eastern orient was barbaric and regressive, therefore justifying Western occupation. However, it was in the wake of 9/11 that the narrative intensified and took on a whole new life. As the Twin Towers came down and the ensuing 'war on terror' began, a political rhetoric started regarding Muslims and how they were seen as a threat to Western democracy. Anything to do with Islam was suspicious, and one of the most visible representations of Islam was the veiled Muslim woman.

Politicians across the globe expressed their distaste, disapproval or openly mocked Muslim women. Australia's prime minister, Tony Abbot, said that 'he wished [the burqa] was not worn', US Congresswoman Carolyn Maloney said that 'women and girls cannot venture outside without a burqa which they are forced to wear', and the UK's former prime minister, Boris Johnson, mocked Muslim women, comparing them to 'letterboxes' and 'bank robbers'.

Comments such as these, from political leaders, opened the floodgates for hate crime, discrimination and changes in policy, but they also consolidated the idea that Muslim women were oppressed. Maloney's comments were said to justify the occupation of Afghanistan, France went on to eventually ban the hijab from educational institutions and the burqa from public spaces, and anti-Muslim hate crime in the UK increased by 375 per cent in the wake of Johnson's comments. When the world's leaders openly vilify Muslim women and discuss their apparent oppression, without giving Muslim women the opportunity to speak for themselves, it sets a precedent, a story gains momentum and here we are, decades later, still listening to the same tired tale and batting away ridiculous questions. In fact, it's little wonder we've arrived here.

I often lack patience or grace when people ask me about the oppression of Muslim women. I want to be thoughtful and compassionate, but I find myself at the end of a tether that has already been stretched too far. In my calmer moments I understand that people are curious and just want to learn more. The rest of the time I find people's questions lazy. It only takes a small bit of research and common sense to understand that the dominant narrative around Muslim women is one rooted in stereotypes, Islamophobia and over-sensationalized media headlines.

The truth is, most people know a Muslim or have close Muslim friends, so they already know on some level that the questions posed are unfair. We've seen it with every single oppressed group and the ensuing movements surrounding them, whether that's with the BLM protests or trans rights. A wealth of information exists at people's fingertips and yet people will choose the easiest option and ask ignorant questions as a quick route to understanding.

The most dangerous part of this is, of course, the risk posed to the safety of Muslim women. When an ill-informed conversation continues, it puts Muslim women in jeopardy. Not only do they risk being attacked or becoming subjects of hate crime, but it also puts their opportunities at risk. It limits the jobs they get, the promotions they can attain, the careers they could have and the lives that could be lived. It changes the very shape of Muslim women's lives, a reality I am all too familiar with. Post-9/11 my life changed irrevocably. I was viewed in different ways, asked more interrogative questions at job interviews, and being a Muslim ensured that the world approached me with caution and fear, or as a project to be worked on and, eventually, freed. The story told about Muslim women changes the story they get to live.

Things are changing, with democratized conversations on social platforms and Muslim representation in entertainment in ways we've never seen before – for example, the recent *Ms. Marvel* series on Disney+ – but they're not changing fast enough. There still isn't adequate representation in entertainment (one is never enough), politics or the media to counteract the damaging stereotypes. In short, the questions keep on coming. While I may roll my eyes, the fact remains that when a person asks these questions, they are othering Muslim women and subscribing to the notion that Islam is oppressive to women. They're placing these women in a box in their head as something strange, different and unfamiliar. It sends the message that you're not one of them, part of this society or socially accepted.

I've spent much of my life as a Muslim woman, especially when I wore the hijab (the material worn to cover our hair) for six years, feeling like an alien with two heads. At one end of the spectrum sits outright Islamophobia and the shouts and hisses you receive in the street, and at the other end are the gentle questions about how free I really am, intended to be inquisitive but instead serving as a reminder that I am seen as someone who needs rescuing. It removes the agency of Muslim women and that is where so much of the problem lies.

Should you come across the phrase 'Islam is an oppressive religion to women', there are numerous responses you can try. First, reply with a question – specifically, why does the person you're talking to feel like Muslim women are oppressed? Turning the question back on the individual forces them to really interrogate their reasons and vocalize statements that, once viewed in the cold light of day, often seem ridiculous. It also opens a conversation, and for me, I find that one of the best ways to avoid a defensive stance. The knee-jerk reaction and temptation to tell people to f*ck off is rarely conducive to any kind of understanding or progress.

Second, explain that according to Islamic theology, it is not mandatory for Muslim women to wear hijab. It's seen as an extra act of religious devotion but if women don't want to, they have zero religious obligation to do so. Therefore, if you see a Muslim woman choosing to wear the hijab, burqa or veil, it's because she has done just that, and *chosen* it.

Third, remind the person you're talking to that for many Muslim women, covering up and veiling their body and hair is an act of feminism. In a world that hyper-sexualizes women, judges women on the way they look and dress, and is obsessed with the appearance of women, covering up removes the focus from female sexuality. In doing so they tap out of the relentless beauty standards and ideals that many women find frustrating and limiting. They opt out of a system that reduces a woman's value to her appearance and how willing she is to play out traditional notions of femininity.

Fourth, and perhaps one of the most important points to counter someone with, is that Islam is inherently a religion that prioritizes, protects and empowers women. It is, however, like all the major Abrahamic faiths, a religion that has been interpreted via a patriarchal scholarship. Globally we are all subjected to the patriarchy, and Islam is no different. Men have used religion for their own purposes and to control women for decades. Islam is not exempt from patriarchal notions and we are all formed by the habits of our environment. The misogyny and derogatory views against women that inform our world, and every society globally, also exist in Islam and the cultures around Islam.

And finally, **a veil doesn't equal oppression**. One of the most common justifications people use when discussing Muslim women as oppressed is the hijab. People will cite hot weather, fashion, discomfort and liberation as reasons why Muslim women may not want to wear the hijab, bolstering their belief that it is forced upon them. However, for many Muslim women, the hijab is an integral part of their identity. It's also important to note that the act of covering hair is not unique to Islam. Nuns cover their heads, Jews and Amish wear head coverings, as do Sikhs.

Prompts for discussion

- Challenge the person you're talking to, to think about the oppression of women worldwide, from every background and religion. Urge them to consider the wider problems of patriarchy, as opposed to something exclusively reserved for Muslim women.
- Ask the person you're speaking to if they know any Muslim women who are oppressed. Also, ask them what the Muslim people they know are like. The chances are they will have friends or collegues who are Muslim, and they probably don't see those people as oppressed.
- Ask them why they believe Muslim women are oppressed specifically. Asking someone to explain their bias is one of the quickest ways to show that the bias isn't built on anything tangible, but rather impressions and vague thoughts that hold no basis for an argument.

Information to remember

- A study based on thirty-five years of *New York Times* and *Washington Post* reports found that journalists are more likely to report on women living in Muslim and Middle Eastern countries if their rights are violated, but are more likely to report on women in other societies when their rights are respected.
- Associating the clothing Muslim women choose to wear with oppression, and arguing that they shouldn't wear hijabs, burqas, veils or long covering clothes, is an oppressive act in itself. Feminism is about choice, and Muslim women are making their choices. It's up to us to respect that.
- A report into UK media coverage of Muslims and Islam found that the majority of articles and broadcast clips have a negative slant, with one in five associating Islam with terrorism or extremism.
- According to Islamic theology, it's entirely the woman's choice to have an abortion. She can make that choice based on her own economic realities, her mental health, or for any other reason she so decides – a choice that is denied to many women in the Western and so called 'free' world.

"The Police Are Here to Protect Us"

It's around midnight, and I'm propped up on the sofa in my parents' living room. It's dark save for the light from a lamp illuminating my corner of the room. I've been half watching television and half browsing the internet, consuming mindless information about celebrities and tumbling down Wikipedia holes. I've been staying at my family home because I'm about to take a break from advertising and move to Greece with my partner, Jordy, to work on boats for a season. It's meant to feel like a fresh start, but I'm not in a great headspace. It's one of those odd nights when I'm only staying up because I don't want to go to bed.

A man I used to go to school with has been harassing and stalking me online. I don't know how to get him to leave me alone. Three days ago, this stretch of harassment began as it always does; with a flurry of messages from people I used to know. Old uni housemates, people from high school I'm no longer in contact with, and a guy my sister used to date all reached out to ask, 'Is this you?'

The question is always accompanied by a screenshot of messages they've received from a profile that looks to be mine, but has actually been set up by my online stalker. He'd stolen my pictures, information about my family and created profiles that, at first glance, would be hard to differentiate from mine, especially if you no longer knew me that well. I felt a trickling sense of dread this was the start of something that would go on for too long, and could potentially put me in danger.

Earlier that day, after one of my friends had replied to this man and called him by his name, the stalker had responded. 'Where is Gina now,' he'd demanded – no question mark. Abandoning the anonymity of the fake account, he'd revealed his interest in my *physical* whereabouts. With those four words, my not inconsiderable concern had crystallized into palpable fear. I had done my best to stay calm and go through my usual process: ask the friend to screenshot the interaction and send it to me, then report and block the account, and stay vigilant for future activity. I dragged the screenshot into the desktop folder I had created for collating evidence should I ever need it, added the username it had come from to my draft email of names he used and began mindlessly scrolling into the evening to distract myself.

Just after midnight I receive an alert that someone is trying to access my emails. Instantly, I know what is happening and change my password to something more secure, but as I do so, I get an email from Apple asking me to verify a login attempt to my iCloud from a different device. I start to panic. I can't change my email password and log in to Apple at the same time, and I have this image of my stalker calmly gaining access to my accounts as I scramble to stop him.

My first thought is that he is after nude pictures. I am

twenty-four and have been in a long-term but often long-distance relationship for three years, so I know that if he gets into my phone, he'll probably find them. I also know how that plays out, and it won't be in my favour. After five or ten minutes of panic, the notifications stop and, in real time, I feel him give up. I stare blankly past the glow of my screen into the darkness of the room, my heart thudding in my ears. 'This is enough,' I think. 'I've had enough.' The next day I count the screenshots in my dedicated folder: there are one hundred. I decide to contact the police.

At this point in my life, I understood policing primarily through its depiction on the news and in TV shows (programmes about high-speed chases or drug busts), and from my own experience with officers, which was negligible. The interactions I'd had with the police were limited to being told by them to get out of the park – nothing serious and nothing that made me feel threatened or frightened. Because of this, I believed the police force to be a heroic institution that worked tirelessly to make society safer. They found the murderers and locked them up, they stopped violence before it got out of hand, and they kept our neighbourhoods safe so that we could all live in peace. The police are here to protect us, right? They held people accountable, the process for which – from my couch in a small, north-western, majority white town – seemed simple: a crime happened, they solved it.

On some level, however, I knew it couldn't be that simple. I knew the police might have to prioritize other cases over mine, which could lead to mine being dropped, so I did my own research before filing the report. I figured that if my stalker had been in trouble with the law before, there would be more of an impetus to convict him.

A few minutes of googling revealed that he had previously appeared in court and been sentenced to four months in prison for harassing and hacking another woman. This new information made me even more worried for my safety, which, in turn, cemented my decision to go to the police and my conviction that they would *have* to do something. Sadly, I now know that again and again survivors and victims of male violence have uttered their belief that the police are there to protect them, only for it never to become a reality.

A few days later, with the support of my parents, I called the local police station, although I didn't have complete faith in them holding men like this accountable. The Crime Survey for England and Wales estimates that 4.9 million adults in England and Wales have experienced stalking or harassment in their lifetime, with women twice as likely as men to experience these crimes. Studies of individuals charged with stalking indicate over 56 per cent go on to reoffend. Stalking may also escalate to other crimes, such as sexual assault or murder. A 2017 report by a joint inspectorate team found that out of a sample of 112 cases of stalking and harassment examined by HM Crown Prosecution Service Inspectorate and HM Inspectorate of Constabulary, none were found to have been dealt with well. More than 60 per cent showed no evidence of a risk management plan for victims. In 95 per cent of the case files reviewed, care for the victim was deemed to be inadequate and three-quarters of the cases were not even handled by detectives. Even though the Protection from Harassment Act (1997) and the Protection of Freedoms Act (2012) can be used to prosecute perpetrators in the UK, the PfHA does not define cyber-harassment, which results in ambiguity, and neither Act provides protection against unidentifiable perpetrators. Couple this with a historical culture of misogyny within the police and you don't have a recipe for accountability, you have one for neglect, even harm.

I still, somehow, hoped they would do the right thing. Later that week, a young male police officer arrived at my family home and we sat together in the living room as he asked question after question. I detailed everything I could remember, and he asked me to forward all the screenshots. Worryingly, there were several moments of confusion over who had made which account and how my stalker had done what he did, and I remember noting that this lack of understanding about how social media operates was going to work in my stalker's favour.

The officer left and I felt strange, not better. I knew that to him this was just another report, and I sensed that he didn't understand the behaviour to be as dangerous as I did. I also didn't feel any more in control of the situation. I had no idea what was meant to happen next, what the process would look like, if there was something else I should be doing to ensure my case got taken seriously, or who to ask if I had any questions. 'I'll pop this down to the station and you'll hear from one of us soon,' was all the officer had said. I was left with the feeling that whether 'justice' would be served would be dependent on happening to have an officer who both understood social media and was sufficiently moved by my experience to make it their business to hold my stalker accountable.

A week later I walked down to my local police station nervous as anything but ready to give a victim-impact statement. I was there for three hours. At no point was I told how important this statement was and what it would be used for, and so I arrived unprepared and emotional. During this process, which felt a lot like a school exam, I mentioned that my stalker had already been in court and asked if that would have a positive effect on the likelihood of conviction.

The officer opposite me paused and leaned forward 'Oh, he has?' I blinked back at him, astonished. 'You didn't know that?' I asked. 'Isn't that on your records? Is that not the *first* thing you check?' He clicked back into professional mode and told me they'd look right into it.

I continued to give my account of the harassment, adding more detail than before, placing emphasis on my stalker's actions and making sure to get every little detail correct. I walked out of the station feeling both angry and totally let down. A day went by and I heard nothing from the police. Another day passed, and another, and after a week or two it became clear that 'justice' was a slow process.

It wasn't until Jordy and I made it to Greece weeks later that I started to receive email communications from the police: 'We are doing the paperwork for the telecoms enquiries.' More moot updates followed as they tried and consistently failed to trace the accounts my stalker was using. They were always four or five steps behind. I continued living my life as he continued to view me as something to control.

Working as part of a lead crew looking after holidaymakers in the Sporades was as stressful as it was idyllic. One day we'd be at sea in raging storms, trying to keep our guests safe, and the next we'd be heading to an island, listening to music and gazing out at the glassy blue water. My old iPhone sat untouched in its waterproof case most days and I discovered the beauty of being disconnected from the world. That being said, the thought that my stalker could be impersonating me or messaging my family and friends while I was busy working on the water was a constant worry. My bubble would burst the second I received a message from a friend saying he'd been in contact, and helplessness would take hold as I realized I was too far away to do anything.

As summer approached, he stopped messaging my family about me and reverted to pretending to be me, impersonating me using fake accounts which he'd populated using stolen pictures of me in a bikini. While catching up with my mum, I found out he'd called her pretending to be Jordy. Then, a friend of Jordy's in Australia told us he'd been in touch to explain that Jordy had come out as gay and was sleeping with other people. I even found out that he was spreading lies about my classmate's dead mother.

When I updated the police, I was told they had tried to arrest him multiple times but, and I quote, he 'hadn't been in'. I remember genuinely thinking – for a split second – that they were making a joke. After a month of attempts, he was eventually arrested in September 2016 and interviewed under caution and admitted to creating two fake accounts pretending to be other people. The officer on my case emailed me to tell me that 'due to lack of evidence linking him to [the accounts] it will be hard to prove it's actually him', and said, because of this, they'd submitted my case to the Crown

Prosecution Service (the public agency for conducting criminal prosecutions in England and Wales), but in April 2017 – almost one and a half years after I'd reported his actions – they declined to take it forward.

With the CPS ruling, I knew my chances of holding him accountable were over. I was heartbroken but unsurprised. It had been implied to me during earlier conversations with the police that until someone got hurt, there was little they could do. This told me, in no uncertain terms, that my case wasn't a priority because I wasn't in 'enough' danger.

There were legal powers they could have used, though, such as the Malicious Communications Act of 1988 – the sergeant at Cheshire police had even recommended my officer report him for malicious communications. He had been charged back in 2011 and, in fact, five years after my case was dropped, they would sentence him to nine years in prison for five counts of stalking. It took 11 years, 10 arrests and over 100 victims to get there. One of his victims slept with a baseball bat. I had a home alarm system for fear he would come to my house. We were in enough danger. This wasn't about a lack of legal powers, this was inefficient policing.

It was just over two months after my case was dropped that I was upskirted at a festival called British Summer Time by a group of men I didn't know. Knowing how the police failed victims of misogynistic crimes – especially if they were non-contact – I did everything I could to prevent the same thing from happening again. The moment the picture was taken, I confronted the guy and took a mental picture of him. I asked for help from everyone around me. I shouted. I grabbed the phone he'd used to take the picture and ran to the police with one of the perpetrators chasing me. I handed the officer the phone containing the picture, and I had witnesses with me, ready to give their accounts.

I was in tears as I recounted what had happened. There and then the police told me they were 'sorry' but that there was not much they could do and that I 'wouldn't hear much' from them. I swear to God, that day something inside me just snapped. I had done *everything* we ask survivors and victims of sexual harassment to do, often in the scariest moments of their lives, and the police couldn't even do what they claim their job is: to protect and hold the perpetrator accountable.

Back in 2017 there was a law they could have encouraged me to use: outraging public decency. Sure, it is a grossly inadequate public nuisance order to use for a sexual offence and involves requirements to prosecute such as 'three or more people' to have seen the lewd incident, but my experience fulfilled those requirements. I wasn't told what the perpetrator did was against the law. I wasn't told I could take it further. I was told nothing other than that I wouldn't hear much from them. They didn't even kick the guys out of the festival, which speaks volumes about how seriously they viewed what happened to me and the danger I was potentially in. There was no reason these officers shouldn't have taken my case seriously.

I started my campaign to change the law the following week and, after it had gained some traction, I began doing news interviews, which would be edited down and posted on the broadcasters' official Facebook pages. In one of the interviews, I critiqued the police's response to sexual-assault victims. Among some comments of support, and some of gross misogyny, were a smattering of demands that I be more respectful to the police. 'The police are here to protect us! It's not their fault!' But it wasn't my job to be respectful in the face of negligence, it was my job to discuss how and why this had happened to me.

As a culture, we are so desperate to humble women – especially those who exercise a degree of agency and speak on topics that critique the gender hierarchy. We socialize women to be quiet and reasonable even when they have been hurt and failed by the institutions that claim to protect them. We don't listen to women's righteous anger. Black women's anger has been systematically rebranded as aggression in order to delegitimize them, while white women's anger has been tied to the patriarchal idea of hysteria, 'a disease of over-civilization' which was seen as indicating nervousness and weakness. Even in our most painful, shameful moments, we are encouraged to show decorum and respect to those who have neglected or failed us.

As I began my campaign, at panels, events, meet-ups and online, I spent time with survivors and victims who were angry, and who refused to be quiet about that anger. I wanted to be my full self and embody my anger too, but I was about to embark on two years of political campaigning in and out of the powerful and oppressive halls of Westminster, where I had to learn to become incredibly diplomatic. In order to get the job done and change the law, I had to become even more palatable to the institution than I was to the media.

Privately, I'd use my anger as fuel to continue, but publicly I appealed to a British public that is uncomfortable with righteous feminine rage. Throughout that work, I'd see the phrase 'the police are here to protect us' pop up again and again, and each time I'd bite my lip, remembering the greater cause, when all I wanted to say was 'But who is "us"? And why do I, and every victim of sexual violence I've met along the way, especially Black, disabled and trans survivors, have a story of when they did exactly the opposite?'

In Response to 'The Police Are Here to Protect Us'

When a dominant community reaps the privileges and advantages of a social hierarchy (for example, in a racial hierarchy this would be white Britons, who make up approximately 80 per cent of the population), a generally held view or perspective can feel, to that community, like the *only* view. This is all the more true when, historically, that view has been encoded by the system and alternatives or evidence to oppose it have been rejected from the mainstream narrative. 'The police are here to protect us' is a fairly robust example of this – it's a phrase used to suffocate any critique or questioning of policing and how it operates as a system.

Popular culture has played a *huge* part in building this mindset. Television shows, documentaries and reality series that depict law-enforcement strategies and policing have been around for as long as television has, and for people holding enough social and financial privilege to live a relatively quiet, police-free life, these programmes can be the most exposure they have to policing full stop.

The UK's first ever cop show, *Telecrime*, was broadcast in 1938. A 'whodunit' that encouraged viewers to unravel grisly crimes, it took inarguably awful acts of violence and depicted morally sound officers risking it all to bring the perpetrators to justice; a classic hero/villain narrative. Nowadays, police dramas such as *Line of Duty* offer slightly more flawed and realistic characters, and reality shows such as *Police Camera Action!*, *Traffic Cops* and *24 Hours in Police Custody* follow actual officers working in their real-life jobs. But even in these cases, the narrative is focused on showcasing the best of the police and reinforcing a binary hierarchy where officers are 'the good guys' and the perpetrators are nameless, faceless individuals who pose a threat to 'us' and 'our society', with 'bent coppers' being outliers.

The viewer is never encouraged to ask why, say, the guy they've just thrown into the back of the van has such an addiction struggle, or why this area left behind by the state is struggling with issues of knife crime and interpersonal violence. In doing so, it becomes voyeuristic dehumanizing entertainment for those of us who want to feel a sense of exceptionalism, and good PR framing for the police, which makes it much easier for the public to believe the idea that 'the police are here to protect us' rather than 'the police are here to maintain a social order' (a situation in which, crucially, some people are more demonized and oppressed than others).

Critiquing the police often leads to defensiveness because we *want* to believe in the fallacy of good and bad. Those of us who haven't been on the receiving end of inequities such as uneven distribution of wealth, gendered violence or removal of rights want to believe that a protective system that keeps things 'just' is more real than it is, and that our problems can be solved by a group of people using force. Or, as their framing would have it, a 'group of saviours'.

The reality, like everything, is much darker and much more complicated, despite what the mainstream media would have you believe. As well as the cultural narrative of police benevolence, pop culture also misrepresents the effectiveness of the force; the volume of serious crimes we see police 'solving' through reality television shows, documentaries and even the Twitter feeds of various forces versus the amount of serious crime they *actually* 'solve' in our society is wildly disparate.

Despite the sweeping and strong legislation the police have at their disposal to arrest perpetrators of serious crimes, the Home Office reported in 2019 that just 7.8 per cent of all recorded offences resulted in a charge or summons. For violent crime that figure was 8 per cent, for robbery it was 7 per cent, for theft it was 6 per cent, and for sexual offences other than rape it was 3.5 per cent. In 2020, an abysmal 1.6 per cent of rapes resulted in a charge or summons, making it almost impossible for survivors and victims of rape to hold their perpetrator accountable. As Laura Bates notes in *Fix the System, Not the Women*, 'When someone has a 99 per cent chance of getting away with a crime with zero legal repercussions, isn't it quite reasonable to refer to it as having been decriminalized?'

Our legal system is not operating as its PR machine would have us believe either. Take a look at the CPS Twitter account and you will see positive tweets full of reassurance: 'We're committed to transforming the way rape cases are handled' and 'See how we're working to deliver justice for more victims of these devastating offences'. Given that, in 2016, the

CPS Inspectorate wrote that when it comes to rape and serious sexual offences, 'All areas are under-resourced for the current volume and even more so for anticipated future increases', it's damning that data released in July 2022 suggests that '[the CPS] is still failing to meet its own targets', according to End Violence Against Women.

Before a case even gets to court, though, the police are failing victims. In a House of Commons Committee report, Project Bluestone lead Professor Betsy Stanko OBE noted that the outcome of 86 per cent of rape allegations is determined by police and their decision-making. In the report, Stanko said, 'That is a huge, huge influence on what gets transferred to the Crown Prosecution Service for decision. That is the first step: do the police transfer a case and actually ask for charges? If it is 86% of the cases, and we know that from the evidence, that means the police largely determine which cases go forward and which do not.' Though some victims and survivors have seen convictions improve their immediate safety – myself being one of them – these numbers show that for sexual offences, outcomes like this are not a given.

For survivors and victims of male violence, the police have a lot to answer for. In 2020, a More 4 study found over a two-year period that, on average, one woman per week came forward to report their partner who worked in the police was seriously abusing them or their children. In this investigation, one former police commander described officer-perpetrated domestic abuse as an 'epidemic' within the force. Some victims blamed a 'boys' club' culture of cover-ups and closing ranks that made survivors feel silenced. This boys' club is likely part of the reason that out of a group of 1,319 officers (from forty-one forces across the UK) with domestic abuse allegations, 80 per cent kept their jobs.

In fact, most crimes reported to the police aren't 'solved'. From 2018 to 2019, less than 4 per cent of offences were dealt with out of court, by way of an on-the-spot fine, caution or community resolution, such as an apology or compensation.

To see conviction as the definitive answer to a happy, healthy community is to ignore prevention as a viable and constructive solution, and to value incarceration – something I no longer subscribe to – instead. When 'the police are here to protect us' comes up, its logic is usually pro-punitive, and even by that logic, the numbers above show that policing is failing. If you were to take an exam and failed to answer over 90 per cent of the questions in each section, it wouldn't just be a fail, it would be an *epic* fail.

As veteran US police researcher, political scientist and professor David H. Bayley noted in his 1996 book *Police for the Future*, 'The police do not prevent crime. This is one of the best kept secrets of modern life. Experts know it, the police know it, but the public does not know it. Yet the police pretend that they are society's best defence against crime and continually argue that if they are given more resources, especially personnel, they will be able to protect communities against crime. This is a myth.'

Given the vast majority of crimes that are investigated aren't 'solved', it probably comes as no surprise to hear that when it comes to racially motivated crimes, things are even worse. There is a lack of recognition of that racial motivation, and cases are grossly under-prioritized. In many instances, they're ignored. In 1993, when teenager Stephen Lawrence was murdered in South London by a group of white men in a racist attack, no arrests were made for two weeks, despite five suspects being named by anonymous informants. Only after an unforgivable thirteen years were convictions brought forward because of the pressure applied by an organization of campaigners and Stephen's family in the wake of his murder. Unsurprisingly, the Macpherson Report – which was published in 1999 in response to the public outcry at the police's handling of the case – found attempts to catch Mr Lawrence's killers were hampered by institutional racism in the Metropolitan Police. From Azelle Rodney, who was shot by police while unarmed in 2005, to the murder of Chris Kaba, an unarmed man who was not a suspect of a crime, yet was stalked by police who hadn't activated their lights or sirens before being boxed in and shot through the windscreen of his vehicle in 2022, the violence historically enacted against Black communities by the police doesn't start and end with neglect of investigation. Though the media frames these patterns as isolated incidents, they aren't caused by under-resourcing or apathy, but by anti-Blackness. In 2020, a Novara Media report found that of the seventy-four people fatally shot by police since 1990, twenty of those have been Black or of another ethnic minority, making these communities proportionately twice as likely to be shot dead by an officer, despite making up only 13.8 per cent of the population. Such data instantly makes clear why eight out of ten Black Britons polled by the charity Hope Not Hate agreed that 'police are biased against people from my background and ethnic group'. Black communities across the UK have been organizing, resisting and campaigning for decades that the police don't, and never have, protected them, and yet this is still the prevailing narrative because it preserves and protects the institution itself.

When it comes to women living under multiple systems of oppression, Black women in particular are being failed by the police at even higher levels. Misogynoir – a phrase coined by scholar and activist Moya Bailey to describe where misogyny and anti-Blackness meet and 'the ways anti-Black and misogynistic representation shape broader ideas about Black women'– is rife in these institutions. The CPS doesn't produce disaggregated stats on prosecution outcomes, so although the Office for National Statistics reports that Black and mixed-race women are more likely to be victims of rape, it refuses to even look at how women who face the cumulative danger of anti-Blackness *and* misogyny are being harmed comparatively with white women.

The Valerie's Law campaign led by Sistah Space – a domestic-abuse charity supporting women of African and Caribbean heritage – made headlines in 2021 for their lobbying to make specialist training mandatory for all police and other government agencies that support Black women and girls affected by domestic abuse. It was named after Valerie Forde, who was murdered by her former partner in 2014 alongside their 22-month-old daughter. Valerie had asked the police for help after her ex had threatened to 'burn down the house with her in it', but, horrendously, this was recorded as a threat to property, not to her.

According to a freedom of information request sent to police forces and the Crown Prosecution Service, Black victims of sexual assault and rape are 1.5 times less likely to see police bring charges against their alleged abuser in comparison to white victims, and research by Sistah Space showed 86 per cent of women of African and/or Caribbean heritage in the UK have either been a victim of domestic abuse or know a family member who has been assaulted.

Male violence against women, trans people and non-binary people is endemic, and because it is hard-baked into policing too, victims don't even feel as if they can come forward. Add to this the institutional racism for which the police force has become infamous and it's no wonder that the same report by Sistah Space found that only 57 per cent of the victims polled said they would report the abuse to the police. How can we expect people to seek protection from an institution that has such a huge issue with domestic violence that in the last five years UK police forces received more than 800 domestic-abuse allegations against its officers and staff? When it comes to misogyny, a cocktail of whiteness, toxic masculinity and disproportionate power creates a terrifying culture that causes harm, so why would people choose to put their hope for protection in the hands of those who most embody those traits? Or as Mary Edwards Walker put it, 'You are our protectors is not true; for if you were, who would there be to protect us from?'

Rejection of the police as 'protector' has long been the default in many Black communities across Britain, but for women who live at multiple intersections of privilege or belong to the upper classes, and don't seek out alternative narratives that disrupt the 'police as heroes', 2021 was the year many woke up to the reality that the police do not protect them, either. After Sarah Everard's murder by police officer Wayne Couzens – who had been investigated three times previously and had exposed himself mere days before he raped and killed Sarah – three of his former colleagues were found to have shared racist, misogynistic, homophobic and ableist messages with him on WhatsApp, and were later charged with sending grossly offensive messages on a public communications network. As part of a wider investigation, a string of other officers were also charged with sex crimes, including one who was charged with forty-one offences, including eighteen of rape.

All of this took place parallel to an IOPC (Independent Office for Police Conduct) report, released in 2022, on nine linked investigations called Operation Hotton, which uncovered 'disgraceful bullying, racism, misogyny and "inappropriate behaviour" within the Metropolitan Police', demonstrated by streams of WhatsApp messages between officers that joked about raping female colleagues, attacking their wives, using knives to get women into bed and hurting Black children.

The Met Police Commissioner – the most senior officer in the country – thought an appropriate response to all of this was to remind women there is the occasional 'bad 'un' in the police. Except there's not just a few. Six hundred sexual misconduct allegations were made against Met police officers between 2012 and 2018.

When concerns about the public's lack of trust in the police reached fever pitch after Everard's death, senior policing figures advised women – who, by the way, have spent their *entire lives* hearing 'just report it to the police' when harassed or assaulted – to 'verify a police officer's credentials' if they want to feel safer in an officer's presence. They also advised women to 'shout to a passer-by', 'wave down a bus' or 'call 999', as if interrogating an officer wouldn't put women – especially those who find themselves at the intersection of multiple systems of oppression – in more danger, or flagging down a bus is a practical option. As if – wait for it – calling the police on 999 makes any sense when the officer is the source of your fear in the first place.

When women took to Clapham Common to remember Sarah – not even to protest the misogyny of the police officers that led to her death – the Metropolitan Police moved in with force, wrestling grieving women to the ground and citing Covid legislation. (The same legislation they later refused to use to charge government officials for hosting indoor parties during restrictions.) An official inquiry found that the police 'acted appropriately' at the Everard vigil, but as author Alex S. Vitale states in his seminal book *The End of Policing*, 'To rely on the threat of lethal force to obtain compliance flies in the face of "policing by consent".' To add salt to the wound, when throngs of male footy fans congregated to watch the Euros three months after the Everard vigil – when restrictions were still in place and Covid cases were higher – no such force was used. How, and when, are women meant to feel like the police protect us?

The violent history of the Metropolitan Police is particularly important when it comes to exploring the culture of policing across the country. The Metropolitan Police was the original blueprint for modern policing and is still the largest force in the country today, with 34,545 officers and a whopping annual allocation of a quarter of the total police budget for England and Wales. In *The End of Policing*, Vitale recounts how Robert Peel created the Met in order to 'to protect property, quell riots, put down strikes and other industrial actions, and produce a disciplined industrial workforce'. This model, which aimed to control and subdue the working and labour classes into industrialization – not keep them safe – was expanded across England, then exported to Boston and, later, New York.

While Peel was building the Metropolitan Police, he was also involved in managing the colonial occupation of Ireland and had previously used the country as a testing ground for the expansion and extraction of resources, creating a semi-armed police force in Dublin that focused entirely on enforcing colonial order. The reality is, the blueprint of policing casts a long shadow and must be recognized as important context when we analyse the institution now, when corruption in the force is widespread.

Speaking of which, the Police watchdog chief found that between 2013 and 2016, more than 8,500 complaints about corruption were recorded by forces in England and Wales, which employed 200,922 officers at the time. 'Corruption' could be anything from brutality or fraud to coercion, sexual assault, torture or general abuse of authority. After the controversy of the Macpherson Report, Cressida Dick – back when she was head of Scotland Yard's diversity directorate – stated that, despite major improvements, the force was unlikely to 'ever not be institutionally racist'. If we can accept that misogyny and racism are not 'a problem we have in parts of society' but part of the material that made it – or as poet Kyle 'Guante' Tran Myhre describes white supremacy, 'not the shark, but the water' – then the individuals who make up the many police forces across the country will, too, not be free of misogyny and racism.

Sexism and racism – systems we used to build and run our country and much of the world (and still do) – are so intricately laced into our systems, brains and structures that it would be impossible for policing not to be defined by them, let alone evade their influence. As an institution, policing is populated by a majority cis-gender, heterosexual, white male workforce that exists in a society that rarely asks it to question social, political and economic inequalities, or how it contributes to or benefits from those inequalities. So, it's easy to see how these issues prevail within the force and outside it. It's completely impossible for policing to be free of these corruptions, just as it is not possible for any of us to be free of them by default.

Understanding this means accepting that the enforcement arm of an unequal legal system has historically used force to dominate less privileged people over whom it has disproportionate power. We also have to accept it often happens in struggling communities where, in the words of sociologist Robert K. Merton, 'some commit crimes because they are responding to a social situation'. And domination is the opposite of protection. When the institutions that claim to 'protect you' repeatedly neglect and hurt you, and perpetuate and reinforce the very culture that is the root of harm affecting you, it's impossible to feel safe. For those of us who haven't suffered police neglect or harm because of our race or gender – or whose lives haven't been disrupted across generations by the police enforcing a social order, which they see us as the bottom of – we erase this harm and neglect when we commit to perpetuating this benevolent image of the police; an institution that is anything but.

It's for all these reasons that when people who are insulated by their class use the response of 'the police are here to protect us', it has to be unpicked or challenged in *some* way, if only to hold up a mirror and offer a sense of reality. For the liberal, white middle class, it can be much more comfortable to see all of society as the 'us' in this phrase, because recognizing how differently we are treated by our institutions and the systems they uphold can make us question ourselves and our role in that inequality.

That being said, it's more honest and helpful to recognize that the 'us' in this phrase generally means the white middle classes. When the white middle classes use it, they are referring to those who our society doesn't marginalize or discriminate against in systematic ways. Because when it comes down to it, those who society marginalizes because of their race, gender, status and socioeconomic background are having to deal with an entirely different type of police force.

It's totally understandable that if you've led a relatively insulated life and had little interaction with the police, your perception would be skewed by your lack of exposure to the force and its depiction in pop culture, but spend some time digging and history will tell you a different story.

Although I previously worked in punitive activism, my work doesn't lie there any more. For me, real protection would look like prevention – I mean, even if the police solving crime looks like success to you, if they solve every crime they investigate, they'd still be showing up *after* the fact. As a victim of sexual assault and stalking, I benefit from my stalker finally being in jail. I am safer and my mental health is much better. However, I also know that this outcome followed ten years of sacrifice from his victims; years of pressure from the women he hurt. My case went across the desks of tens of officers before it found one who cared enough to make it their business. This isn't a sustainable solution and I will always advocate for preventing men like him from becoming radicalized into exerting power over women, rather than removing him from society because of his actions only to reintroduce him to it years later.

When someone tells me 'the police are here to protect us', I answer honestly and I don't try to protect their image. If this phrase comes up for you, try giving a couple of facts about the impact the police actually have in material terms. Bring up the difference between how the police are framed in the media and the history of the force – what it was created for, and how it exists to retain social order rather than to protect or save us. Ask the person to whom you're talking to define who 'us' is. Talk them through the force's deeply troubling history of misogyny and racism, and explain how its disproportionate power allows it to evade the very accountability to which it claims to hold perpetrators. Remind them that, historically, the safest communities are the ones with the most reciprocity, social values, responsibility and community resources, not the largest police presence.

Prompts for discussion

- Ask the person to whom you're speaking to define who 'us' is and discuss the realities of other communities.

- Think about how many times you have had interactions with the police. If you can count them on one hand, consider how these encounters may not be representative of the force as a whole.
- Ask whether an enforcement institution that was invented to control the working classes can ever work in the interest of the working classes and those treated as less by society. Explore other ideas about the police's role. Ask the person you're talking to what they think about the concept of prevention instead of punishment – do the police prevent crime in a real sense? And how much crime is birthed from struggle?

Information to remember

- Policing is about social order, not protection and benevolence. It was created in order to stop the working classes rioting, and to create a new industrial workforce.
- The Home Office reported in 2019 that in the year to March 2019 only 7.8 per cent of all recorded offences resulted in a charge or summons.
- A More 4 study found that, on average, one woman comes forward every week to report their partner who works in the police is seriously abusing them or their children. Eighty per cent of police officers with domestic abuse allegations kept their jobs.

Nova Reid is a thought leader, TED speaker, writer and producer. Nova's sought-after online academy – Becoming Anti-Racist with Nova Reid – and bestselling debut book, *The Good Ally*, have consistently been described as life-changing, making her an award-winning (Black Magic Network's Top 100 Black British Women, Precious Award for Social Impact), renowned agent of change.

"I Don't See Colour"

Nova Reid

My reflex whenever I hear someone say, 'I don't see colour' is, 'You're an absolute liar.' Growing up in the eighties and nineties, 'I don't see colour' was as common as hair scrunchies, NASA jackets and Trolls (the original plastic kind with pink hair, not the internet ones). I stopped counting the number of times I heard this statement from children and adults alike. I remember the physicality of wincing every time I heard it back then, not really knowing how to respond to what always felt like a disingenuous and manipulative comment that left me feeling winded and, at times, still does.

I observed early on that this statement almost always came from white people who declared in one shallow breath that they were 'not racist'. Yet, by deferring to this statement – like some kind of PR move – to position themselves as a 'good white person' (and not one of those 'dodgy ones running amok' over there), ironically, it signalled to me that they were, and are, in fact, racist and, most definitely, not honest.

When you're Black and in a white majority environment it's a strange thing having to learn to balance on this precarious tightrope of being hyper-visible and yet also invisible. I've always found it more than odd and incredibly disconcerting that people go to such great lengths to try to ignore or pretend they don't see such an obvious, often hyper-visible and important part of my identity.

When I was a child and first heard this statement from an adult (it's an odd power play having a white adult attempt to centre themselves, alleviate their guilt and prove to a Black child that they're not racist), even though I didn't have the language to articulate this type of pervasive racism, I knew how it made me feel.

Unsafe and less than human.

Sadly, decades later, this phrase *still* hasn't died out. Adults and their offspring are still clumsily using it with a dysfunctional sense of misdirected pride. 'I don't see colour' is a red fucking flag. It communicates a lack of engagement in anti-racism, concerning discomfort around race and difference. And to be frank, it is nothing more than a self-serving self-declaration. It's less about doing something meaningful to address racism and more about positioning oneself as 'not racist', perhaps to feel better – or a little less guilty about – our 'colourful' colonial history, shall we call it, and the incessant white supremacy in society that persists.

I mean, when you break it down, this statement falls into the category of one of those weird phenomena that Brits (who generally and culturally speaking have a dysfunctional relationship with honesty) have mastered; when they don't take responsibility for past harms and say the opposite of what they *actually* mean. Because, unless you have a visual impairment such as colour vision deficiency or are blind, then, yes. You *do* see colour. And even so, fascinating research by Professor Osagie Obosogie, published in his book *Blinded by Sight: Seeing Race in the Eyes of the Blind*, shows us that racism even persists in blind people in the same way it does with sighted people.

This is because racism isn't merely about 'seeing colour', it is about what we learn, consciously and unconsciously. It is about how we are socialized. It is about what we are taught, verbally and non-verbally, about groups of people who may be different to us, and how we subsequently interact with one another socially and culturally. So, while many – perhaps even you – like to maintain with a full, puffed-out chest that they don't discriminate based on skin colour, our behaviour often tells a very different story.

Racism is not innate, it is learned behaviour. We are not born hating or automatically fearing or associating negative attributes with one group of people over another based on skin colour. But children learn racism from adults pretty damn quickly. Studies show that children as young as three years old start to express racial bias in the playground. Further research shows that parents and caregivers who teach children a 'colour blind' approach not only perpetuate racism, but create stigma, as it teaches children there is 'something wrong' with people's skin colour. And more to the point, research confirms this approach actually has the opposite of the desired effect and children raised 'not to see colour' grow up to be adults who are not only unsophisticated at talking about race but also unable to recognize racial discrimination, let alone tackle racism.

To be crystal clear, this approach is *NOT* working. (Allow the shame to come and go, now you know.)

Being anti-racist is an active practice. And when I think about how 'helpful' statements such as 'I don't see colour' actually are when it comes to actively tackling anti-racism – it's not remotely helpful, it is inconsequential. Unless of course it's being weaponized as a shield, in which case it's entirely malignant. It is less about addressing racism or seeing someone as a full human being and more about personal brand management. About making oneself look 'good', absolving guilt and shame (some inherited, some probably your own) from centuries of past and present horrors enacted under white supremacy.

This isn't about denigration, this is about being honest and getting curious about your own behaviour. Ignoring race and pretending not to notice skin colour does not, has not and will never do anything to meaningfully tackle racism. I wouldn't be writing this chapter, or an entire book on the subject, if it did. I'd be resting, living in peace somewhere on a Caribbean island, free from racism and free from the irony of being asked to teach white people how not to be racist.

Racism, though powerful, is entirely illogical, and it does this strange thing where it stays stuck in a time machine and simultaneously evolves. So, while petrol bombs and faeces in letterboxes for most (certainly not all) are now rare, overt racism was and, let's be honest, still is a social practice, a 'norm'. Racism, specifically anti-Blackness, was allowed; it formed a global industry, it became the bedrock of pseudoscience, and from the seventeenth century it was written in law, often by the British, to justify treating Africans worse than animals because of pigmentation. It persisted for centuries and centuries. For too long it was perfectly acceptable to enact violence under white supremacy and refuse work and basic human rights to somebody because of the colour of their skin. Only in 1965, in the UK at least, did it become illegal to discriminate against someone based on race.

Read that last line again.

The cultural and social practice of racism, and specifically the dehumanization of Black folk based on who we cannot help but be, doesn't just miraculously disappear with a (less than adequate) law change. What was once acceptable socially, quite simply, now isn't. For the most part – and clearly this is debatable for some – it's 'generally' no longer socially acceptable to be overtly racist. However, racism continues to exist in many ways, from pay inequity to the disproportionate number of Black people killed in police custody, violent public attacks, Black women being four to five times more likely to die in childbirth, to racism at work, in the therapy room, sliding into WhatsApp groups dressed up as 'banter', and across the family dinner table. The consequences were, and still are, devastating. And deep down you know this, hence your guilt reflex to declare you're not racist whenever you see someone Black. Racism persists, but rather than be acknowledged and addressed, it is suppressed, shut down and hidden.

We have learned racism and we have also learned how to suppress it, and statements like 'I don't see colour' are examples of what happens when we do not intentionally address and face our racism, and specifically our anti-Blackness. It still leaks out in the most seemingly unremarkable of conversations. Because as much as we try, we cannot hide generations' worth of unaddressed racism under a dusty old rug. The social practice of white supremacy and its offspring, racism, can't disappear with a law change. It also doesn't just exist in a 'few bad apples' in the police force, the Ku Klux Klan, Britain First, or individuals who 'want their country back'. Racism has never solely existed in these small microcosms, it's cultural, it's social and it's political – it's everywhere, it's systemic, it shapeshifts and constantly takes on new formats.

Formats such as racial microaggressions. A racial microaggression is a type of covert everyday racism; comments and often uncivil behaviour that happen both intentionally and unintentionally, consciously and subconsciously. Either way, the impact remains the same. They communicate that Black folk and people of colour are misplaced somehow. They are the subtle ways in which people in racially marginalized identities are regularly not treated the same, from comments such as 'I don't see colour', to unwanted hair touching, lack of eye contact, regular racial profiling, the clutching of a handbag and avoiding sitting next to a Black or East Asian person on public transport, for instance.

Of course, in isolation, this small list of examples I've used to illustrate can seem 'relatively' harmless, but that's what makes racial microaggressions so insidious; they are anything but small in impact, because many of us receive racial microaggressions several times a day, every day. On our daily commutes, in the workplace, on the street, during a neighbourly exchange, at the playground, in education, in spiritual spaces, while shopping, in healthcare settings, in friendship circles, and for many, even in families and intimate relationships. It is this consistent and persistent exposure to othering and everyday racial stress that shows up time and time again in research as causing more harm than overt acts of hate. It is the cumulative effects of racism that lead to increased levels of stress hormones, which creates a type of wear and tear in the body that leads to physical and/or psychological distress or illness. To be clear, experiencing racism *is* trauma, and regular exposure to racial stress such as racial microaggressions can and does show up in Black bodies as trauma.

As a result, it is not surprising that fellow Black peers (and I include myself in this) will often say they would rather come face to face with an out-and-out racist once than have to deal with constant exposure to everyday racism from liberals who become so enveloped in their own guilt, embarrassment, shame, or maybe even superiority, that they will not take responsibility for their racism.

Regardless of intent, words have impact and our intention is not more important than the impact of our words or behaviour. Focusing on intention also conveniently absolves you of taking responsibility for your actions and racism. If you're reading this and need unhooking from your 'but it wasn't my intention' reflex, I like to think of it in basic terms: if we accidentally crash into someone else's car, we don't spend the next hour harping on about how 'it wasn't our intention' to hit the car. We exchange insurance details, and take responsibility for the damage to make it right.

If you genuinely want to be actively anti-racist, one of the first things you need to do is accept, in the same way we have been socialized to be sexist, you've been socialized to be racist and may do or say racist things. That doesn't mean you're a bad human being or inherently flawed, but it does require honesty and taking responsibility for your racism when it shows up, again and again. If you're not willing to do that, then stop taking up space and declaring that you're anti-racist.

'I don't see colour' is not only unhelpful, it's harmful. It makes the people with whom you are professing to be in solidarity with feel gaslit, invisible, irritated, exasperated, harmed and untrusting of you, so why would you knowingly want to continue using this statement?

You should see colour.

Seeing colour or any other defining part of someone's identity is not and has never been an issue – it is part of our humanity. It is beautiful and worth seeing and celebrating. If you treat someone unfairly and discriminate *because* of their colour, then we have an issue. And that's the key difference. Blackness isn't a dirty little colonial secret to hide under a rug. It's legacy, it's survival, it's beautiful, it's creation.

White supremacy has done a number on all of us, and while our work looks **very** different, we all have our work to do and have a responsibility to heal so we don't keep passing this BS on to children. Your discomfort at seeing us, *really* seeing us and our beautiful Black skin is a direct reflection of your discomfort with your own racial identity. Only you can reconcile that.

Racism was built on so many lies. So be honest.

Racism was also built on much inhumane treatment. So humanize us.

See us. See colour. See all of our humanity. Celebrate it. But see your colour too. Get curious about what it means to be white in a society built on patriarchy and white supremacy. Make peace with your identity. If there's shame, don't panic; instead, take that as a cue to deal with it, process and understand it, not to be overrun by it; take control of it, address your knowledge gaps, take responsibility for what you can do today to reduce racism, figure out your role.

When you learn new information that challenges core values, it can feel hard, but you have a choice: cling on to old information (and white supremacy) for dear life to appear to be 'right', or adapt and do better. You get to decide. So, decide.

Prompts for discussion

- Instead of just blurting out 'I don't see colour', what would it feel like to pause and simply just listen?
- Or if you must say something, consider, 'I try not to discriminate based on skin colour, but sometimes I get nervous and say the wrong thing, and I recognize that I might. I'm working on being actively anti-racist and am open to being given feedback if I do or say something racist.'
- Resist the urge to defend your position or declare you're anti-racist, or to get tangled up in perfecting what words to say. Quite simply, this is about being

honest. We will know you are anti-racist by how you behave, not by perfecting an 'anti-racist' vocabulary.

Information to remember

- Children as young as three years old start to express racial bias in the playground.
- Caregivers who teach children a 'colour-blind' approach perpetuate racism, and this approach also has the opposite of the desired effect. Children raised 'not to see colour' grow up to be adults who are less able to recognize racial discrimination.
- Racism even persists in blind people in the same way it does in sighted people.

"You Can't Say Anything These Days"

It is February 2020 and I am seated at the desk of a tiny recording studio in the BBC's Broadcasting House. In normal times I would be at the BBC 5 Live studio, opposite veteran DJ and presenter Nihal Arthanayake, but because of a new virus, we've decided it isn't necessary for me to travel to Manchester, where the show broadcasts from. Instead, I am co-presenting from a small, soundproofed, temporary studio in London. I am video-linked to Nihal, who is an hour into hosting his four-hour flagship show. He, as always, is in the Salford home of the station, looking relaxed and in control.

Nihal has been doing this for decades and he's a true professional: funny, warm, casual and someone who makes hosting mainstream live radio look like an absolute breeze. However, as I've found out, it's a very specific skill that requires thinking about so many things at the same time: what point you're making, where the conversation is heading, how much time you need to fill, and retaining journalistic balance. During this particular broadcast, I realize that hosting is even harder when you're not in the same room as your co-presenter, especially when you've been thrown in at the deep end.

I first met Nihal about six months ago when I was invited on to his show to talk about and promote the release of my debut book, which I wrote as a toolkit for activism as the Voyeurism Act came into effect. After I leave the studio, his producers approach me about doing a limited series of one-hour slots during which Nihal and I would offer a platform for people who are trying to make a difference in society. I obviously jumped at the chance, and by this point we are six shows in. The focus of this particular episode is a campaign to stop street harassment, something sister duo Maya and Gemma Tutton were spearheading, and they've joined me in the studio along with Rose Caldwell from an organization called Plan International. All three women want street harassment to be outlawed in legislation, but they also want a cultural shift in how readily we accept harassment as a normal part of women's and marginalized genders' existence.

Halfway through the show, we've discussed the reality of what it's like to be a woman or girl navigating public space: the catcalling, the leering, the shouting, the groping and the sexual violence. We've discussed the fact that one in three schoolgirls is harassed on Britain's streets despite their uniform being a very visual signifier of the fact they are underage.

During the break for the news and sport updates, in preparation for being back on air, I reshuffle my notes, which tell me 'Nihal to read texts after news' will be the next segment. As always, a green light clicks on in the studio to tell us we are live, and the sound of the introductory jingle comes through my headphones. Nihal re-introduces the show and hands over to me to give a recap of the issues we've been discussing before we move on to listeners' questions.

The texts are supportive and thoughtful, which surprises me slightly as the station's listenership is primarily male. Pleasingly, though, some fathers have texted in and commended Maya and Gemma for their work. A 54-year-old woman tells us of a lifetime of street harassment: being followed, being flashed and being assaulted in the street. She describes how she gave up her life's passion of cycling because of the comments men made about her body. She also tells us how, at the age of twenty-one, the police failed her when a man assaulted her and tried to hit her with his car, and how she is witnessing her sixteen-year-old deal with the same type of attention now.

'John from Dagenham has texted in,' Nihal announces, and I detect a slight sigh in his voice. As he reads, I listen intently while staring down at my legs, my brow furrowed. According to John, there are so many rules nowadays that it's impossible to speak to women and long gone are the days when the BBC was unbiased. Nihal reclines in his chair and takes a breath.

'Respectfully, I don't think you've listened to the discussions today, John,' he begins. 'I know the BBC is all about balance, but what would the "balance" be for this topic?' He draws a pair of air quotes as he lingers over the word 'balance'. 'It's OK to harass women – and children – in the street? That's not "balance".' Nihal laughs and moves on to the next text.

I look at Maya, scrunch up my nose and nod in approval.

She, Gemma, Rose and I are bonded by the shared experience of existing as women in the world, and we all feel some satisfaction at Nihal's respectful takedown of a listener who clearly can't distinguish street harassment from consensual and respectful conversation.

After the show wraps, we pack up and leave the studio. I say goodbye to Maya and tell her that I am always around if she needs anything. I reassure her that she's done a great job on the show, but she brushes off the compliment, explaining that she is exhausted. I understand so deeply what she means by this.

I walk out through the impressive circular entrance of BBC HQ and catch an Uber home, replaying the show in my head as I always do. I pick apart what I didn't do well, and agonize over how I could have found a better way to articulate myself in a certain section, or how I spoke over Nihal slightly during another. I find myself mulling over the responses we had from listeners and feel a familiar sense of hope that we might have changed just one person's opinion. Maybe a father who was listening will now choose to speak out the next time he witnesses something he thinks doesn't look right. In spite of this, I notice that rather than focusing on the positive and supportive texts, I can't help but think about John. His text is stuck in my mind and has left me feeling exasperated.

Whenever social-justice topics come up in conversation, whether it's on a radio show or sat around the dinner table, it's normal to hear a comment like John's. It might be worded differently, but it reflects a defensive response that people often have when our culture is progressing: 'You can't say anything these days!' It's from the same playbook as phrases such as, 'why does everything have to be so politically correct?', 'everyone's so offended these days' and 'the world's gone mad!' They usually indicate that someone feels their rights are being infringed upon because they can't say the same things they've always said. John certainly isn't alone in his response; in fact, he's part of a club of millions.

In the Uber, I keyword search the show to see what the response has been on Twitter. The official BBC 5 Live account has posted a cut-down video of our discussion, and one of the first comments underneath it reads, 'Genuine question: Is there an acceptable way to pay someone a compliment?' I tap the speech bubble and type out my answer. 'Yes. Respectfully (not sexualizing them) and in the right environment.' I drop my phone on to my lap and vow not to respond to any more comments. I sit back and look out the window as we crawl along in traffic down Oxford Street.

In Response to 'You Can't Say Anything These Days'

This statement – and others like it – are everywhere. It is an expression of defiance that always seems to come up during discussions about political topics, and it's most commonly used by those in society who are benefiting from systems of oppression – namely straight, cis white men, or straight, cis white women. Anyone who has started using people's pronouns just to hear 'this has all gone too far', who has mentioned that monikers such as 'darling' or 'love' make them feel patronized and had been told to 'lighten up', or who has called out sexual harassment and been met with 'you used to be able to flirt with women' can attest to this. Personally, when I hear someone complain that 'you can't say anything these days', I always want to ask, 'and what is it exactly that you *want* to say?'

The mainstream media has been forced to dedicate more coverage to social-justice issues because of grassroots and online campaigns, and powerful media figures have increasingly found themselves answerable to the general public who, by and large, will offer agreement, critique or condemnation on social media. 'Cancel culture', or more importantly, the rebranding of accountability that certain people perceive as 'cancel culture', is something repeatedly cited by media figures who are uncomfortable with the feedback they receive in a digital age.

I'm not talking about thoughtful and meaningful discussions about trial by social media here; rather, the likes of Elon Musk, Joe Rogan, Piers Morgan, Katie Hopkins and Andrew Tate, who will criticize 'cancel culture'. What they are actually rallying against is being exposed to the reaction their opinions elicit. All of these individuals have discussed how they have been 'cancelled' or 'silenced' for their opinions. To be cancelled, though, is to be completely removed from one's platforms, unable to engage in your work and removed from your position of power. That these people claim to be 'silenced' in their mainstream newspaper columns, on their active social platforms (with hundreds of thousands of followers) or on their number-one global podcast (with heavyweight corporate partners) is a ridiculous irony that shouldn't be lost on any of us.

In fact, due to new media – the ability to create your own channel or platform yourself – and social media, celebrities and commentators currently have more outlets than ever before, so it could be argued that they can be more publicly vocal than ever. And while performative online slanging matches or trial by social media will rarely be an effective way to encourage these individuals to meaningfully evaluate their language or opinions (real growth takes time and happens away from the digital sphere), it's also true that the biggest cheerleaders of free speech are also often those who are quickest to condemn and attempt to silence any negative response to their work.

Whether you're a celebrity or not, thanks to social media our views and language are visible in a way that they never have been before. We are exposed to others critiquing our way of thinking on a regular basis, and in a very public way, all day, every day. And being pulled up on your use of language or opinions in a public way is confronting for some people. For those who are committed to expanding their worldview, eager to learn about the experiences and realities of others, and who choose to exist in spaces (either online or offline) where that is supported and valued, being challenged on their language might be received as helpful, welcomed and eye-opening, just as it is necessarily uncomfortable. However, for those who have had little exposure to discourse that reconsiders or challenges the social norms, hierarchies and language they've previously enjoyed or continue to enjoy, being called out (or even better 'in' – a version that includes conversation, compassion and context and is advocated for by Professor Loretta J. Ross) can feel like a personal accusation that you are 'out of touch' or ignorant. And perhaps it is.

This reaction is partly dependent on whether those individuals have developed the necessary tools to handle such a conversation. If they're part of a dominant community that created social norms and still benefit from them, or if they come from a background where those norms weren't challenged, their skillset may be underdeveloped. That might be especially true if they're of a generation that didn't have the same level of access to alternative discourse online.

When parts of society are being forced to recognize or, even better, understand the experiences of those who have historically been disenfranchised, we often enter a period of unrest. Growth of any kind is uncomfortable, especially when it's collective. When people who have been marginalized push back and speak up, movements are started and culture begins to shift. Ultimately, as well as listening to, and supporting, the work marginalized communities are *already* doing, dominant communities should be working on their own personal healing and making social, political and economic changes that accommodate progress.

Often those changes start small, such as in the language we use every day. Certain words and phrases that the dominant group previously deemed acceptable are rightly branded as harmful, and although this change is the result of an ongoing and gradual cultural shift – permeating the consciousness of individuals and institutions over years – it can feel sudden to some people. Think, for example, of how using others' pronouns has become the norm in certain industries and progressive communities. Or how some women are pushing back against being referred to as 'females' by men (and transphobic women), because it is a scientific descriptor originally rooted in the enslavement of Black women by white European colonizers in the 16th century that reduced Black women's personhood to their biology in order to justify their subjugation and the using of their reproductive systems as a means of production. Disruption of language like this in dominant communities has been a long time coming and is the result of decades of work from marginalized communities, but once any part of these conversations reaches the mainstream media, the public perception is that it's 'too much, too soon'.

The dominant culture feels entitled to what it's previously enjoyed and is entirely unused to being asked to make any type of allowances for new ways of operating – even emotional allowances such as not even being tasked with challenging your thinking, but instead just controlling your anger at a certain topic when around people it affects. It therefore perceives the shift as a threat, and fears its 'freedoms' being taken away in some respect. We see this when white people respond to diversity quotas by saying that 'it used to be easier to get jobs', inadvertently revealing their disappointment that their careers no longer benefit from racism. Similarly, in the gun-safety debate in the US, restrictions on who can carry guns – the biggest killer of US children and an almost uniquely masculine form of violence – is seen as an infringement of liberties, and in discussions around male violence, men reject ideas involving any restrictions being put on them ('male curfews would be inhumane!'), while maintaining that restricting women's lifestyles or movements is the answer to keeping them safe ('don't run late at night!').

This scarcity mentality makes people respond defensively. For example, cis people may view identifying language (which, let's face it, if not self-defined, is arbitrary anyway) as evolving to a slightly new place because they are seeing more representation of trans and non-binary people in the media. From this they may feel that the way they speak is no longer the accepted norm, and in being asked to use language that is new to them, can feel undermined or somehow 'silenced'. But language, slang, nomenclatures and the way we talk about each other has to evolve if we are to change the collective consciousness and make more people feel included and safe, and dominant cultures must be part of that change.

Language is a tool for self-identification and self-expression, so it needs to progress in order to accommodate our evolving understanding of ourselves. Things are fluid and ever-changing, and language is a way to share ideas and information about ourselves, each other and our world. So, it will be essential to listen and be willing to accommodate the ways in which language changes if people are to feel accepted.

A real problem we have is that most people don't think that the things they say *mean* anything, and don't think their words have an effect. It might sound like a big, trite cliché but it's true. Whether you're writing a disparaging tweet about someone you think will never see it, or you're making an outdated joke at home with your family, you're putting it out into the world, and it's being read or heard by someone. However small the audience, you are normalizing whatever you're saying and making it seem acceptable.

Whether you're being flippant or deliberately provocative, if the words you use dehumanize others or delegitimize their experience, then you are contributing to their further marginalization. And when someone utters a pejorative as a 'joke', uses outdated or offensive language, or employs a phrase such as those explored in this book, they can be informing or framing someone else's thinking in the process. If you hear it once, you'll probably wince. Twice? You might awkwardly laugh. But fifty times? Well, you won't even react any more. People say something, no one questions it, it spreads, ad infinitum – that's how language endures and perspectives become normalized.

Language also serves as a shorthand for how you think about people in your own psyche. I know this because I see the process in my work all the time. My peers and I are always trying to progress our language as we learn new things. And often, the usage will change the mindset. If you're receptive to it, language has the power to help us reframe our thoughts and perceptions in a more inclusive way.

And yet, rather than seeing the potential of language to inform and improve our understanding of each other's experiences, many in dominant groups respond by centring themselves and viewing this evolution as a threat to *their* expression. Online you'll often see 'you can't say anything these days' coupled with a reflection on the importance of 'free speech' – the idea being that it is highly sacred. And sure, a sign of a healthy democracy is that citizens are able to communicate their thoughts and beliefs without state intervention or violence, and a sign of an oppressive regime is the restriction of opinion. That being said, freedom of speech is not a right without limits – something that is often conveniently forgotten by those who use the right to freedom of speech to justify regressive or harmful use of language that leads to people fearing for their safety.

Hate speech is defined as abusive or threatening language that expresses prejudice against a particular group, especially on the basis of their race, religion or sexual orientation. But many would recognize this as a limiting definition. Even when language doesn't technically constitute 'hate speech', it can lead to harm, and often 'the right to free speech' is invoked to justify something that comes very close. In fact, 'free speech' is cited to cover a whole host of unsavoury, bigoted attitudes.

Take Piers Morgan's behaviour towards Meghan Markle. It's a great example of the thin, grey space between free speech and hate speech. Writer Laquesha Bailey explored Morgan's obsessive reporting about the Duchess of Sussex in her article 'A Statistical Breakdown of Piers Morgan's Obsession with Meghan Markle' because, as she puts it, 'It is easy to dismiss one-off occurrences and anecdotal evidence, but data points gathered over an extended period allow for a fuller view of the issue.'

Piers mentioned Meghan 834 times between 27 November 2017 and 20 May 2021. Out of 741 (!!) mentions across Twitter, 52 segments on *Good Morning Britain* and 41 *Daily Mail* columns, 97.6 per cent of them were critical in nature. In his criticism of Markle, Morgan cited well-trodden stereotypes of Black women, accusing her of 'race-baiting' and of being 'scheming and manipulative', 'two-faced', 'whiny', 'desperate' and a 'social climber'. Bailey argued that Morgan's 'continuous public criticism of Meghan Markle is distinctly personal given its volume and frequency', and that he 'hides behind the title [of journalist] while spewing vitriol and abuse that lack the journalistic ethical standards of accuracy and impartiality'.

As someone who has experienced harassment, and who currently has a police case out against someone for it, I can say Morgan's behaviour feels a lot like harassment to me. The power dynamic at play between Morgan and Markle also suggested misogynoir – a term coined by Black feminist writer Moya Bailey to describe the meeting of misogyny and anti-Blackness – but to rebrand it as free speech seemed to get him off the hook. In a 97-page ruling, Ofcom found that Morgan's comments on *Good Morning Britain* that he 'didn't believe' Markle about being suicidal were 'potentially harmful and offensive' but were permissible given that his views had been challenged by other presenters on the show, and that any restriction of such views would have a chilling effect on freedom of expression. Ofcom did, however, say it had concerns over Morgan's comments about suicide and mental health.

Meanwhile, Meghan Markle was told that during 2019 'she was the most trolled person in the entire world', which led her to become suicidal. I have been on the receiving end of thousands of hate messages a day for weeks at a time – nothing near what Markle experienced – and I can tell you that abuse censors you. It makes you fear for your safety, so you don't react. It forces you to be smaller and quieter, to start hesitating and questioning yourself. I can't imagine what it must have felt like for her, dealing with that level of abuse, but I will say that Morgan's 'freedom of speech' led almost directly to Markle's censorship, and that in itself makes it conditional logic. Freedom of speech for him, censorship for her.

The reality is that many people who feel censored and use the phrase 'you can't say anything nowadays' aren't intent on harassing someone into silence. Most of us know individuals who, though they don't promote hateful discourse, are overwhelmed by the sheer volume of 'new' language to learn and are struggling to understand why language that has been normal throughout their life is suddenly viewed as unhelpful or harmful. Because of how fast society moves in the information age, they may have lost their instincts on which phrases are acceptable and which are problematic. They may also never have been encouraged to think critically about the language they use in the first place.

Whether it's your dad using a problematic word in a 'joke' or your nanna making fatphobic comments, let them know that their language is harmful. If their response is 'you can't say anything nowadays', explain that engaging with the evolution of language makes room for more people to feel and be safe and at peace. If they push back on this and cite free speech, let them know that their response and attitude towards the evolution of language is shoring up harmful movements.

Tell them that their sexist joke invokes the same culture of misogynistic language used by men who believe that women owe them sex – consensually or not; that when someone refuses to use another person's pronouns, they fortify the stance of cis people – or transphobes – who refuse to accept trans women's identity, contributing to a cultural shift that has led to a rise in hate-crime attacks; that these groups are increasingly defensive because they are no longer being given a free pass to say whatever they want, and that creating cultures where those groups feel emboldened leads to dangerous behaviour, be it sexist, racist, transphobic, or ableist. Remind them that when we refuse to zoom out and connect the dots between our own words and these harmful cultural movements, we're not being honest.

As is not the case with someone who is ignorant of the harm their words cause, if you're responding to someone who thinks things have 'gone too far' – that they should be able express a problematic view without rebuttal – they're likely to think you're being over-sensitive, or unfair if you try to correct them. If they respond in this way, breathe. Explain that, historically, women of all backgrounds have been socialized to believe they communicate in the wrong ways – that they are 'too emotional', 'too hysterical', 'too aggressive'. If this person feels they 'can't say anything nowadays', it's important that they remember that some groups have, for a long time, felt inhibited and silenced, and lived in fear of how they will be treated when they do speak about the things that matter to them.

If the person you're talking to says that 'not being able to say anything these days' is making *them* feel silenced in some way, remind them that their views are actually the mainstream. That they can turn on the TV and see these ideas whenever they want. Remind them that the people who are actually silenced are often the subjects of their jokes and views. If they deny that marginalized groups are being silenced, ask them to name a handful of famous non-white, disabled or LGBTQIA+ reporters, journalists or presenters. Then ask them to name similar figures who share their views.

Finally, offer – with compassion – an opportunity for them to consider the ways in which they are actively contributing to the silencing of others. Explain that, traditionally, when people from dominant cultures are faced with uncomfortable truths – usually during political discussions – they avoid accountability and attempt to retain control by silencing marginalized communities. Remind them that if society marginalizes you because of your gender, or you are forced to navigate stereotypes and prejudices every day because of your religion, not being able to speak freely is an everyday reality. And so, continuing to do so in the face of adversity is essential but also dangerous. Explain that people are being denied a voice and are in actual harm's way for speaking about their experiences, and that regressive and problematic language contributes to the culture that allows this to happen.

If all else fails, just ask them what they *want* to say. Offer lots of room to talk and encourage them to be specific. Ask them to deconstruct their joke or idea as if you don't understand it. If they are hesitant to do so, ask why. Wait for them to lay it out for you. Explore it with them in its simplest terms, so the underlying message is revealed. Then ask them why they wanted to say it. What it feels like when they say it. What it does. Tell them that no one can stop them saying what they want, but that the reaction may be uncomfortable or combative, and if 'free speech' must be protected, that they must accept those responses, too.

Draw attention to those whose voices are really silenced

in

and be clear that a culture that moves towards
clusive, self-determining, intentional language
is one you would want to be a part of. If they don’t feel that way, then it’s time for them to ask themselves why, and you’ll be there to discuss that with them if they can show up honestly.

Prompts for discussion

- Explain the difference between freedom of speech and hate speech. Explain how hate speech doesn’t have a global definition but is broadly: ‘offensive discourse targeting a group or an individual based on inherent characteristics (such as race, religion or gender) and that may threaten social peace’. Explain that freedom of speech does not mean freedom from consequences . . . Yes, you can say whatever you want, but that doesn’t mean people have to accept it, agree with it, or even respond to it. Especially if it’s harmful or inappropriate.
- If the person you are talking to is receptive to a discussion, draw attention to who in society is actually silenced – those who are really having their free speech infringed are marginalized individuals. Give examples.
- Ask them to explain what they stand to lose from not being able to say said phrase. Ask them if their words could potentially cause people harm, even indirectly. Would they choose to continue? Remind

them that changing a word or two in your vocabulary is a small price to pay for a better society.

Information to remember

- Amnesty International revealed that women journalists and politicians from the UK and US receive abuse on Twitter every 30 seconds, with Black women being disproportionately targeted, showing that online access gives people unrestricted ability to say what they want to who they want.
- From Article 10, Freedom of Expression of the Human Rights Act definition: 'Everyone has the right to freedom of expression. This right shall include freedom to hold opinions and to receive and impart information and ideas without interference by public authority.' It doesn't state that those opinions can't be challenged. In fact, by definition, it supports this.
- Eighty-one per cent of students think that freedom of expression is more important than ever, with 86 per cent specifically concerned that social media is enabling people to express intolerant views – mirroring trends in the UK population overall (78 per cent and 84 per cent, respectively).

Cathy Reay (she/her) is a writer and speaker on disability rights and her experiences as a polyamorous queer disabled woman. She is a single parent and is passionate about improving the experiences of single parents. She lives in the UK with her two kids and very cheeky cat.

"You [Disabled People] Are Such an Inspiration"

Cathy Reay

My distressed four-month-old was screaming so loudly I could barely hear anything over the wails. I was too busy desperately trying not to drop her as she thrashed about in my arms.

'Sorry?' I shouted a little exasperatedly over the jarringly high-pitched noise, feeling incredibly hot, flustered and very much not in control of the situation at hand.

'I said, I don't know how *you* do it,' the woman almost shouted, gasping softly in admiration as I managed to wrestle my child into her buggy and strap her in. When I stood up, my back cracked ominously and I winced. Beads of sweat had formed on my face. I blew cool air up at the fringe that had stuck to my brow and thought about how I'd really like to be at home under a cold shower, rather than in front of this stranger who seemed determined, for whatever reason, to engage me in conversation.

Begrudgingly, I glanced in her direction properly for the first time and noticed that her face was scrunched up in a cute expression; the kind of 'aww' look you might offer a shaggy dog (if you like dogs) or a sweet child (if you like children). Not so much the look you offer a thirty-something woman.

Although my own expression was frosty, she decided to continue. 'You're just . . .' She paused and glanced over her shoulder at the non-existent crowd that had formed behind her, before gesticulating in my direction proudly. It felt like I was a museum exhibit she was unveiling to collectors. 'You're doing so well, you know . . . considering.' Her enunciation was so deliberate, so thick, it was difficult to distinguish admiration from condescension. Whatever the intention of her comment, disguised as a compliment, it felt violent.

Leaving me no time to respond, she tottered off, pushing her sleeping baby in their spotless iCandy Peach, her steaming Starbucks sitting in the attached matching coffee-cup holder. She was wearing a cute floral dress and a wide-brimmed sunhat. Everything about her mum aesthetic was irrefutably and annoyingly perfect. She moved quickly, no doubt satisfied she had done her good deed of the day, likely not wanting to hang around in case my baby kicked off again and I actually had the gall to ask for help.

Lightly pushing my grumbling child back and forth in her buggy, I watched the woman's frame gradually become smaller and smaller until she disappeared round a corner. I took a few deep breaths. I felt hot, sweaty, tired, achy, frustrated and drained, but most of all I felt small.

Sure, SuperMum3000, I'm doing so well (as she'd already left I was replying to her in my head, thinking of the quick-witted comebacks I could've, should've said; a coping strategy I've formed for times exactly like these). *I expertly sailed through that library Rhyme Time session while you watched on, smiling dotingly at your placid child as my own wailed through nursery rhyme classics like 'Wind The [Bloody] Bobbin Up' the first, second and third time we sang it. Now I'm off home for a three-hour crying session as I attempt to coax my spirited baby to nap. The tears will stream from both our eyes as our coupled exhaustion and frustration ebbs and flows. After this joyous bonding time, I plan to make her some dinner, most of which will end up on the floor. My back will twinge as I clean it up. I then need to bathe her (here comes the back pain again), give her milk (and again), burp her (and again) and rock her to sleep (and again!). My entire body will be in agony by 8 p.m. She won't sleep, obviously, so we'll have another three-hour crying marathon together before we both conk out on the sofa, only to wake up an hour later for our scheduled middle-of-the-night cry. Because my body can't handle the physical strain that comes along with solo parenting, I won't be able to walk without being in severe pain tomorrow and will have to parent largely from my bed.*

Sure, SuperMum3000, I'm doing so well. Because I have no other choice. Because there's nobody else here. Because, just like you, I'm doing my best.

See, we're not all that different, SuperMum3000 and I. We're both in our early thirties with one child around the same age. Going by her selection of buggy and outfit, it's probable that she has more disposable income than me. The only glaringly obvious difference, though, is that only one of us is physically disabled.

Perhaps something inside her felt urgently called to draw attention to the fact that, in her mind, this whole situation just isn't *normal* for people like me. It's not *normal* for people like me to be able to complete daily tasks and enjoyable activities. It's not *normal* for people like me to have a child. Hell... is it even normal for Disabled people to have *whispers* sex?

There was a time I didn't think so, when I was younger.

I was the first person with dwarfism in my average-height family. A child of the early nineties, I turned preteen just as the middle elite started getting dial-up modems at home. We were connected, but boy was 56k slow. My exposure to other people with dwarfism doing cool, amazing and plain old ordinary things was majorly limited.

Porn, magazines, books, movies and TV shows that featured romance and sex scenes never included people who looked remotely like me. On the rare occasion they did, we were posited as objects of desire, freaks of nature, and never as fully rounded romanticized and sexual beings. In my teens, I was resigned to the idea that sex would never happen for me, and I could definitely forget marriage and kids. To this day, I'm still shocked (and immediately suspicious) when someone reveals that they fancy me. *Me?* A little freak like me?

It struck me then how SuperMum3000 had probably never met a parent who has dwarfism before. Like most people of our generation, her limited exposure to us was probably in pantomime – in *Charlie and the Chocolate Factory* or *Snow White*. Maybe she'd seen a person with dwarfism competing in the Paralympics. But it's rare for most people to see us doing ordinary, everyday things. Things like taking our baby to a Rhyme Time class.

So, her saying 'I don't know how you do it' suddenly made a little more sense. Because she genuinely doesn't – because she's never encountered someone like me parenting before. Because she can't wrap her head around how I'm able to do the same thing as her; because she finds it incredible that I can. Maybe to her I'm a rare breed, a one-off, someone who broke the mould. Maybe she thinks I smashed down barriers nobody has ever dared cross. I start picturing myself pushing my kid's buggy in a Wonder Woman outfit and I can't help but smile.

Disabled people are often so hidden from public life that non-disabled people forget we exist outside of the lens of being charity cases and 'superhumans'. As the late, great comedian and disability rights activist Stella Young said: 'For lots of us, disabled people are not our teachers or our doctors or our manicurists. We're not real people. We are there to inspire.'

I couldn't tell you the first time someone told me I was an inspiration because it's something people just say when I'm doing things that are decidedly ordinary and non-inspirational all the time. Things like going to school, learning to ride a bike, learning to swim, having fun with other kids my age, getting a degree, working, getting married, becoming a parent. Being present in society. It's a phrase many like to dress up in other ways, parroting chestnuts such as, *I don't know how you do it! You're doing so well! I can't believe you can do that – how amazing!* Or the simply put *WOW!* often expressed from the lips of well-intentioned young children as they watch me cross the road safely all by myself.

Sometimes these words are proffered as people watch me struggling to do something, like SuperMum3000 did, in situations where I actually could use a little help (after consent is established, of course). Alternatively, they're a stock response to any achievement I've made, no matter how insignificant. Occasionally, they're just given by strangers that are so baffled by my existence that they have to say something – anything – to explain the fact that I am on the street, in public (!), doing my weekly shop.

You might be reading this thinking, 'Oh, come on, people are just trying to be nice!' and I get it – believe me, I get it – but even if niceness is the intention, treating me as inspiring doesn't make me feel so nice. It feels objectifying and othering. It's a reminder that, because I'm Disabled, society will always perceive me as different. It's also heavily rooted in the medical model of disability, which teaches us that our impairments are what set us back from participating in society. So, dwarfism is the reason I can't access a high bar stool. It's the reason many men don't fancy me. It's the reason I can't participate in a netball tournament with other women my age.

That doesn't really hold up for me. Sorry, you're telling me it's because I was born this way that I can't do all those things? That feels pretty shitty. I subscribe – for the most part – to the social model of disability, which shifts the argument to say that we are disabled by society itself rather than the disabilities we have. Inaccessibility is the reason the bar stool is so high. Ableism is the reason many men don't fancy me.

Inaccessibility is the reason I can't take part in that netball tournament.

The social model doesn't work for everything – there are medical reasons, for example, that someone like me might not want or be able to have children. However, for the most part, I truly believe that if society shifted its opinion and value of Disabled people, we'd suddenly find the world a lot more welcoming and accessible to us than it is now.

It's a very strange paradox being Disabled. On the one hand, society constantly tells us we're worthless. And on the other, people are applauding us in the street just for being alive. Sometimes when people treat me as inspirational, it makes me think they're doing it just because they don't want to help, like SuperMum3000. They see independence as the goal of my existence and don't want to interfere with it. Doesn't every good Disabled person want to achieve things by themselves?

I'm a big fan of interdependence. The kind of society where, when we need to, we draw on each other's strengths and work together; the kind of society where we don't see it as a failing on someone's part if they're unable to complete something on their own. Like non-disabled people, I have strengths completely unrelated to my disability (though my double-jointedness is my favourite party trick) and, also like non-disabled people, there are things I might need help with from time to time too. Putting Disabled people on pedestals for our achievements removes our agency to lean on others for support if we need to. We're not a failure if we need back-up – nobody is.

Stella Young hit the nail on the head when she coined

the term 'inspiration porn' in her 2014 TEDxSydney talk. Non-disabled people finding Disabled people inspirational for – what the non-disabled perceive to be – 'overcoming' their disabilities is othering. Through this lens, our existence is solely to make non-disabled people feel good, or better. We're incorporated into 'get up and work' mantras ('if that Disabled person can do it, you have no excuse!') and we're put on pedestals for simply being.

I only have to scroll a little way down my Facebook feed to find examples of the type of inspiration porn that often goes viral on social media. A photo of a girl who has no limbs painting a picture with the brush in her mouth, and the words 'Disability didn't stop her – what's your excuse?' plastered across the bottom. A picture of a child who has Down's syndrome smiling and putting their thumbs up, with the age-old phrase 'the only disability in life is a bad attitude' around their frame. A photo of Stevie Wonder at a piano with the text 'every Blind man's hero' underneath. Less than a decade after Stella told us about inspiration porn, we're still encountering it and subject to it, both online and off.

So the next time you witness a non-disabled person referring to a Disabled person or something they've done as inspirational or putting us up on a pedestal just for existing, help them to understand we deserve the same agency, privacy and humanity as everyone else. Highlight that their words reduce us to our diagnoses when we are so much more than that. Talk about why it's problematic to offer unsolicited compliments such as these, particularly for everyday tasks, and talk about why the reaction to someone like me doing the thing is different to someone like them doing it.

Like Stella said, 'Disability doesn't make you exceptional, but questioning what you think you know about it does.'

Prompts for discussion

- Think about your own experiences, both when you were a child and now, of seeing Disabled people doing ordinary things like shopping, working, admin. How is it different to your experiences seeing non-disabled people doing similar things? How do you think this difference contributes to the way you feel when you see Disabled people in society?
- Draw attention to the fact that we don't tend to find non-disabled people doing their shopping, working, being in relationships and simply existing, inspiring. Think about the kind of response you might have to a Disabled person doing those things and compare.
- Think about the phrase 'you're so inspiring' and how you might feel receiving this when you're in the middle of doing something, particularly from a stranger. What reaction would you have? Would it be positive or negative – why?

Information to remember

- There were at last count at least 14.6 million disabled people in the UK (Family Resources Survey, 2020–21). That's more than one in five people.

- Assuming Disabled people cannot do things non-disabled people can do is infantilizing. Assuming Disabled people have some kind of superpower when they can do things non-disabled people can do is infantalizing. Don't assume anything.
- Being Disabled isn't synonymous with living a sex-free, romance-free, child-free life. Many of us want, are able to and go on to experience fulfilling romantic relationships and raise awesome kids. It's also totally fine if none of that is our thing either.

“The Government Are Doing Their Best”

I'm strolling across Hampstead Heath with my partner, Jordy, wearing the same T-shirt I slept in last night, but I've put on clean leggings and underwear, which is a first for this week. I know I look exhausted. My eyes are puffy and my skin is sallow and blotchy. I've scraped my hair up into a knotted greasy bun, and the thought crosses my mind that if anyone who knows me sees me today, they won't recognize me.

The heath is peaceful and beautiful. The sky is a misty pastel blue and completely free of plane trails, as it often is these days. It's fresh but warm, with people milling about, walking their dogs and taking advantage of the one-walk-per-day rule. I am feeling a little broken, but it's OK because Jordy is holding my hand. He picks a dandelion clock, passes it to me and tells me I should blow it for Grandma, and I do.

It's weird how much care I take in doing this. I think it's because I know I won't be able to hold my dad, who spent last week desperately and horrendously dealing with the reality of not being able to access his mother while she was bed-ridden with a deadly virus. A mother he never got to say goodbye to.

I won't be able to dress in my best clothes and sit in a pew, clutching an order of service with Grandma's face on it, next to the people who loved her. I won't be able to cry alongside them. I won't be able to share stories about her at the funeral, either. The rituals of losing someone we loved have been taken from our family and so many others, so I blow the fluffy needles of the dandelion into the wind, and make a wish that my dad and my auntie (who lives in Spain and is stuck there) will be OK.

As Jordy and I make our way towards the exit of the park, I spot a group of nine or ten twenty-somethings lounging on the grass, uncomfortably close to one another. Around them lie bikes, and there's a speaker playing music as they laugh and chat, smoke and drink. Gatherings like this aren't legal. At any other time in my life, I would have taken pleasure from watching them enjoy spring in London, but today I feel anger rise up inside me and I want to shout at them. I imagine myself strolling past and casually, calmly saying, 'My grandma just died from this virus alone in a hospital bed, but please, do carry on with your fucking essential socializing.'

It's April 2020 and we're a month into what much of the British public think will be our only lockdown. Covid-19 has spread across the planet like wildfire and London is adjusting to the pandemic. Walking home from the park you can see it everywhere: windows decorated with kids' drawings of rainbows, to show support and thanks to the NHS; masked people swerving past each other on the pavement.

When we get home, Jordy makes me a cuppa and I go through the motions of scrolling on Twitter. It's flooded with coronavirus updates from the media, people sharing their experiences and stories, and the hot takes are coming from every direction. There is something comforting about seeing so many people feel the same way that I do about this unprecedented experience, but of course, my timeline has been carefully curated – by both me and the algorithm – to serve me content I enjoy and agree with.

If you were reading just my Twitter feed, you'd be forgiven for thinking that the entire country was outraged at the government's handling of the deadliest pandemic since the Spanish flu. However, each time I click on a news article and read the comments underneath, I'm smacked by the realization that that's just not true. Time and time again, the same comment – written slightly differently – pops up: 'the government are doing their best'.

The days and weeks after we lose Grandma see me shuffling around the house, not doing much except having long conversations with Jordy and my housemate, Zoe. I cry randomly, take naps, and toggle between watching Disney+ to soothe myself and obsessively scrolling through Twitter, Apple News and Instagram to gain some kind of understanding – or maybe control – of the spiralling situation the world finds itself in.

I'm the kind of person who allows grief to set in. I fit everything else around it. It comes first and I don't try to distract myself with everyday life. I can't. Instead, I feel it, let it wash over me and then move on to being productive when I am strong enough. This time it's pretty different. I can't move on to being productive because people are going through exactly the same thing that I am every day. I know I'm sharing this experience with so many strangers right this second.

The grief over losing my grandma is mine, but it is also collective and feels huge. I can't escape it, either.

I'm also terrified that my mum – who is immunocompromised – will fall ill, and that my grief will be compounded. I can't leave the house to see anyone, so there are no distractions. I can't switch on any of my devices without seeing commentary on what killed my grandma, so I have no choice but to sit with my grief.

There is so much anger in me. Anger that – although I can't put my finger on it yet – is directed at something specific. Anger that this virus hasn't been contained and suppressed in the way it should've been. As the days drag on, the phrase 'the government are doing their best' sloshes round my head uneasily. I hear political commentators and even government ministers using it during panel debates on mainstream TV. I hear radio hosts of phone-in debates asking Londoners making their morning coffee: 'The government may be doing their best . . . but is it enough?'

By mid-April, I've seen enough to know that the Conservative government are not doing their best to suppress and reduce the number of Covid infections in the UK. By this point, the estimated number of care-home patients – just like my lovely grandma – who have died from coronavirus stands at one in twenty. I've read about how the prime minister is alleged not to have attended the initial five COBRA meetings on the crisis, missing out on vital findings from government scientists that could have curtailed the spread. I've watched, agog, as he headed to Kent for a holiday after raising the threat level to 'moderate'.

That same week I'd stood in Zoe's doorway, looking at her

yellow skin as she lay on a sweat-soaked mattress, coughing and breathing heavily. She had looked at me nervously and explained that she couldn't believe how bad she felt. I'd had to reassure her that she wasn't going to die, but she subsequently ended up in A&E, terrified by her symptoms, and was diagnosed with an 'unknown upper respiratory infection'.

I'd read that both Boris Johnson and the health secretary, Matt Hancock, failed to dial in to a conference call with EU leaders and health ministers to discuss coronavirus response planning, despite being invited. I later discovered that over the course of the next six weeks they failed to participate in a further seven calls. I also remembered how lockdown didn't start until after a quarter of a million people were allowed to attend the Cheltenham Festival.

Before losing Grandma, I had been aghast at these failings but after losing her and seeing, first hand, my loved one be de-prioritized, my horror morphed into a clear sense of my family being personally neglected. The horrendous reality that thousands of other families were and had been facing long before the pandemic – living under a government that would let their loved ones die – was now a personal experience for me. One that my many privileges had allowed me to escape up until this point.

As the year ticked on and summer arrived, the government offered discounts to *encourage* people to eat out inside public dining spaces while this airborne virus was still rife, and cases grew again. By winter, a wave of infections bigger than the first saw my friends lose loved ones, and yet time and time again, that phrase resurfaced about Boris Johnson and his cabinet: 'The government are doing their best.' Meanwhile, my social feeds showed disabled people, immunocompromised people and epidemiologists writing impassioned and sometimes rallying cries for the public to demand better ventilation, more masks, better financial support from the government. Yet this platitude about the government's perceived efforts continued to be offered up even when the evidence in front of us illustrated, at best, that they were unable to safeguard sufficiently against their citizens dying and, at worst, an alarming detachment from their suffering and an urgency to prioritize the economy and the profits of their cronies over lives.

I'd spent the best part of a year staying inside and being the 'difficult' friend who said no to every social engagement to make sure that I wouldn't be responsible for someone else going through what my family and I had. But as the frostier months appeared and our government encouraged people to go out and do their Christmas shopping, cases rose once more, and I felt so hopeless about this devastation affecting even more families. The festive period of 2020 came and went, and January 2021 saw the worst number of daily Covid cases on UK record. As that harrowing month drew to a close, the prime minister issued a half-apology during a press conference from Downing Street. 'What I can tell you,' he said, 'is that we truly did everything we could, and continue to do everything that we can, to minimize loss of life and to minimize suffering.' It was almost a year to the day since the World Health Organization had alerted the UK government about the virus, yet only around the time of this speech did the Department of Transport close travel corridors to the UK for the first time since the pandemic began.

A year after all of this, I would almost lose one of my best friends to Covid, aged twenty-nine. She was rushed by ambulance to hospital and cared for in the ICU as she hallucinated her late mother was comforting her.

But here's the thing – this particular nightmare wouldn't have been so horrendous for so many people had the government been 'doing their best' to combat the fundamental issues facing our society that had led to such difficult living conditions and realities. Had fewer people been on zero-hour contracts, there would have been less financial precariousness for so many families. Had council housing been invested in properly, and domestic violence numbers been taken seriously, the government's woefully trite 'home is safe' messaging might have meant something. Had unemployment provisions and *adequate* sick pay been a basic workers' right, rather than low statutory sick pay – an insufficient amount on which a third of the population rely, and to which two million people aren't entitled at all – then 'stay at home' might have been a more viable option for workers.

Greater support for public services would have seen state schools – which teach the country's most underserved children – with more resources to support at-home learning (i.e. they'd have been able to afford to provide laptops and software specifically for this purpose). That could have alleviated some of the stresses of working parents juggling being a caregiver, teacher, provider and living through a pandemic all at once, under the same roof.

At the time of writing, 2.1 million people in the UK are experiencing self-reported long Covid including long-term damage to the heart, lungs and kidneys. Long Covid experts identified the pandemic as a mass-disabling event, and given our government's solid history of failing to uphold disability rights (the 2017 UN inquiry revealed it had failed to fulfil its commitments to the UN convention on disabled people's rights), it's painfully unsurprising that disabled and immunocompromised individuals were treated as expendable. This is perhaps most powerfully illustrated by the horrendous offering of Do Not Resuscitate orders to Covid patients with learning disabilities. Similarly predictable is the fact that any government provisions that were offered did little to alleviate the material impacts of the virus, and that they were later withdrawn. Our government's response was very much same shit, different day, but one can't help but ask questions about what could have been.

If we'd worked on ensuring a higher living wage, we could have seen fewer individuals working two jobs to stay afloat in an economy that, since 2010, has seen wages stagnate and the cost of living soar. In fact, let's take the opportunity to look at inflation. The Bank of England analyses prices on seven hundred products yearly (from milk to football tickets) and found in 2018 that, on average, those prices had increased by 2 per cent since 1997, which was 21 years before the report. Keeping inflation to 2 per cent is a government recommendation, but it is enough to cause serious issues for both unemployed and working people. For the unemployed, benefits have not risen in line with inflation, and many of those living on benefits are unable to afford basic living costs.

As of July 2022, inflation reached a whopping 10 per cent for the first time in 40 years amid a cost-of-living crisis that is bringing Britain to its knees. UK domestic gas prices rose nearly 96 per cent in early summer 2022, while electricity prices shot up 54 per cent. UK households face some of the highest prices in Europe – nearly double those in France. At the time of writing, 700,000 people have signed up to Enough Is Enough, a campaign founded by trade unions and community organizations to fight the cost-of-living crisis. Things are really, really bad and people are searching for solutions.

These fundamental issues – housing, wages, inflation, workers' rights, education, disability rights, flexible working for parents, preventing gendered violence – are the scaffolding that, if dealt with efficiently by the government, support the people of this country and make their lives better, safer, more comfortable. This could make, oh I don't know, living through a pandemic more doable, manageable, less soul-destroying? The pandemic – which we are still experiencing, if the life-changing impacts of long Covid are anything to go by – isn't just hard because of the virus, it's hard because of multiple structural failings that show that the government are certainly not, and have not been, doing their best.

In Response to 'The Government Are Doing Their Best'

To me, this expression is *the* political platitude of our time, and it's a sign we're not living under fair or effective leadership. As a phrase, it may sound somewhat thoughtful – especially in the context of a pandemic – but it's used too frequently to be thoughtful, and its prevalence is frustrating.

In response, we have to ask this first: doing their best *for whom*? If the person saying it is suggesting that the cabinet is working in the interests of their corporate donors or those from a similar economic background then pat them on the back. We're done here, because they'd be correct. What a constructive conversation! However, if they're intimating that the work that comes under 'their best' is in aid of British society – which includes disabled people, unemployed people, working people, people marginalized for their gender or race and those living below the poverty line (a pretty big majority of the population!) – then, no.

The pandemic and the government's woeful response to it has pushed the total number of people in the UK living in poverty to more than 15 million – 23 per cent of the population – according to the Legatum Institute, and recent data shows that as of October 2022 – as the UK's cost-of-living crisis deepened – more people, including children, are going hungry than during the first weeks of Covid lockdown as one in five families reported experiencing food insecurity.

'The government are doing their best' is a brilliantly benign way for someone to express their opinion on a huge, complex topic without having to really engage meaningfully; either because politics is intimidating or because apathy is easier. It offers a vague assertion of belief in those who run the country, but rarely comes with evidence as to *how* the government are working so hard to do their best. It's neither combative nor divisive, so is a perfect way to put an end to a conversation. 'Their best' is entirely unquantifiable. Win! Political discussion averted!

Outside the halls of Westminster, 'he's doing his best' is something you might say about your son as you watch him stuff up an open goal during his first five-a-side, or as he falls trying to land his first pirouette in class (we’re not pushing gender stereotypes in this book). In a professional capacity, ‘they’re doing their best’ could *maybe* be a fair assessment of your colleague’s performance in a high-pressure situation, such as trying to close a deal with a high-value client. But let’s say ‘their best’ *did* lose the company a client. Would that excuse work for that person in the post-pitch meeting with their boss who is demanding to know what went wrong? Probably not.

Under capitalism – a system that runs on human labour and profit over humanity and emotional needs – I’m not sure that much space is ever held for ‘I’m doing my best’ as an adult. Whether or not that’s healthy could be the subject of a whole other book, but the point is, in our working society we’re expected to shoulder the responsibilities and burden of the role we’ve chosen. If we make an error, we get warned, disciplined and we lose money or responsibilities. If we are part of a more traditional workforce during a period of economic turmoil such as a pandemic – especially one where staff can be viewed as disposable and replaceable – then messing up, even if there is a valid reason for our mistake, will often mean losing our job and therefore our income, leading to precarious financial security.

In this economy, plenty of people are losing their jobs without messing up. There is a punishment for ‘not working hard enough’, and it shouldn’t be more of a threat to someone whose life is made consistently harder as a result of inequality and economic struggle (Unequal division of domestic labour! Expensive childcare! Expensive bills!) than it is for the influential wealthy elite who are creating and compounding those inequalities. In reality, beyond your childhood years, using 'I'm doing my best' as a justification doesn't cut the mustard 99 per cent of the time. So why should it work for the elite?

The structural imbalances they create and uphold are also reproduced in our education system, which was created in the context of our class-based society. In *Natives*, Akala ruminates on whether 'education should be a site of power, a place to reproduce the social societal norms or a place to question and attempt to transcend them'. It seems, so often, it is the former. Children coming from difficult financial backgrounds do not, and have never had, the same education as children from wealthy families or backgrounds. For example, in a state school the career opportunities that are presented to you are often reflective of those typically associated with your class. The experience at Eton – a college that costs over £48,500 per term (£10,000 more than the UK's average income) and has produced 20 of the UK's 55 prime ministers – prepares wealthy boys from privileged backgrounds for the opportunity to serve in public life in particular types of leadership roles such as law, finance and entertainment.

With that in mind, it wouldn't be leftfield to assume that Alexander Boris de Pfeffel Johnson's education at Eton, and then Oxford, prepared him for a public career defined by leadership and rooted in power. One that has seen him be a political journalist, an elected MP, Mayor of London, Shadow Minister and finally (phew!) Foreign Secretary – all positions that would have prepared him *more* than adequately for one of the highest-ranking and most powerful positions in the country.

We could say that when he was sworn in as prime minister, he was – according to the systems and structures built by men like him, and how we measure competence – as ready as one could ever be. However, a government isn't reliant only on the PM, so what about his cabinet of senior ministers who lead on policy? Well, two-thirds of them were also privately educated. This statistic is stratospheres above the number of Britons who are afforded the opportunity to attend a private school, which stands at only 7 per cent, and is reflective of our current PM at the time of writing – Rishi Sunak's – cabinet. (At this rate it's anyone's guess who will be PM when this book is published.) Therefore, by Britain's own standards of academia and education, our government should be made up of some of the brightest minds in the country.

Now, whether you believe that or not is up to you (I, emphatically, do not), but the point is these ministers are as prepared as one can be within the current education and political system, and have willingly accepted the ultimate responsibility: to keep people safe, well and living. This is why when people die, systems fail, preventable disasters happen and inequality skyrockets, 'the government are doing their best' is actually offensive.

If we want to talk about those who are 'doing their best' and are worthy of that evaluation, then we should take a look at people living under systems of oppression – those who are unemployed or on low salaries or zero-hour contracts, single parents, Gypsy Roma and travelling communities, immigrants, disabled people. The majority of these individuals are having to create personalized, strategic ways of navigating systems riddled with challenges that are rooted in the intentional de-prioritization of their needs. The Department for Work and Pensions, which decides if people are 'fit to work' and therefore eligible for benefits, was linked to 590 suicides in England between 2010 and 2013 after reports by coroners showed 'clear evidence that there's potential for the assessment process to cause some very major adverse effects on mental health'. These real structural, systematic failures – or choices, if you realistically consider who the government is trying to squeeze out of the services it offers – affect every waking moment of the lives of those who sit at the lower end of the class system or at multiple intersections of marginalized identity, and mean that 'doing our best' doesn't result in better living conditions because those improvements are way beyond their control.

You can't 'do your best' out of living in poverty or being oppressed by a system because you're doing so within the parameters and rules it sets. One in three of us doesn't have a safe or secure place to live and across the UK more people from Black, Asian and other backgrounds of the global majority are likely to be in poverty (i.e. have an income of less than 60 per cent of the average household income) than white British people. Not having a home that is permanent, comfortable and affordable means less security and having to move more often, therefore making it more challenging to foster relationships and find support systems and a place within your community. And while our collective mental health is struggling (since Covid there has been a 150 per cent increase in helpline calls to leading mental-health charities), we also know children and adults living in households in the lowest 20 per cent income bracket are two to three times more likely to develop mental-health problems. Disabled people are also four times more likely to report feeling lonely 'often or always' and experts have warned that the mental health of the UK's transgender community is in crisis. Research by the UK government also revealed that nearly two-thirds of people of South Asian origin in England experienced mental-health problems as a result of the pandemic.

These are not unintentional consequences or accidental situations. They are the result of the state's resources being moved away from what people need for their lives not to be centred around struggle. Take working parents in Britain: our childcare is the second most expensive in the world, prices have increased 27 per cent since 2009 (following David Cameron's government and successive years of Conservative austerity), and now the average cost of sending a child under two to nursery for a full working week is £14,000 per annum – almost 50 per cent of the average UK wage. If half of your income goes on childcare in order for you to continue your career, you're essentially earning half of what you would have before you had a child. This devaluation is compounded by the fact that, thanks to gender inequality, most workplaces don't prioritize mothers, which means missing out on career progression. Across many industries there is a distinct lack of workplace flexibility for mothers, but also for employees who undertake care roles in other respects, such as those who care for disabled or ageing relatives or partners.

The Motherhood Penalty is very real. Financial precariousness or struggling to pay the bills monopolizes your time because efforts to save money require leading a less efficient lifestyle; you wait for public transport, you rely on an underfunded NHS and can't go private for prompt treatment, you spend hours budgeting. Working full time while being strained under the cost of parenting – leaves no time to care for yourself, and potentially puts a burden on your mental health.

You see, empathy and understanding is a perfect response to someone 'doing their best' in the face of structural inequality. It fits. It's relevant. Because they're fighting something bigger than themselves. But empathy and understanding are less relevant when the individual in question has the most opportunity, power and access in the country, and is making life harder for those without. It isn't relevant when their primary challenge is ... just doing their job, and they are not only insulated from much of the societal struggle the majority of the population faces, but also to blame for a great portion of it. Working people are living and dying by the decisions made by our government while, by contrast, many politicians remain protected from the realities they create by way of their own privilege and wealth.

At worst, a controversial policy decision leads to public criticism and online abuse. If that politician is non-white and/or is a woman, the kind of abuse they receive is especially harmful in that it feeds into multiple systems of oppression. By and large, though, the policies they write do not negatively affect them structurally, whereas a policy decision can push their citizens into poverty, lead to lifelong struggle and even death. Policy and legislation lay the groundwork for much of the wealth inequality that exists in our country or, as the saying goes, 'Every billionaire is a policy failure.'

Just take the fact that Shell – who received rebates of more than £100m from HM Revenue and Customs in 2021 – made £8.2bn in profits between July and September 2022. Eight billion in three months. And they paid zero windfall tax in the UK despite making record global profits of nearly £26bn while British people – who are facing increasingly frequent extreme weather events brought on by climate change – are dealing with their energy bills doubling.

This bullshit is why it's imperative that we engage in constructively holding our government to account during the tough times. We have to decide if we want to hold space and show disproportionate empathy for our wealthy elected cabinet who don't extend empathy or support for those struggling, and who, in the face of collective challenges (such as Covid), won't have to deal with the worst consequences and hardship, or even have to abide by the rules they set to address them (hi, Partygate!). Responding to 'the government are doing their best' means asking if we are looking at rare mistakes by an otherwise welfare-based cabinet, or consistently poor decision-making, de-prioritization of marginalized people's needs and gross negligence.

If a family member says 'the government are doing their best', tell them that this phrase diverts attention away from the myriad valid criticisms being directed at these ministers, and is encouraging us to accept whatever they're doing as 'all they can achieve'. Even if that means hundreds of poor people of colour dying in community housing because government bodies cut costs by using flammable cladding. Even if that means sending workers – who, again, are most likely to be working class and/or people of colour – back into care homes without being tested for a killer virus. Even if that means partying while we died, and forcibly removing migrants who have lived here for years.

Tell them this phrase asks us to assume the best of an government that has shown us anything but compassion, and which (at the time of writing) is set to approve a huge new oil field named Rosebank, which will produce as many emissions as 28 countries, despite having signed the climate agreement stating that no new oil, gas or coal development can be approved if we are to keep global warming below the 1.5 degree Celsius threshold. Offer an example by noting that organizers like #StopCambo – who are aiming to stop new oil fields – are more likely to be doing their best. Say that disability activists who are fighting for justice in the face of systems that are killing people are doing their best.

In her piece for the *Guardian* on the Cummings' whistleblowing scandal, journalist Nesrine Malik notes, 'The structure of a healthy political system has separate branches with distinct responsibilities, so that "checks and balances" will prevent the concentration and abuse of power.' She recognizes that this alone isn't enough to ensure a healthy democracy, that the media has continued to prop up, and failed to challenge, our government's decisions. 'When we ask about the impunity this government continues to enjoy, we are not talking about a passive and uninformed public, but a public poorly served by those whose job is to oppose and challenge the government.' The cabinet is answerable to its public, and in a fair society nobody is above criticism.

In unprecedented times we do see fight and fury by brilliant and courageous communities, organizers, advocates and more, but we also see apathy, and this can come from a sense of feeling overwhelmed. So many huge, impossible-to-control and terrifying situations are present in our everyday lives, humming along in the background like an extractor fan you've *almost* forgotten is still on. They sit outside of what feels manageable mentally, and can be exhausting and traumatizing to endure. Especially if you're someone who sits at multiple intersections of oppression, and therefore experiences a number of compounding threats to your life and livelihood.

Because of this grinding feeling of a lack of control, we can cling to moments of hope – or even just the idea of it. But feeling hopeful and taking action to address the issues that we face are not mutually exclusive. The only thing that has ever progressed regular people's lives is regular people recognizing they are being underserved, naming the issue and working with others across identity lines – originally created to weaken and divide us – to build movements that force change.

In real moments of shared struggle, such as living through a global pandemic, fighting the realities of the climate breakdown or confronting structural racism, to disengage and assume the best of those who are actually making our lives harder is to spread the mistruth that our government are doing all they can. They are not. Disengaging is what a government *wants* us to do when it is prioritizing its own power and status. Examining the activity of our current cabinet over the past three years shows us that they are doing what is best for *them* and what is in their class interest, not ours.

So, next time someone says this phrase in response to, say, the cost-of-living crisis or in reference to the handling of the pandemic, tell them it is wishful thinking, and an easy way to 'tap out' from political conversations (as if a political conversation is anything other than just a discussion about peoples' lives). Offer that you understand it can feel as though we have no power to hold the government accountable, but while regular people are struggling under the weight of their policies, the only challenge government ministers have is their job description. Ask the person you're talking to whether, if they messed up in their own job to the degree any number of government ministers have, would they still have it?

Tell them that you know that apathy is easier than fighting, but we all have a right to be angry, and to listen to that anger. Tell them that defending an elite, powerful group who would have you homeless and struggling in a second, will get you nowhere. Tell them that marginalized people are the ones doing their best and that the government couldn't possibly be doing the same, because if this is their best, what does their worst look like?

Prompts for discussion

- Explain the concept that power, wealth and influence insulate you from a slew of practical life problems. For example, a politician (hi, Matt Hancock, Suella Braverman) isn't guaranteed to lose their job following a long list of failures. Then contrast this with the fact that a working-class person living under systems that make their lives practically harder every day is likely to lose their job, income or opportunities for much smaller indiscretions.

- Ask the person you're talking to about something they are struggling with. Are they frustrated that their bills have gone up? Start there and discuss how the government and big business are profiting from it.
- Scroll through some news stories with them: wealth inequality, poverty in Britain, the rise in reliance on food banks, the death toll of Covid and the outcome of Brexit. Ask them if they think that is indicative of a government doing their best.

Information to remember

- The prime minister and 65 per cent of his cabinet were privately educated at the best institutions in the country. A mere 7 per cent of Britons can afford a private education. By this metric we can hypothetically assume the cabinet is made up of some of the most educated individuals in the country and therefore should be held accountable to a proportionate level.
- In January–February 2022 the Trussell Trust found that food-bank usage was up 22 per cent compared to the same period in 2020. Low-income families

experienced what the UK's biggest food-bank charity called 'historic' levels of need.

- In July 2022, 91 per cent of UK households reported that their cost of living had increased in the previous month due to higher food, electricity and fuel costs, while the UK has the greatest number of billionaires on record and the government awarded £10.5bn worth of contracts without scrutiny during Covid.

Ione Gamble is a writer and editor based in London. She is the founding editor in chief of *Polyester* zine, an intersectional, independent arts and culture publication. With a focus on contemporary feminism and identity, she is also the host of The Polyester Podcast. Her debut book, *Poor Little Sick Girls*, a collection of essays exploring unacceptable women in all their forms, was published in 2022.

"Stop Glorifying Being Unhealthy"

Ione Gamble

We don't arrive at the assumption that all fat people are unhealthy for no reason. You'd be hard pressed to walk down the street without seeing a bus-stop advertisement urging us to 'fight obesity'. It's impossible to watch any number of morning TV entertainment shows without being drawn into a segment on weight loss; from miracle foods to exercise that will change our lives and why being fat will, ultimately, make us die younger. We've replaced 'the circle of shame', once seen in gossip magazines, with heavily manipulated selfies and sponsored Instagram adverts telling us how to perfect intermittent fasting.

From birth, women and marginalized people are taught to hate themselves. This indoctrinated disdain towards our bodies grows with us, mirroring where we are at any given moment in our lives to ensure we will never be truly at peace with ourselves. We're forced to scrutinize every part of our bodies; whether our skin is too spotty, or our hair too straggly. If our features are the 'right' shape and if our bodies are too big or too small. But while advertising, and the media at large, does its utmost to cultivate insecurity among women of all ages, when it comes to fat people the hatred is government mandated.

Health anxiety has been bubbling in the public consciousness over the course of the Covid-19 pandemic, regardless of weight. But while the British government made mistake after mistake when it came to handling the health emergency, they decided to blame one group in particular – fat people. Early on in the pandemic, then-prime minister Boris Johnson caught the virus, and after a short stint in hospital decided that the severity of his stint with Covid was due to the fact he was overweight. He then declared a war on obesity, placing the pressure on 'obese' individuals to overhaul their lifestyle or face the burden of blame for Britain's death toll due to the pandemic.

Once the vaccine rollout began, and fat people were prioritized for inoculation, public outrage mounted as to why people who 'refuse to look after their health' could jump the queue for medication that could save all of our lives. This government-sanctioned fatphobia leads to a downward spiral in quality of life for all fat people; it makes us depressed, it subjects us to street harassment or online abuse, and it tells us we aren't worthy of a happy existence. Outside of the context of a global pandemic, fat people still find themselves ostracized. Seemingly each week our lives are targeted in varying ways. From debates in Parliament as to whether children should be weighed in school to keep their weight from ascending, and sugar and junk-food taxes aiming to eradicate any weight gain whatsoever, to the number of fat people living in the UK being considered an epidemic by the politicians that run our country.

Until the 2010s took hold, our weight, and the judgement towards it, was largely constructed by brands who wanted our money, and celebrities who benefited from peddling the idea of a perfect body. At the turn of the century, in the early noughties, rhetoric around why it was bad to be fat was based around aesthetics. To be super-skinny was the look *du jour* with celebrities such as Paris Hilton, Nicole Richie and Victoria Beckham paving the way for a beauty standard that dictated the smaller you are, the better. Teenage girls and adult women alike grew up consuming TV adverts that urged us to eat Special K cereal instead of dinner to lose weight, or to glug weight-loss shakes and join diet groups with mandated, ready-meal plans and weekly weigh-ins. Yes, the pressure to be skinny was all-encompassing. It engulfed my teenage years – I attempted one fad diet after another, hoping it would rid me of the baby fat that encased my organs. But for all the damaging mindsets early-aughts diet culture manifested, by and large it felt as though the government stayed out of our business when it came to the size of our frames.

The rationale for our disdain towards fat people has shifted over the past decade – but one constant remains. If you're plus size, you're taught that you're a failure, that you're a human that's unworthy of respect and a woman that is abjectly unattractive. But at the same time, as younger millennials came of age, and after seeing all of the damage the diet industry caused our mothers long into adulthood, we decided to ditch the diets, meal plans and beauty standards that urged us to shrink ourselves or be ignored. Ignited by the invention of social media, body positivity taught millions of young women that our worth was not dependent on the size of our frame. Suddenly, the companies who had spent the last century selling women insecurity were having an identity crisis. No longer were we willing to starve ourselves under the false promise that a thigh gap would make our lives better, and no longer would we buy their products as long as they promised to help us lose weight.

Online, young women were finding ways to destigmatize the parts of ourselves we had always been taught to hate. Rolls of fat, cellulite and stretch marks became badges of honour, and the subject of thousands of selfies. Searching for a way to ensure we would never be happy in ourselves, and therefore keep buying the products that promised to make us look and feel better, corporations cottoned on to wellness. Unable to ostracize fat people based on desirability alone, they paired our hatred of fatness with the increasing cultural pressure to be as healthy as possible, and created a monster. Now, you can be fat, to a certain degree, as long as you can prove it does not put your overall health at risk. Fat people are granted permission to exist publicly as long as they eat salads, exercise regularly, and tell the world all about it online.

No matter how much our elected officials want us to believe that fatness is inherently unhealthy, the actual scientific evidence is not so straightforward. There is a long history of research that proves weight does not necessarily correlate to wellness. Unfit skinny people have been proven to develop diabetes at double the rate of healthy fat people, and the

BMI index, the framework largely used to determine how healthy an individual's body mass is, was invented by a mathematician, not a scientist or medical doctor. Other studies have found that up to three-quarters of obese people are in fact metabolically healthy.

However, rather than spending days, months and years debating if being fat is healthy or not, I would rather we consider why being healthy has come to replace being a morally sound, good person in modern society. It seems to have become an accepted fact that, with the exception of committing a serious crime, being unhealthy is one of the worst things a human can be. The fact that so often fat people are accused of glorifying being unhealthy – solely because of the size of their bodies – is proof of this in and of itself. There is not one single reason why an individual should have any business caring, let alone passing judgement, about the weight of anyone else.

Yet our state-sanctioned fatphobia, combined with wellness becoming the prominent lifestyle pursuit of the twenty-first century, has made us believe that fatness is everyone's problem – even those who don't inhabit it themselves. Fat people are blamed for the increasing pressures on our National Health Service, as we accuse them of taking up doctors' time that could be better spent looking after individuals who attempt to look after themselves.

As climate change makes each summer hotter than the one before, TV hosts wax lyrical about how the heat would not affect us so badly if we weren't a nation that was overweight. Fat people are often used as a scapegoat by people in power to divert attention from the larger issues in which government intervention is required to make any tangible difference, such as the strain on our NHS being blamed in part by the government on fat people not looking after themselves. With fatphobia so ingrained in the modern human experience, no matter how many 'body positive' advertising campaigns showcase a fat woman, the reality is that our hatred towards bigger bodies is the same as it ever was; we've just found a new rationale for it.

As our health anxiety has grown exponentially over the last five years, being the best, most physically well version of yourself has become a universal plight. To know which vitamins supposedly aid our ailments is not niche knowledge, TikTok videos are constantly diagnosing us with different disorders, and athleisure is a legitimate style choice for every day, rather than just for the gym. Our obsession with weight transformed from a fixation on 'shallow' notions of traditional beauty, to a focus on public health, via personal optimization. In actuality, it's impossible to tell if somebody is healthy just by looking at them. Of course, there can be physical indications of disability or long-term illness. But if we're considering health in the context of lifestyle being a determining factor as to whether somebody is well or not, it's an absolute farce to assume that somebody's body shape can tell us anything about what's going on beneath their skin.

My own personal relationship between health and weight has been skewed ever since I was diagnosed with the auto-inflammatory condition Crohn's disease when I was nineteen years old. After spending the majority of my teenage years attempting to shrink my waistline by whatever means necessary, I began to lose weight without even trying. Living independently for the first time, I could suddenly see the outline of my ribs, could fit into smaller clothes, and found myself receiving daily compliments on my figure.

However, my life as a skinny woman was not long for this world. After a few short months, I was rushed to hospital, and discovered that my narrowing frame was all down to the fact my body was ravaging itself from the inside. I wasn't just unhealthy, I was close to death. To kick-start my recovery, I was fed steroids through an IV; side effects of which include weight gain, and a bloated 'moon' face. As quickly as I lost the weight, I put it on in spades. But as I began to heal, I started to realize, the more weight I gained, the healthier I would be. It was at that moment that I came to the realization that our worldview on health and body size is nothing but a farce, used to control people but also to make examples of those that refuse to conform.

Arguments that place fatness as unhealthy ignore people like me, who live with chronic illness that not only makes it difficult for them to lose weight, but for whom doing so would also mean a noticeable decline in health. With the popularity of body positivity rising alongside our obsession with wellness, the two have morphed into a singular beast, in that we are told we can only love our bodies as long as we are also healthy. Not only that, but by positioning the validity of fat people's existence on the contingency that they must be healthy, those who are both chronically ill and fat are left feeling entirely ostracized by society.

On my good days, I love being fat. It means my body is doing the best it can with a stomach that literally wants to kill me from the inside out. It ensures I can enjoy the food I love, rather than spending days in excruciating pain. It shows that I have come through treatment, and that my body is no longer at war with itself. But it's all too easy to allow myself to be swallowed up by the fatphobic sentiment that engulfs all of our lives. Ultimately, I am no longer interested in attempting to perform health when, deep down, I know it's impossible for me to do so. I refuse to post each salad I eat on Instagram, share workout pictures, or pretend I'm taking the steps to be healthy when in reality I will never be considered so by a society that not only hates fat people, but also fears unwell women.

When told to stop glorifying being unhealthy, I urge all of us to stop trying to pander to those who benefit from our self-loathing. There are many reasons for skinny people to believe that fat people are glorifying being unhealthy, but deep down the motivation always remains the same – being fat is an idea that is loathed by our society. Our health anxiety has been used as a convenient veneer to leverage more hatred towards fat people, rather than see us as a group of people worthy of respect just like anyone else. Instead of dignifying their hatred with a response, we should be interrogating why other people's health – or body weight – matters so much to us in the first place.

Prompts for discussion

- What made you believe being fat is unhealthy?
- Have you ever felt being unhealthy makes someone less worthy of respect?
- Where or how did you learn that being fat was bad?

Information to remember

- Nearly half of *3- to 6-year-old girls* say they worry about being fat.
- A 2016 study that followed participants for an average of nineteen years found that unfit skinny people were twice as likely to get diabetes as fit fat people.
- There is only a 0.8 per cent chance of a woman classified as 'obese' achieving a 'normal' weight.

"It Was a Different Time":

As an Excuse for Harmful Language

I'm on the sofa of my Archway flat in London. My legs are draped over my dad's as he sits comfortably nestled into the corner cushions, ankles crossed, holding a glass of red wine. Mum is just to the left of him on a brown leather Scandi armchair. My family is a bunch of night owls, and hanging together at home under cosy low lighting, drinking wine and spending the evening laughing our heads off or deep in conversation is our favourite thing to do.

From what I've seen of my friends' situations over the years, I don't think every family talks in the same way mine does; my parents, both in their sixties, are very open-minded. We've discussed the language younger generations use and why, trans rights, the Black Lives Matter movement, sexism in comedy, sexual abuse, victim-blaming – all kinds of topics that I'm sure many people my age actively avoid discussing when they're with their mum and dad. Often, the conversation will start out being about something random; a story one of us has heard or something that has happened that week. Then, as I offer my perspectives, which are heavily defined by my work and which they don't share, it'll evolve into something deeper and more far-reaching.

This evening has been no different, and as we huddle and chat, the discussion turns to mental health. For some reason, when I talk to my dad about social-justice topics, which I feel I have a clear view on, I am more mindful of articulating myself clearly than when I talk to my sister, mum or my partner, Jordy; a feeling that doesn't make that much sense to me. If you saw Dad and me together, you'd see that we are the closest thing a father–daughter relationship could be to a friendship. There is so much love between us – and not just familial love, but respect too. I see him for the man he is, not just my dad, and he sees me for the woman I am, not just his daughter. He's not difficult or intolerant. In fact, he's quite the opposite – open-minded and compassionate. He sends me links to podcasts with Laura Bates, he shares pro-choice stories on his socials and he challenges conservatives in Facebook comments. I'm ridiculously proud that he's *my* dad, but on certain things, he can be more stubborn and set in his opinions.

My dad and I were raised in different generations. Not only that, we were raised differently according to expectations of our genders by both our parents and society. Having lived under the patriarchy, my mum and I have shared experiences (both said and unsaid, whether the relentless pressure of beauty standards that she has mentioned or experiences she had with men) of being on the receiving end of misogyny or sexism, and a more instinctive understanding of the way these prejudices operate in our society. My dad hasn't had those equivalent experiences, and although he has encountered difficulty and struggle in his life, it hasn't been imposed on him because of his gender. This means it sometimes takes a little bit more for him to understand these topics.

Add to this the fact that we have different styles of communication (I operate from an emotionally vulnerable place, him from a practical one) and our shared stubbornness, and you get a clear sense of why we sometimes reach an impasse during conversations. It's why I feel pressure to ensure that I'm articulating myself as clearly as possible when we don't instantly align. I feel it's my job to support my dad in understanding issues with some sense of intersectionality, because I am an access point that he respects, and so I want to get it right.

This evening, as the conversation veers towards mental health, I can sense an opportunity for discussion. I mention that so many of my generation are dealing with stress, with little understanding of it and no mental-health support. I tell my parents that poor mental wellness in young people is an epidemic, and I describe a graph I've studied that illustrated the correlation between social-media use and mental-health issues; the upward lines mirrored each other, demonstrating just how closely the two are linked. Dad looks gently confused.

'I just— I don't get that. I think about my parents, and your mum's dad, like, pulling people out of burning buildings, losing friends in the war and coming home ... and there was none of this "they're struggling from mental health" stuff. It didn't exist . . .'

I understand his feelings, but I disagree. 'It did exist, just no one knew what to call it. They didn't have the language. It wasn't a cultural conversation so these feelings weren't validated.'

His brow is still furrowed. 'But it wasn't like everyone had "depression" or "anxiety",' he says, making air quotes with his fingers. 'The things they saw in the war . . . the horrors . . . They just had to get on with life.'

I want to pause and engage properly, not snap at him for what I read as him downplaying people's mental-health struggles or insinuating that their prevalence was being exaggerated. I think about how Dad is imagining these immediate, indisputable horrors, such as the experiences of war, and comparing them with a mental image of someone on their phone.

'From what I've seen and read in my work,' I start, 'I see mental health as more of a dial – like a fuel gauge in a car – and it's constantly shifting depending on situations, trauma, health, et cetera.' I hold my hand up as I speak and mimick the gauge jittering and falling to the left and right. 'Just like their physical health being good or bad, everyone has struggled with their mental health at some point. Grandad probably did too, but there wasn't any precedent for talking about it. They didn't have the tools. To me it's not that "everyone suddenly has mental-health issues" but rather that they have always existed. The difference is that now we can identify them, and everyone's mental health is on that gauge, somewhere.'

Dad listens intently and nods.

'Nobody talked about it at all then,' Mur

even a *thing*. It was a different time.'

Dad nods again. 'A *completely* different time.'

We continue to sip our wine and chat. Our conversation moves to climate anxiety and the Western condition of the paradox of choice, where you are so overwhelmed by options that you become anxious or apathetic, before the discussion becomes light-hearted again.

That phrase stays with me, though, as I lie on my sofa bed, falling asleep: 'It was a different time.' A little warm from the wine, I consider why their use of it didn't anger me in the same way it did when I heard it in other scenarios. Most commonly, I'd heard it uttered by people from generations before mine as a way to justify harmful attitudes or language, not as a way to explain them.

In Response to 'It Was a Different Time'

The phrase pops up on the news and in podcasts. You'll come across it on Twitter in threads about the pulling down of statues, celebrities using outdated language, offensive movies, or in discussions about historical sex allegations. You may even have used the phrase to justify or excuse racism or misogyny in your own family and consign it to a bygone era, rather than challenge it or compassionately explain why it's harmful. For some, it seems that the cultural context and time when a single pejorative or view was deemed ‘acceptable’ by certain demographics is justification enough to exonerate the person for using or holding it. Even, weirdly, if they still do.

The context in which this phrase is often used is what makes it infuriating, and that is dependent on whether the intent is to explain, or to justify or excuse. After trying to understand the differences between generations and their mental-health struggles, my parents employed it to agree with me that the cultural context of my grandparents’ era may have restricted them from evaluating or communicating their feelings. On the other hand, using ‘it was a different time’ to excuse homophobic, racist, sexist, ableist language or harmful behaviour is all too common. It’s a platitude mostly parroted by those who belong to dominant communities, in order to exculpate themselves from the harm their words or actions have caused or are still causing. It’s not a particularly sophisticated approach, but that hasn’t stopped it from becoming a neat excuse to avoid or skirt critique of perspectives that might otherwise be challenged by those around them. I think the suggestion that we shouldn’t address problematic behaviour or language because it originated in the past is ludicrous at best and damaging at worst.

Whether or not we feel we can respond to this phrase speaks to a deeply held question that so many of us have: Can people *actually* grow and change? I personally have questioned others’ ability to do so, and I’m sure most of us have felt that way about some of the people in our own lives. Sometimes, it can be hard enough to know if your peers care about the inequity and struggle in society deeply enough for them to interrogate their use of language or reflect on their conditioned biases, let alone whether your 80-year-old great-auntie (who you don't even get on with) would.

But people do grow. They might make a conscious choice to re-evaluate and expand their learning when it comes to holding outdated or harmful views and attitudes. They might be forced to grow through personal experience, although experience doesn't automatically equal growth.

On the flip side, some people resist change, and have never been encouraged to reckon with their views. Maybe they simply don't want to face that reckoning or perhaps they benefit from not doing so. Most frustratingly, even when people have had a personal experience that could have shifted their perspective for the better, they can remain committed to ignorance. Often, people cling to the views that uphold their relative power and the systems from which those views stem, even if they don't know they're doing it.

The idea, however comforting, that everyone *wants* to change is just not reality; most of us know many people who refuse to reach outside of their orbit to explore perspectives and ideas that don't directly relate to, or affect, them. But what *is* true is the idea that everyone is *capable* of changing and growing.

We tend to see history as a smooth arc of progress, instead of the messy, stuttering, repetitious and complex journey it is. Such a view significantly simplifies and flattens our understanding of the past. Equally, when we evaluate and define history through a single lens, we lose perspective. White nostalgia is an example of that. White dominant communities often refer to 'simpler times' or 'the good ol' days' when describing past decades, wistfully branding them as 'better' or 'freer'.

At the time of writing, there are 1.1 million posts under the hashtag #borninthewrongera on TikTok, a trend where Gen Z content creators recreate aesthetics from the twenties, fifties or eighties. But while they praise bygone eras for their creativity, freedom of expression and culture, these videos always fail to recognize that these periods weren't 'better' for huge swathes of the population who were poor, working-class, Black, LGBTQIA+, disabled, women, or any combination of the above. For these communities, who were pushed to the margins of society, denied basic rights and relegated to low social status by the dominant communities that outlawed them or claimed they didn't exist, these times were harder, and the collective amnesia from those in positions of privilege that removes these millions of people from history is all over the media and social media. It also replays that way in our minds.

When we belong to a group that has experienced myriad social privileges and ranks high up on constructed social hierarchies, our memories of the past are framed entirely by the privileges that we – or people we imagine to be like us – experienced during that time. If we think back – recalling movies, TV shows, radio broadcasts, music, fashion, celebrities – we might feel wistful or sentimental, as our memories come to us through the lens of our personal experience and worldview at the time. It's similar to how, if you had a peaceful childhood, you might see the world as 'simpler' back then, only because you're seeing it through a child's naive and simplified lens.

Even if we try to think about past eras more objectively, we will struggle to do so because of what *didn't* get shown in the media, who *wasn't* included in mainstream discourse and what was missing from our laws and policies. When we evaluate our society of the past, we do so within the context of *our* exterior world, *our* immediate environment and *our* experiences, all of which were informed by our background, socioeconomic status, class and more. For example, an upper-class, older white man living in London would recall the fifties very differently to how a twenty-year-old working-class Black woman living in London during the same decade would.

The frame of reference and cultural context becomes even more limited for those thinking back to a time when there was comparatively low access to information, as it was for generations that came before us. The question is ultimately, when we look back at past decades, are we looking at what that time was *actually* like? Or what it was like for *us*? Could it be that holding on to old opinions and outdated language is part of emotionally holding on to a bygone era when members of a dominant community could hold social status unchallenged and remain unaccountable for those opinions?

When it comes to the phrase 'it was a different time', I have a hard time responding, because ... obviously. Every single person we know, and will ever know, grew up in a decade or era 'different' to the ones they will be living in as they grow older. That much is obvious. But to use that as a justification for harm makes little sense. Yes, time moves on, and cultures develop and grow. But people do, too. They grow in huge, life-changing ways – they become partners, or might become parents; they develop themselves as professionals. Their lifestyles evolve and they have to shift with them, too. They buy new phones, learn new software, apps, ways to communicate. They might learn languages or take up hobbies. Sure, there are some blocks when you get older, such as struggling to master new technologies or processes, but you turn to your support system for help.

All this is to say that there is a willingness from most people, as they age, to learn, shift, grow and change in myriad different ways; from lifestyle choices and technological advancements to embracing new opportunities. 'Moving with the times' doesn't seem to be an issue for people, but for some reason, being able to let go of language or ingrained perspectives that used to – or still – make someone feel powerful, or 'better than', is. That's because it takes real self-reflection and honesty, which is work that many people don't feel they need to do.

Even for those who appear much less overtly harmful or bigoted, the way we are socialized to view, evaluate and judge people who don't look or sound like us is a hell of a drug; how willing we are to overlook others' problematic behaviour is testament to this. For a long time, I couldn't understand why people I thought of as well-meaning would be resistant to, or defensive about, even altering one measly word or phrase in their vocabulary. Through reading the work of Reni Eddo-Lodge, Koa Beck, Emma Dabiri, Nova Reid and bell hooks, I realized it's not that they're resistant to changing a word, it's that they're resistant to the challenging of their position, a worldview; the 'healing', as Reid states, comes from confronting their complicity and challenging the systems from which they benefit. To overhaul your attitude on something – especially a prejudice as ingrained as misogyny, racism or homophobia – is to admit to yourself that you have been causing harm. In turn, this forces you to reckon with the concept that you're not exactly who you thought you were, which therefore undermines your understanding of yourself as a 'good' or 'kind' person (as if good people can't cause harm). Questioning your nostalgic beliefs and ideas doesn't come easily when your ego is being fed by them, and you are benefiting emotionally and socially from *not* doing so.

To offer 'it was a different time' as a defence of misogynistic or racist language is to say such language was 'more acceptable' during the past decades, but to *whom*? Asking someone this question during your conversation can be helpful in gaining clarity. The misogynistic language that dominated adverts in the fifties and sixties – talking of 'chesty blondes', 'keeping her where she belongs' and reminding us that 'women don't leave the kitchen!' – may have been normalized, but that didn't make it acceptable to many women at the time. Slurs white society used to dehumanize Black people were never acceptable and definitely weren't to the people they were forced upon. There is no such thing as 'acceptable' discrimination because systems of prejudice have only ever been acceptable to the demographics that benefit from them.

Acting as if previous decades were wholly accepting of certain language and ideas is to act as if society at the time was composed only of those who created and espoused that language and those ideas. It reveals that you're evaluating a period of history purely on the standards of the dominant community and oppressive culture to which you belonged, because the ability to freely use harmful language without accountability was only possible due to the political, economic and social systems that kept people marginalized, disenfranchised, disempowered and subjugated.

When we use phrases like ‘it was a different time’, the continual, tireless opposition from oppressed but courageous people who fought for their livelihoods and rights – who always knew that what was happening to them was wrong, unfair and constructed – is erased, as are the efforts of those who fought alongside them. Whiteness, straightness and cisness will always refer to itself as the default, removing from the conversation those upon whom its language has the most impact. Discriminatory language has never been acceptable to the communities it harms. How does it make sense that those perpetrating harm get to define the parameters of acceptable community conduct?

When you are trying to hold on to hope that people can grow, the thing to remember is that it is not just a generational divide but an ideological one; there are plenty of people in older generations who are willing to change and learn, and those who continue to fight for change. There’s the grandfather of a young person coming out as non-binary on TikTok who comforted them and told them he’d ‘just read about it’. At the 2022 London Pride parade, 72-year-old Ted Brown, one of the co-founders of Gay Pride, celebrated its fiftieth anniversary by retracing the exact route that was walked in 1972, surrounded by veterans of the movement, including 70-year-old Peter Tatchell. When you witness individuals like this who have fought to make society more accepting, you realize how much hope there is, and how the concept that age equals bigotry is not only untrue in many cases, but also self-fulfilling. If you throw up your hands and give up on people, you can guarantee that age will equal bigotry.

It can feel hard to challenge that prejudice sometimes, but it's on members of the communities that historically created these social hierarchies and still benefit from them to challenge our family and friends with compassion. To reply effectively to 'it was a different time' is to ask why. Then why again, until the basics, themselves, become a little clearer.

It was a different time!
Why?
You could say that stuff back then!
Why?
Because it was accepted!
By whom?
Society!
Which parts of society?
Just . . . society!
All of society?
Yes!
Even [insert demographic or community that society marginalized here]?
Well . . . No, probably not.
So [insert only dominant community here] then?
Well . . .
Why not [marginalized community] society?
silence

If you can get to the place in the conversation where the person to whom you're speaking can acknowledge that the words or views they hold were harmful *back then* that's half the battle, because the aim of this phrase is to rebrand the words or attitude as harmless because they originated in a different era. If the person responds by challenging that these things were 'more accepted then', it's probably time to ask, 'By whom?' Then point out how 'accepted' and 'acceptable' are not the same thing. Note that much of what is happening right now is ostensibly seen as normal and is therefore sadly accepted by many – women in many parts of the world, including Northern Ireland, don't have access to abortion services, for example; hundreds of thousands of people don't have a home in the UK. That doesn't mean these things are OK.

Remind the person you're talking to that something that was harmful then is still harmful now – although the time may be different, *the human impact is the same*. Offer that it might have been different for *them* – in that their perspective or attitude was accepted – but that it was no different for those whom their views or words affected and are *still* affecting. Remind them that discrimination is still hurting, disenfranchising and killing people as it was back then, and appeal to their compassionate side by saying that you know they recognize and care about this. If they make the argument that growing up pre-internet made it harder to access other perspectives, experiences and new information, follow their logic and make the argument that it is now the *easiest it has ever been* to do that, and that this is, actually, exactly what you are trying to do for them by responding.

Finally, tell them that a culture is only as fair as the people, language, norms and values that define it, and that every person who chooses not to do better hurts someone else. If all else fails, challenge them by making it known, in a calm but clear tone, that you don't think it's kind or acceptable language, that it never was, and that you won't respond to it because it makes you very uncomfortable. If they want to discuss the reasons for that with you, tell them you'd be happy to explain. Whether you compassionately correct them or just make your discomfort known, it may take a few goes until they get the message. Persevere, because their words aren't welcome now. It's just a different time.

Prompts for discussion

- Ask the person to specify a 'different time' and then 'who' exactly the language was acceptable to 'back then'.
- Note the difference in meaning between 'acceptable' and 'accepted'. Something can be accepted as a norm and still not be acceptable because it causes harm. Name another example of something accepted as normal now that the person you are talking to would find unacceptable.
- If the person is using the language now, and someone is justifying it because they got it from another era, challenge them with their own logic – that language no longer belongs in this era because it is a different time.

Information to remember

- Sociology shows us that shared language often forms the basis of a community and the words we use to refer to people change how we treat those people. Using the right words helps to reinforce the community objective.

Daze Aghaji (she/they) is an environmental justice activist who advocates for regenerative cultures in the writing, speaking and artwork she creates. Her campaigning consists of high-profile political actions like running for the European Parliament, suing her government and being a strategist for Extinction Rebellion.

"Climate Change Is Coming"

Daze Aghaji

I write this during a time that will never be forgotten. The summer of 2022 – a period of political turmoil, the death of our country's longest-reigning monarch and, most importantly, the hottest summer on record in British history. If this is not the moment that the phrase 'climate change is coming' scares you – a phrase used so commonly and carelessly – then I'm not sure what will. Personally, it scares me more than outright climate denialism.

The only time that 'climate change is coming' has arguably been an accurate statement was in the 1800s, when scientists first issued warnings about our pending atmospheric issues. As far back as 1823, scientist Joseph Fourier calculated that a planet the size of Earth, at its distance from the sun, shouldn't be as hot as it was. Almost 200 years later, this narrative remains pervasive, yet the statement itself is completely untrue; climate change is not coming, it is already here.

To appreciate quite how damaging this phrase is, it's crucial to understand how the public perception of climate change and climate denial has evolved over time. Curiosity in our atmospheric issues was piqued in the nineteenth century thanks to the work of scientists such as Fourier, John Tyndall, Svante Arrhenius and Guy Callendar, but in the twentieth century, as the fossil-fuel industry boomed, the public began to openly embrace the warming of our planet. Over the course of the next hundred years, the expanded use of fossil fuels had an impact on everything. For a while, the effects were beneficial; from improving the economy, providing better standards of living and even greater access to food.

It wasn't until scientist James Black met with executives at oil and gas company ExxonMobil in 1977 that the consequences of this billion-dollar industry became clear. His report, *The Greenhouse Effect*, marked an overwhelming consciousness-raising moment which should have irrefutably changed our understanding of the climate crisis for ever. Black's damning presentation outlined his theory that there was a direct correlation between the carbon emissions created by the industry and the unusual warming of the planet. He warned that continued warming could potentially have dire effects on all life on Earth, stating, 'In the first place, there is general scientific agreement that the most likely manner in which mankind is influencing the global climate is through carbon dioxide release from the burning of fossil fuels.'

At first, industry executives took Black's warning extremely seriously. Exxon put their money where their mouth was and funded millions of dollars' worth of research to enable them to better understand his hypothesis. The results, however, were far too damning. They found out that by the time the public noticed a rise in temperatures, 'it could be too late to take effective counter measures to reduce the effects or even stabilize' the climate. The fossil-fuel industry knew that if they continued to unravel the truth, they would no longer be able to extract coal, gas and oil in the same way, and would therefore generate substantially less profit. This, of course, was the sticking point for fossil-fuel companies. As has been proven to us time and time again, under capitalism, profit and growth matter far more than human life.

The leading fossil-fuel companies went on to take drastic steps to protect themselves and their profits. Defunding the research to which they'd previously committed millions of dollars, they also buried as many of their findings as they could. What had already been leaked to the public, they set about trying to undermine with publicity campaigns of misinformation. They founded the Global Climate Coalition, a group that 'promoted' climate action on the surface, but in reality worked to complicate our understanding of climate change by funding misleading reports and lobbying lawmakers to reject environmental bills.

The aim of these companies was to create enough doubt in the public's mind that we would question whether climate change actually existed, or whether it was just a figment of James Black's imagination. This move marked a new era in our understanding of the climate crisis – it became something we could deny the existence of rather than something we shouldn't ignore.

Although it still lingers today, climate denial was common until 2018, when the narrative was once again shaken by a new report, this time issued by the Intergovernmental Panel on Climate Change (IPCC). It warned that we had just twelve years to drastically change our relationship with energy, industry, building, transport and cities in order to prevent global warming from exceeding 1.5 degrees Celsius, or we risk a climate that will no longer sustain human life. We risk making our only home uninhabitable.

The report stressed the need for unprecedented and ambitious change to avoid the trajectory of extreme heat, drought, poverty, flooding and other terrifying impacts of climate change. In doing so, it planted a seed of urgency in the public's mind and inspired the global community to demand action. We began to see people rising up, from youth activists organizing marches as part of Fridays for Future, to movements such as Extinction Rebellion, a network of lovable activists (including myself!) using civil disobedience to highlight the need for change and rapid climate action.

The IPCC report and the subsequent general uprising undermined the legitimacy of climate denialism, forcing the fossil-fuel industry to return to the drawing board and devise new ways to spread confusion and misinformation. Rather than denial, their message became one of delay – recognizing the reality of climate change while trying to make it a problem of the future, not of the current moment; whether by setting sustainability targets so far in the future that they require no action now, or even blaming consumers for the climate crisis and pushing small incremental change in the full knowledge that systemic change is needed. And so, in 2022, we have come full circle and Fourier's warning that 'climate change is coming' remains all too common.

The narrative of climate delayism does the same now as climate denialism has done in the past. And just as we responded to climate denialism then, we must respond to climate delayism now. We must strip it of its social acceptability, refuse the greenwashing agenda of the fossil-fuel industry and allow it to spur us into collective action. Delaying action is fatal, and we must push ourselves to have difficult conversations which respectfully challenge this belief, even if held by the people we love. We must understand that even people who comprehend the climate crisis often fall into the delay mentality because this is the narrative that has been fed to us consistently and insistently for decades. It's also much easier to contemplate than the urgent reality. It's crucial that we support and hold people through this journey, to provide space for their grief and to help them take action. I'm a true believer in softness, and having a conversation about climate delay is a perfect place to practise this.

At this moment I feel deeply connected to the fear that induces people to believe that 'climate change is coming'. It's far easier to get on with your life when you believe it's a problem for later. But this year, in the global North, and Europe in particular, we have experienced the very vivid effects of the climate crisis in unprecedented ways. This summer, I watched the land I love on its knees, experiencing heatwaves, wildfires and drought. Reaching temperatures in excess of 40 degrees Celsius, it was dubbed 'the coolest summer of the rest of our lives'. The reality is that since 2001, the UK has experienced seventeen of the eighteen warmest years since records began 136 years ago. So, if this isn't climate change then what is? If this is not enough to convince people that we cannot delay taking action, I don't know what else will. As I write this, my heart beats fast and heavy. I am petrified. If it weren't for the way activism keeps me grounded, I could easily see myself falling into a delay or outright denial mindset.

As we come to terms with our own realities here, we must also consider the global South: the frontline of the climate crisis. 'Climate change is coming' does not acknowledge or honour what climate-vulnerable people have faced already. Living on the frontlines of the climate crisis means flooding of low-lying islands, extreme temperatures that cause drought and food insecurity, and more. We need to recognize that ridding ourselves of the notion that climate delayism is acceptable is also an act of solidarity with and support for the people who are already being confronted with the worst effects of the climate crisis.

We need to help people recognize the signs of a collapsing ecosystem, and the only way we can do that is by strengthening our bond with the natural world. In the same way we can pick up on small and subtle changes in our best friend's behaviour if something is wrong, we should have the same deep love for the planet, which will allow us to notice the subtle signs of climate distress. Whether that's the early blooming of spring flowers or the autumnal orange leaves that littered our pavements during the peak of summer this year. Let's reconnect with nature so we can be present when nature is giving us warning signs.

Let's face this crisis – the greatest that humanity has ever encountered – in a way that makes people feel supported. This could be by holding spaces and events to discuss our collective fear, hopes and wants for the future, or as individuals, by processing our emotions through journalling or another creative output.

Next time you hear someone say 'climate change is coming', meet this in grief, hold them through the discomfort and fear of seeing the reality, and support them in taking action that can help them face the hard truth of the situation we find ourselves in. For me, the action was finding my community in the Extinction Rebellion and finding ways to show my love for, and connection with, the natural world. For you, the action you take may look different. As long as it feels good for you and you are deeply rooted in love for all life, trust me, it will create the change we desire and need to see.

Prompts for discussion

- How do you feel about the effects of climate change?
- How can we support each other to face the fear that causes delay/denial?
- What can you do in the climate movement?

Information to remember

- Seventy-one per cent of all global GHG emissions since 1988 can be traced to just 100 fossil-fuel producers.
- In the past sixty years, carbon dioxide levels in the atmosphere have increased 100 times faster than during the end of the last ice age.
- Three-point-five per cent of the population is actively participating in the protests to ensure serious political change.

Conclusion

Whether you read this book cover to cover, dipped in and out or even just read one chapter and passed it to someone after a hard conversation, I hope it encouraged you to consider how much our language – and the things we *choose* to say – define us as a community, as a collective and as a society. I hope it has shed light on the fact that our words have distinct power to preserve dominant narratives and hierarchies, to uphold attitudes and beliefs within our sphere of influence, and to entrench dominant or harmful views in our own psyches.

If you're not someone who regularly evaluates dominant narratives, I hope these pages have reminded you that questioning and unpicking what you hear around you is the first step in disrupting ideas and being part of offering alternative ones. I hope this project, in some way, has encouraged you to reckon with how much you are showing up and advocating for others in your day-to-day conversations. If you're not already doing this, I hope that it gave you a push – and hopefully some confidence – to do more and to do better. And if you already dedicate time and energy to this work, I hope you found things in this book that challenged you, added to your learning and perhaps introduced you to brilliant writers, educators and activists whose work you will seek out to continue your growth.

In 2022, during the course of writing this book, I, like you, witnessed huge political and social unrest. In the UK, three different Conservative PMs headed into Downing Street, our right to protest was restricted while the police were given more power, and we faced a horrendous cost-of-living crisis. In Pakistan, we saw devastating floods while rivers ran dry in Europe, and China experienced the longest and most severe heatwave since national records began. In Iran, we saw rebellion and protests against misogyny and state brutality turn into a fight for a democratic revolution, and in the US we saw abortion rights rolled back after the overturning of Roe v Wade.

All of this shows us that, more than ever, we have to be active in fighting for our collective futures. On a daily basis we must disrupt dominant narratives, resist oppressive white-supremacist forces and hetero-patriarchy. Crucially, we must remember how much our liberation is intertwined – that our struggles are intimately connected and so our strategies and solutions will need to be – and that bridges are only built when dominant groups don't abandon conversations simply because they're difficult or confrontational.

This book was a fairly ambitious project, and the process of pulling it together has challenged and taught me in ways I couldn't have predicted. Through research, I discovered ideas that made certain things click into place. The months I spent listening more intently than normal to how these phrases come up in conversation led to moments of inspiration and reckoning. At times, the work forced me to confront my own flaws; the snap judgements I internally make of those who use these phrases, for example. The exceptionalism I have been working on in therapy came up again, and during parts of the writing process I felt myself come untethered from my instincts about how to handle this project; when we make work that challenges people with privilege, it's ultimately about healing and so we have to find the balance between creating something helpful, but not soothing their transgressions – for me, that was a new challenge. Ultimately, I have grown while working on this book, which feels fitting as the concept of growth – and our collective capacity for growth – was one of my main reasons for wanting to embark on this project in the first place.

When it comes to challenging the limiting and dominating ideas that underpin our society, we are all on a lifelong journey and, wherever you are in your journey, I hope this book is just one of many that you read or listen to. Seek out the work of others and books that explore these subjects and themes with the clarity, wisdom and urgency that comes from experience. Read fiction and jump into other people's lives. If you don't know where to start, begin with the writers in this project and don't stop.

Given how much the word 'hope' features in this conclusion, you can probably tell that this has been one of my main motivations for writing this book. I want you to recognize that most people are capable of growing, of doing better and of learning. That we can't and must never shy away from harm or the diversions and distraction that protect it, and that the act of questioning is rooted in hope and faith in our capacity to learn from each other, which begins with our conversations. Listen carefully to the things we (especially dominant communities) say, think hard about them and read about them. Build your confidence, plant your assertions in humanity and welfare, know how you want society to look and then open your mouth. Speak and facilitate. Be fair, but be honest. Be courageous in challenging and be honest in questioning, and always, always ask 'But *why*?'

Notes

"Boys Will Be Boys"

14 **a 'get out of jail free card':** https://www.ted.com/talks/ben_hurst_boys_won_t_be_boys_boys_will_be_what_we_teach_them_to_be?language=en

16 **it was the West that first introduced a 'binary sex' model:** Thomas Laqueur, *Making Sex*, (Harvard University Press, 1990), p. 196

16 **'consider the changes that colonization brought':** https://globalstudies.trinity.duke.edu/sites/globalstudies.trinity.duke.edu/files/file-attachments/v2d2_Lugones.pdf

16 **'why should we believe in fixed constructs of gender . . .?':** https://twitter.com/glamrou/status/1543586689632931842?lang=en

21 **perpetrators of violent offences were most likely to be male – 82 per cent, in fact:** https://www.ons.gov.uk/peoplepopulationandcommunity/crimeandjustice/articles/thenatureofviolentcrimeinenglandandwales/yearendingmarch2020#extent-of-violent-crime

25 **we have gendered human emotions:** https://www.independent.co.uk/life-style/toxic-masculinity-international-mens-day-2018-gender-stereotypes-man-up-a8641136.html

25 **pressured to 'man up' as a result of damaging gender stereotypes:** https://futuremen.org/future-men-2018-survey/

25 **Most can categorize their own gender by the age of three:** https://www.mayoclinic.org/healthy-lifestyle/childrens-health/in-depth/children-and-gender-identity/art-20266811#:~:text=Most%20children%20between%20ages%2018,time%20they%20reach%20age%203

"Feminism Is About Women Having the Same Rights and Power as Men"

29 **Amazon, ranked the fourth most profitable:** https://www.forbes.com/the-worlds-most-valuable-brands/#5539646119c0

29 **not letting warehouse workers take bathroom breaks:** https://nytimes.com/2022/04/02/business/amazon-union-christian-smalls.html

29 **advocated for in my country for a century:** Koa Beck, *White Feminism*, (Simon & Schuster, 2022), pp. xvii-xviii.

30 **a presence beyond the domestic sphere:** ibid., pp. 5–7.

30 **traditional domestic labour as housewives:** ibid., p. 30.

30 **Lean In:** ibid., pp. 103–5.

30 **#GIRLBOSS:** ibid., pp. 145–8.

30 **a way to change power distribution:** ibid., p. 121.

30 **in larger numbers than white women:** ibid., p. 193.

31 **corporate figures became conflated:** ibid., pp. 82–3.

31 **professional choices possible with their labour:** ibid., pp. 142–3.

31 **advocate for clean water access:** ibid., p. 36.

31 **a rich history of gender variance:** ibid., pp. 51–4.

31 **steadfastly socialist in its theories and approaches:** ibid., pp. 96–7.

31 **challenging a presumed state of wellness:** ibid., pp. 51–4.

32 **'unhealthy' before even taking their vitals:** ibid., pp. 88–90.

32 **disputed the Western conviction:** ibid., pp. 93–7.

34 **women assumed 512 billion of those hours:** https://www.unwomen.org/en/digital-library/publications/2022/09/progress-on-the-sustainable-development-goals-the-gender-snapshot-2022

34 **about 44 million women and girls by the end of 2021:** ibid.

34 **The lack of clean water:** ibid.

"To Play Devil's Advocate": In Response to Discussions on Misogyny

46 **'impulsive reactive responses':** Nova Reid, *The Good Ally*, (HQ, 2021), p. 127.

52 **'Learning to wear a mask':** bell hooks, *The Will to Change: Men, Masculinity, and Love*, (Simon & Schuster, 2005), p. 153.

56 **a third of men who took part:** https://www.ipsos.com/en/one-three-men-believe-feminism-does-more-harm-good

56 **deep-rooted ideas about traditional masculinity:** https://www.gov.uk/government/publications/what-works-in-preventing-violence-against-women-and-girls-review-of-the-evidence-from-the-programme

"Children Shouldn't Be Allowed to Transition Because What if They Change Their Minds?"

59 **a rate that is already disproportionately high:** https://publications.parliament.uk/pa/cm201516/cmselect/cmwomeq/390/390.pdf

61 **ran over 300 articles – almost one a day – on trans people:** Shon Faye, *The Transgender Issue* (Allen Lane, 2021), p. 6.

61 **the number of people who detransition:** https://www.stonewall.org.uk/about-us/news/dispelling-myths-around-detransition

62 **GenderGP's survey:** https://www.gendergp.com/detransition-facts/

"If You Don't Want Attention, Cover Up"

76 **'You know what you're getting into':** https://nationalpost.com/entertainment/celebrity/pamela-anderson-you-know-what-you-get-into-if-you-go-to-a-hotel-room-alone

76 **'She was open to meeting someone':** https://www.theguardian.com/uk-news/2018/nov/15/thong-protest-in-belfast-raises-concerns-over-trials#:~:text=Suggesting%20the%20complainant%20%E2%80%93%2017%2Dyear,the%20jury%20lasting%2090%20minutes.

76 **'normalisation breeds acceptance':** Laura Bates, *Fix the System, Not the Women*, (Simon & Schuster, 2022), p. 35.

77 **actual experiences of violence:** https://vc.bridgew.edu/jiws/vol11/iss4/8/?source=post_page

77 **perpetrated by men against other men:** https://www.nytimes.com/2013/06/24/us/in-debate-over-military-sexual-assault-men-are-overlooked-victims.html

79 **more than 90 per cent of rape and sexual assault victims:** https://www.bbc.com/news/uk-scotland-43128350

80 **'players have to respect the game and the place':** https://sportscommunity.com.au/all-players-including-serena-williams-must-show-respect-to-umpires/

80 **'the over-policing of black women's actions':** https://www.teenvogue.com/story/serena-williams-catsuit-ban-french-open-racist

82 **'I have never met a patient':** https://www.dw.com/en/combating-sexual-violence-is-chemical-castration-a-valid-method/a-56839505

82 **'an appropriate and accepted expression of masculinity':** *Denying Rape but Endorsing Forceful Intercourse: Exploring Differences Among Responders,* https://www.liebertpub.com/doi/pdf/10.1089/vio.2014.0022

84 **it is men – not clothes – who are responsible:** https://www.cdc.gov/violenceprevention/pdf/nisvs_report2010-a.pdf

85 **the *What Were You Wearing?* exhibition:** https://media.un.org/en/asset/k16/k16igyxy27

86 **sexually harassed in public spaces in the UK:** https://www.unwomenuk.org/safe-spaces-now

86 **reduces the chance they will seek help in the future:** https://neurostimtms.com/blaming-the-victim-and-mental-health/

86 **48 per cent of Amish, Mennonite and other Plain children:** https://www.themisfitamish.com/post/update-child-sexual-abuse-in-amish-mennonite-hutterite-anabaptist-other-religious-communities

"Men Aren't Doing Anything to Help Feminism"

89 **only about 32 per cent of men:** https://www.ipsos.com/sites/default/files/ct/news/documents/2022-03/International%20Women%27s%20Day%202022_0.pdf

90 **subjected to physical or sexual partner violence:** https://www.unwomen.org/en/what-we-do/ending-violence-against-women/facts-and-figures

90 **paid anywhere from 76p to 95p for every £1 earned by a man:** https://www.theguardian.com/world/2022/apr/06/uk-gender-pay-gap-women-paid-90p-for-1-earned-by-men

93 **globally, women take up over 75 per cent of unpaid care work:** https://www.ilo.org/global/publications/books/WCMS_633135/lang--en/index.htm

93 **girls spend 40 per cent more time:** https://www.kcl.ac.uk/news/womens-unpaid-care-work-has-been-unmeasured-and-undervalued-for-too-long

94 **'. . . the intensely painful feeling':** *I Thought It Was Just Me (but it isn't): Making the Journey from 'What Will People Think?' to 'I Am Enough'*, Brené Brown, (Gotham Books, 2007), p. 29.

"Not *All* Men"

103 **98 per cent of victims who had experienced rape or assault:** https://www.ons.gov.uk/peoplepopulationandcommunity/crimeandjustice/articles/natureofsexualassaultbyrapeorpenetrationenglandandwales/yearendingmarch2020#:~:text=Age%20and%20sex,In%20the%20years%20ending%20March%202017%20and%20March%202020%20combined,)%20were%20male%20(98%25)

104 **only 1 in 100 rapes were recorded by police:** https://rapecrisis.org.uk/get-informed/statistics-sexual-violence/

104 **5 in 6 women who are raped don't report it:** https://rcew.fra1.cdn.digitaloceanspaces.com/media/documents/Statistics_about_sexual_violence_and_abuse_-_sources_RCEW.pdf

104 **almost twice as likely to have experienced sexual assault:** https://www.ons.gov.uk/peoplepopulationand

community/crimeandjustice/articles/sexualoffencesvictimcharacteristicsenglandandwales/march2020#disability

104 **'strong evidence that disabled women':** https://www.theguardian.com/world/2021/nov/25/the-everyday-assault-of-disabled-women-its-inappropriate-sexual-touching-at-least-once-a-month

104 **the daily challenge:** https://static1.squarespace.com/static/5f7d9f4addc689717e6ea200/t/604179671c37f52e3d9985f5/1614903663825/2020+%7C+The+Decriminalisation+of+Rape.pdf

105 **Amongst the reasons women cited:** https://hull-repository.worktribe.com/preview/955161/2018-07-28%2013752%20Harrison.pdf

105 **For the year ending March 2020:** https://www.gov.uk/government/publications/supporting-male-victims/supporting-male-victims-accessible

105 **Every 10 minutes, somewhere in the world:** https://www.unwomenuk.org/safe-spaces-now

112 **perpetrators of violent crime were most likely to be male:** https://www.ons.gov.uk/peoplepopulationandcommunity/crimeandjustice/articles/thenatureofviolentcrimeinenglandandwales/yearendingmarch2020#:~:text=perpetrators%20were%20most%20likely%20to,of%20violent%20incidents%20(82%25)

112 **6.5 million women in England and Wales:** https://rapecrisis.org.uk/get-informed/types-of-sexual-violence/what-is-sexual-assault/

112 **310 out of every 1,000 sexual assaults:** https://www.rainn.org/statistics/criminal-justice-system

112 **Worldwide, 1 in 3 women have experienced physical or sexual violence:** https://www.who.int/news-room/fact-sheets/detail/violence-against-women

"We Need Fast Fashion for Poor People"

114 **three times more likely to rent than 20 years ago:** https://www.theguardian.com/money/2020/feb/10/home-ownership-ons-rent

115 **'I think people have been sitting at home':** https://metro.co.uk/2020/12/22/rishi-sunak-asking-us-to-spend-our-savings-proves-hes-out-of-touch-13790394/

115 **George W. Bush encouraged Americans to get back out there:** https://www.vox.com/the-goods/22662889/september-11-anniversary-bush-spend-economy

117–8 **According to the Resource Generation, it's 2 per cent:** https://resourcegeneration.org/breakdown-of-class-characteristics-income-brackets/

122 **100 billion items a year:** https://cleanclothes.org/fashions-problems/waste-and-pollution

122 **68 items of clothing per year:** https://cleanclothes.org/climate-change

123 **2.1 billion tons of greenhouse gas emissions:** https://www.mckinsey.com/~/media/mckinsey/industries/retail/our%20insights/fashion%20on%20climate/fashion-on-climate-full-report.pdf

123 **Approximately 80 per cent of garment workers are women:** https://labourbehindthelabel.org/the-women-who-make-your-clothes/

"I Don't Do Politics"

128 **the aim was to 'create . . . a really hostile environment':** https://www.theguardian.com/uk-news/2018/aug/27/hostile-environment-anatomy-of-a-policy-disaster

129 **'go home or face arrest':** https://www.theguardian.com/politics/2013/oct/22/go-home-billboards-pulled

129 **women use more public services:** https://www.ohchr.org/sites/default/files/Documents/Issues/Development/IEDebt/WomenAusterity/WBG.pdf

130 **the abolishment of the Disability Living Allowance:** https://www.theguardian.com/commentisfree/2017/may/15/theresa-may-cathy-britain-disabled-people

140 **the largest increase in gas and electricity prices ever:** https://commonslibrary.parliament.uk/research-briefings/cbp-9491/#:%7E:text=The%20monthly%20increases%20in%20both,series%20going%20back%20to%201970

142 **'Every time we engage in the conversation':** https://fee.org/articles/don-t-do-politics-think-again/

143 **the UN Youth Envoy X Body Shop campaign:** https://www.thebodyshop.com/en-au/about-us/activism/be-seen-be-heard/global-youth-report/a/a00079

"They're Really Just Illegal Migrants"

156 **61 per cent of people crossing the Channel:** https://www.theguardian.com/uk-news/2021/nov/17/most-people-who-risk-channel-boat-crossings-are-refugees-report

156 **85 per cent of people who crossed the Channel:** https://committees.parliament.uk/oralevidence/11390/html/

156 **73 per cent of people are waiting longer than six months:** https://www.refugeecouncil.org.uk/latest/news/new-figures-reveal-scale-of-asylum-backlog-crisis/

156 **People seeking asylum receive £5.84 per day:** https://www.unhcr.org/uk/asylum-in-the-uk.html

156 **69 per cent of refugees stay in a neighbouring country:** https://www.unhcr.org/refugee-statistics/, https://

migrationobservatory.ox.ac.uk/resources/briefings/migration-to-the-uk-asylum/

"Innocent Until Proven Guilty": In Response to Sexual Assault Allegations

161 **operating as a sexual predator:** https://www.mirror.co.uk/news/politics/tory-mp-andrew-griffiths-lewd-12919733

163 **'most things about disabled women's lives':** https://www.theguardian.com/commentisfree/2018/mar/08/disabled-people-metoo-womens-movement-inclusion-diversity

163–4 **In 2022 Kelly was eventually found guilty:** https://www.abc.net.au/news/2022-09-15/kelly-found-guilty-on-multiple-counts-in-sexual-abuse-trial/101441784

165 **false claims are extremely rare:** https://assets.publishing.service.gov.uk/government/uploads/system/uploads/attachment_data/file/217471/understanding-progression-serious-cases.pdf#page=35

165 **an abysmal 1.3 per cent:** https://www.theguardian.com/commentisfree/2022/apr/19/uk-courts-rape-civil-prosecution-rates

165 **men are more likely to be raped than to be accused of rape:** https://assets.publishing.service.gov.uk/government/uploads/system/uploads/attachment_data/file/217471/understanding-progression-serious-cases.pdf#page=35

165 **nearly twice as likely as women to be victims of violent crime:** https://www.menandboyscoalition.org.uk/statistics/

169 **'the presumption of innocence':** Amia Srinivasan, *The Right to Sex*, (Simon & Schuster, 2022), p. 35.

170 **'a distinctly European concept':** https://oxfordre.com/criminology/display/10.1093/acrefore/9780190264079.001.0001/acrefore-9780190264079-e-650;jsessionid=0B868697DFDA57A0228B9A42ADDD03C2

171 **'For me, the lesson of history':** The Secret Barrister, *The Secret Barrister: Stories of the Law and How It's Broken*, (Macmillan, 2018), p. 269.

173 **even though C.K. *himself* had admitted they were true:** https://www.bbc.com/news/entertainment-arts-41950043

175 **waiting an average of eight to nine months for a trial:** https://www.bbc.com/news/uk-61061365

175 **a record 179 trials were ditched in 2021:** https://www.dailymail.co.uk/news/article-10705957/Sex-attack-victims-forced-wait-average-eight-years-justice.html

175 **'survivors have faced appalling treatment when reporting rape':** https://www.womensgrid.org.uk/?p=18255

175 **'spaffing money up the wall':** LBC, 13 March 2019, https://www.youtube.com/watch?v=U_FSqfXyUFk&t=2s

175 **almost 99 per cent of rapes reported to police:** https://rapecrisis.org.uk/get-informed/statistics-sexual-violence/

179 **figures show it's closer to 60 per cent:** https://www.ipsos.com/en-uk/perils-perception-2018

180 **1.3 per cent of rape cases result in a charge:** https://www.bbc.com/news/uk-61061365, https://assets.publishing.service.gov.uk/government/uploads/system/uploads/attachment_data/file/901028/crime-outcomes-1920-hosb1720.pdf

"Islam Is an Oppressive Religion to Women"

188 **journalists are more likely to report:** https://academic.oup.com/isq/article/61/3/489/4609692?login=false

188 **the majority of articles and broadcast clips have a negative slant:** [https://cfmm.org.uk/wp-content/uploads/2019/07/CfMM-Quarterly-Report-Oct-Dec-2018.pdf

"The Police Are Here to Protect Us"

192 **over 56 per cent go on to reoffend:** https://post.parliament.uk/research-briefings/post-pn-0592/

192 **In 95 per cent of the case files reviewed:** https://www.theguardian.com/uk-news/2017/jul/05/stalking-and-harassment-crimes-routinely-badly-handled-uk-report-says

193 **the PfHA does not define cyber-harassment:** http://irep.ntu.ac.uk/id/eprint/30468/1/8253_Griffiths.pdf

198 **'a disease of over-civilisation':** https://www.jstor.org/stable/30041838

201 **just 7.8 per cent of all recorded offences:** https://www.theguardian.com/society/2021/may/23/fewer-than-one-in-60-cases-lead-to-charge-in-england-and-wales

201 **'When someone has a 99 per cent chance':** Laura Bates, *Fix the System, Not the Women*, (Simon & Schuster, 2022), p. 74.

201 **Take a look at the CPS Twitter account:** https://twitter.com/CPSUK/status/1583066828439429126?s=20&t=VuJOrApJBI_XZv5NgQTuyw

202 **'[the CPS] is still failing to meet its own targets':** https://www.endviolenceagainstwomen.org.uk/cps-data-survivors-failed-record-number-sexual-offences/

202 **the outcome of 86 per cent of rape allegations:** https://publications.parliament.uk/pa/cm5802/cmselect/cmhaff/193/report.html#footnote-333

202 **one woman per week came forward:** https://www.channel4.com/news/more-than-100-women-accuse-police-officers-of-domestic-abuse-alleging-boys-club-culture

203 **80 per cent kept their jobs:** https://www.theguardian.com/uk-news/2022/mar/17/80-percent-of-uk-police-accused-of-domestic-abuse-kept-jobs-figures-show

203 **less than 4 per cent of offences were dealt with out of court:** [https://www.bbc.com/news/uk-49986849

203 **'The police do not prevent crime':** David H. Bayley, *Police for the Future* (Oxford University Press, 1996), p. 26.

204 **'police are biased against people from my background':** https://hopenothate.org.uk/wp-content/uploads/2020/08/BAME-report-2020-08-v3-00000003.pdf

205 **this is still the prevailing narrative:** https://novaramedia.com/2020/06/01/the-uk-is-not-innocent-police-brutality-has-a-long-and-violent-history-here/

205 **Misogynoir:** https://www.brown.edu/academics/race-ethnicity/events/moya-bailey-%E2%80%9Cmisogynoir-transformed-black-women%E2%80%99s-digital-resistance%E2%80%9D

205 **Black and mixed-race women are more likely to be victims of rape:** https://www.ons.gov.uk/peoplepopulation-andcommunity/crimeandjustice/articles/sexualoffences victimcharacteristicsenglandandwales/march2020

206 **86 per cent of women of African and/or Caribbean heritage:** https://www.theguardian.com/society/2020/jul/11/hackney-domestic-violence-charity-faces-fight-to-stay-in-premises-sistah-space

206 **'You are our protectors is not true':** https://books.google.com.au/books?id=EfSJDwAAQBAJ&printsec=frontcover#v=onepage&q&f=false, p. 88.

207 **three of his former colleagues were found to have shared:** https://www.theguardian.com/uk-news/2022/nov/02/met-officers-jailed-for-sharing-offensive-messages-with-wayne-couzens

207 **one who was charged with forty-one offences:** https://www.independent.co.uk/news/uk/crime/met-police-david-carrick-sex-offences-b2038272.html

207 **nine linked investigations called Operation Hotton:** https://www.policeconduct.gov.uk/sites/default/files/Operation%20Hotton%20Learning%20report%20-%20January%202022.pdf, https://www.vice.com/en/article/4aw4zb/metropolitan-police-whatsapps-operation-hotton

207 **there is the occasional 'bad 'un' in the police:** https://www.theguardian.com/uk-news/2021/jun/08/cressida-dick-admits-there-are-bad-uns-in-the-metropolitan-police

207 **Six hundred sexual misconduct allegations:** https://www.theguardian.com/uk-news/2021/mar/20/revealed-the-grim-list-of-sex-abuse-claims-against-metropolitan-police

207 **'verify a police officer's credentials':** https://www.theguardian.com/uk-news/2021/sep/30/wayne-couzens-lies-raise-fears-over-how-to-identify-rogue-officer

208 **'shout to a passer-by':** https://www.independent.ie/irish-news/crime/british-police-criticised-for-flag-down-a-bus-safety-advice-for-women-in-wake-of-sarah-everard-murder-40908771.html

208 **'To rely on the threat of lethal force':** Alex. S Vitale, *The End of Policing*, (Verso, 2017), p. 1.

208 **still the largest force in the country today:** https://www.met.police.uk/police-forces/metropolitan-police/areas/about-us/about-the-met/structure/

209 **8,500 complaints about corruption:** https://www.theguardian.com/politics/2012/may/24/police-watchdog-corruption-complaints#:~:text=The%20report%2C%20which%20also%20called,were%20recorded%20by%20police%20forces

209 **'not the shark, but the water':** https://guante.info/2020/11/22/nottheshark/

210 **'some commit crimes because they are responding':** https://www.studysmarter.co.uk/explanations/social-

studies/famous-sociologists/robert-k-merton/#:~:text=According%20to%20Merton%2C%20social%20inequality,pressurise%20individuals%20into%20committing%20crimes

213 **only 7.8 per cent of all recorded offences:** https://assets.publishing.service.gov.uk/government/uploads/system/uploads/attachment_data/file/817769/crime-outcomes-hosb1219.pdf

"I Don't See Colour"

217 **the opposite of the desired effect:** Evan P. Apfelbaum, Kristin Pauker, Samuel R. Sommers, and Nalini Ambady, 'In blind pursuit of racial equality', *Psychological Science*, 2010.

223 **children as young as three:** Andrew Scott Baron and Mahzarin R. Banaji, 'The Development of Implicit Attitudes', *Psychological Science*, 2006.

223 **Children raised 'not to see colour':** Evan P. Apfelbaum, Kristin Pauker, Samuel R. Sommers and Nalini Ambady, 'In Blind Pursuit of Racial Equality', *Psychological Science*, 2010.

223 **Racism even persists in blind people:** Professor Osagie K. Obasogie, *Blinded by Sight: Seeing Race in the Eyes of the Blind*, (Stanford University Press, 2014).

"You Can't Say Anything These Days"

235 **Laquesha Bailey explored Morgan's obsessive reporting:** https://medium.com/illumination/a-statistical-breakdown-of-piers-morgans-obsession-with-meghan-markle-f38e270cf5c5

240 **'offensive discourse targeting':** https://www.un.org/en/hate-speech/understanding-hate-speech/what-is-hate-speech

241 **receive abuse on Twitter every 30 seconds:** https://www.amnesty.org.uk/press-releases/women-abused-twitter-every-30-seconds-new-study

241 **'Everyone has the right to freedom of expression.':** https://www.equalityhumanrights.com/en/human-rights-act/article-10-freedom-expression

241 **Eighty-one per cent of students:** [https://www.timeshighereducation.com/news/most-uk-students-dont-think-free-speech-under-threat-campus

"You [Disabled People] Are Such an Inspiration"

246 **'For lots of us, disabled people are not our teachers':** Stella Young TEDxSydney: https://www.ted.com/talks/stella_young_i_m_not_your_inspiration_thank_you_very_much

250 **14.6 million disabled people in the UK:** https://www.gov.uk/government/statistics/family-resources-survey-financial-year-2020-to-2021/family-resources-survey-financial-year-2020-to-2021

"The Government Are Doing Their Best"

257 **the Prime Minister issued a half-apology:** https://au.news.yahoo.com/uks-johnson-takes-full-responsibility-214818679.html

258 **on which a third of the population rely:** https://www.centreforprogressivechange.org/campaigns/sickpay

258 **long-term damage to the heart, lungs and kidneys:** https://www.ons.gov.uk/peoplepopulationandcommunity/healthandsocialcare/conditionsanddiseases/articles/coronaviruscovid19latestinsights/infections

259 **the 2017 UN inquiry revealed it had failed:** [https://www.mountsinai.org/about/newsroom/2022/long-covid-experts-and-advocates-say-the-government-is-ignoring-the-greatest-mass-disabling-event-in-human-history

259 **the horrendous offering of Do Not Resuscitate orders:** https://www.openaccessgovernment.org/blanket-dnr/122280/

259 **prices had increased by 2 per cent since 1997:** https://www.bankofengland.co.uk/knowledgebank/how-have-prices-changed-over-time

260 **UK households face some of the highest prices in Europe:** https://www.energypriceindex.com/price-data, https://commonslibrary.parliament.uk/research-briefings/cbp-9428/#:~:text=From%20September%202021%20to%20September,to%20cuts%20in%20Russian%20supply

261 **number of people in the UK living in poverty:** https://www.theguardian.com/society/2020/nov/30/almost-700000-driven-poverty-covid-crisis-uk-study

261 **one in five families reported experiencing food insecurity:** https://www.theguardian.com/society/2022/oct/18/millions-forced-to-skip-meals-as-uk-cost-of-living-crisis-deepens

263 **'education should be a site of power':** Akala, *Natives*, (Two Roads, 2019), p. 77

265 **very major adverse effects on mental health:** https://www.disabilityrightsuk.org/news/2022/june/

dwp-ignored-%E2%80%98hugely-alarming%E2%80%99-research-linked-wca-600-suicides-mps-are-told

265 **more people from Black, Asian, and other backgrounds:** https://www.insidehousing.co.uk/news/news/black-people-70-more-likely-to-be-impacted-by-housing-crisis-than-white-people-70830

265–6 **more likely to develop mental-health problems:** https://www.mentalhealth.org.uk/explore-mental-health/mental-health-statistics/poverty-statistics

266 **the mental health of the UK's transgender community:** https://www.theguardian.com/world/2022/apr/08/trans-people-mental-health-crisis-point-uk-warn-experts

266 **cost of sending a child under two to nursery:** https://www.daynurseries.co.uk/advice/childcare-costs-how-much-do-you-pay-in-the-uk

268 **£8.2bn in profits between July and September 2022:** https://www.theguardian.com/business/2022/oct/27/shell-doubles-its-profits-to-95bn, https://www.bbc.com/news/business-63409687#:~:text=Shell%20has%20reported%20its%20second,the%20same%20period%20last%20year

269 **a huge new oil field named Rosebank:** https://www.weforum.org/agenda/2022/10/fossil-fuels-incompatible-1-5c-goal-energy-climate-change-study/

269 **'The structure of a healthy political system':** https://www.theguardian.com/commentisfree/2021/may/31/nothing-sticks-to-this-government-dominic-cummings

273 **'historic' levels of need:** https://www.trusselltrust.org/2022/04/27/food-banks-provide-more-than-2-1-million-food-parcels-to-people-across-the-uk-in-past-year-according-to-new-figures-released-by-the-trussell-trust/

273 **cost of living had increased:** https://www.statista.com/topics/9121/cost-of-living-crisis-uk/#topicHeader__wrapper

273 **government awarded £10.5bn worth of contracts:** https://www.theguardian.com/politics/2020/nov/18/ppe-suppliers-with-political-ties-given-high-priority-status-report-reveals

"Stop Glorifying Being Unhealthy"

275 **declared a war on obesity:** https://news.sky.com/story/pm-targets-checkout-sweets-and-buy-one-get-one-free-deals-in-national-obesity-plan-12037000

275 **debates in Parliament:** https://www.independent.co.uk/news/health/child-obesity-weight-health-bmi-parents-a8844996.html

276 **sugar and junk-food taxes:** https://researchbriefings.files.parliament.uk/documents/CBP-9049/CBP-9049.pdf

277 **weight does not necessarily correlate to wellness:** https://www.ncbi.nlm.nih.gov/pmc/articles/PMC4731253/

278 **invented by a mathematician, not a scientist:** https://elemental.medium.com/the-bizarre-and-racist-history-of-the-bmi-7d8dc2aa33bb, https://www.npr.org/templates/story/story.php?storyId=106268439#:~:text=The%20BMI%20was%20introduced%20in,the%20government%20in%20allocating%20resources.]

278 **up to three-quarters of obese people are in fact metabolically healthy:** https://www.ncbi.nlm.nih.gov/pmc/articles/PMC4731253/

282 **Nearly half of *3- to 6-year-old girls*:** https://stars.library.ucf.edu/cgi/viewcontent.cgi?article=4747&context=etd

282 **unfit skinny people were twice as likely to get diabetes:** https://www.ncbi.nlm.nih.gov/pmc/articles/PMC4731253/

282 **only a 0.8 per cent chance of a woman classified as 'obese':** https://www.healthline.com/health-news/obese-people-have-slim-chance-of-obtaining-normal-body-weight-071615#Losing-Weight-Is-Often-a-Losing-Battle

"It Was a Different Time": As an Excuse for Harmful Language

293 **The misogynistic language:** https://rarehistoricalphotos.com/offensive-sexist-vintage-ads/, https://www.ebay.com.au/itm/383664995612, https://scoop.upworthy.com/photographer-reimagines-sexist-ads-from-the-1950-s-and-60-s-with-switched-gender-roles

"Climate Change Is Coming"

300 **'In the first place, there is general scientific agreement':** Black, James F. (June 6, 1978). 'The Greenhouse Effect (https://ia601806.us.archive.org/20/items/aQwayback/exxon/James%20Black%201977%20Presentation.pdf) Exxon. Retrieved 30 January 2016.

301 **'it could be too late':** https://www.documentcloud.org/documents/4411090-Document3#document/p4/a415539. It was unearthed by Jelmer Mommers and the journalism platform De Correspondent and was first released on the site ClimateFiles.com

306 **Seventy-one per cent of all global GHG emissions:** https://www.theguardian.com/sustainable-business/2017/jul/10/100-fossil-fuel-companies-investors-responsible-71-global-emissions-cdp-study-climate-change

306 **carbon dioxide levels in the atmosphere:** https://www.climate.gov/news-features/understanding-climate/climate-change-atmospheric-carbon-dioxide

306 **Three point five per cent of the population:** https://www.nonviolent-conflict.org/resource/success-nonviolent-civil-resistance/

Conclusion

308 **China experienced the longest and most severe heatwave:** https://www.newscientist.com/article/2334921-heatwave-in-china-is-the-most-severe-ever-recorded-in-the-world/

Further Reading

Baldoni, Justin, *Boys Will Be Human: A Get-Real Gut-Check Guide to Becoming the Strongest, Kindest, Bravest Person You Can Be*, HarperCollins, 2022

Barber, Aja, *Consumed: The Need for Collective Change: Colonialism, Climate Change & Consumerism*, Brazen, 2021

Bates, Laura, *Men Who Hate Women: From Incels to Pickup Artists: The Truth about Extreme Misogyny and How It Affects Us All*, Simon & Schuster, 2020

Beck, Koa, *White Feminism, From the Suffragettes to Influencers and Who They Leave Behind*, Simon & Schuster, 2021

Craggs, Charlie, *To My Trans Sisters*, Jessica Kingsley, 2017

Dabiri, Emma, *What White People Can Do Next: From Allyship to Coalition*, Penguin, 2021

El-Wardany, Salma, *These Impossible Things*, Trapeze, 2022

Gamble, Ione, *Poor Little Sick Girls, A Love Letter to Unacceptable Women*, Dialogue Books, 2022

hooks, bell, *All About Love: New Visions*, William Morris & Co., 2000

Further Reading

hooks, bell, *Feminist Theory: From Margin to Center*, South End Press, 1985

hooks, bell, *The Will to Change: Men, Masculinity, and Love*, Atria Books, 2003

Hull, Eliza, *We've Got This: Essays by Disabled Parents*, Scribe, 2023

Johnson, Ayana Elizabeth and Wilkinson, Katharine K., *All We Can Save: Truth, Courage, and Solutions for the Climate Crisis*, One World, 2020

Kendall, Mikki, *Hood Feminism: Notes from the Women White Feminists Forgot*, Bloomsbury, 2020

Khan, Mariam (ed.), *It's Not About the Burqa: Muslim Women on Faith, Feminism, Sexuality and Race*, Picador, 2019

Reid, Nova, *The Good Ally: A guided anti-racism journey from bystander to changemaker*, HQ, 2021

Woozer, Laila, *Not Quite White: A Memoir*, Simon & Schuster, 2022

Yeboah, Stephanie, *Fattily Ever After: A Black Fat Girl's Guide to Living Life Unapologetically*, Hardie Grant Books, 2020

Acknowledgements

There are two people who have watched me struggle through the personal process of creating this book and have offered only warm hugs, honest words and reassuring – and sometimes uncomfortable but needed – advice. Thanks to my partner and husband Jordy for staying up late with me when I couldn't sleep for worrying about decisions that needed to be made, for proactively supporting and listening to every thought that went into this project and for never wanting to debate or question but simply learn. Thanks to Stevie, my big sister, for encouraging me throughout the process with voice notes, chats and hugs, and for being my best friend in the world.

Thanks to my gorgeous mum and dad for continuously defending and supporting my right to use my voice both in public and behind closed doors. Without your encouragement I would have made myself smaller a long time ago. You are the only place I can go when things feel too hard.

Thank you to Lyns, my manager, for being the type of manager who allows me absolute autonomy to decide. It sounds like it should be the default, but it isn't, and with you I actually have control over my career and future, which I have never felt with others. Thank you for your patience, positivity and your consistent protection of me, my time and my head. Northern lasses for ever.

Acknowledgements

Big thanks also to Kim, Justin and the extended team at Diving Bell, who manage in a way others don't and should be used as a model for how to take care of your roster. And specifically to Kim for having the most reassuring voice of anyone on the planet.

Thank you to Abi of Bergstrom Studio for helping me navigate the publishing industry, one that intimidates me and is still slightly a mystery to me. The fact that I feel confident in these spaces is testament to you as an agent. Thank you also for your continued honest feedback, for taking a chance on me as a writer and for being patient with me always.

Big thanks go to Zoe of Transworld. I was unmoored for a little while, but it was worth it to land with you as an editor. You are the type of editor that elicits a sigh of relief from me every time I talk to you, and that is not taken for granted. Thank you for being open and understanding to the changes, shifts and hard decisions I had to make through this process and for knowing that doing what was right was more important than doing what was easy.

Thank you also to Izzie, Sophie, Katrina, Barbara, Beci, Phil, Rich, Tom, Laura, Ashleigh and the wider Transworld team for bringing this book to life.

Thank you to Nova Reid for calling me in during the process of this book. I became unmoored from my instincts and the grace, honesty and intention you exhibit allowed me to own up to my shit. I don't take the opportunity to learn from you – both in private from your work and in person – for granted. This project is better because of your honesty.

Cathy Reay, thank you for pulling me up on why there was

no disabled representation in this book and for jumping at the chance to participate. Thank you also for being the most flawlessly professional writer and contributor I've ever worked with (you basically almost provided the essay before it was even briefed!!). I can't wait to read what you write in the future.

Thank you to my friend Aja who remains a soft place to land, a moral compass and a great friend. Your advice always shifts things for me and I'm so lucky to know you.

About the Author

Gina Martin is a gender equality activist, speaker and writer whose work focuses on gender, misogyny and sexual violence. She is a proud ambassador for UN Women UK and Beyond Equality.

Gina hosts workshops for teachers on sexual violence and misogyny, speaks in schools across the UK and is currently training in facilitation.

She is a monthly columnist for *Glamour UK*, and has written for *Vogue*, *GQ*, *Stylist*, *Grazia*, the *Telegraph*, the World Economic Forum and others.

In 2019, Gina spearheaded the campaign which changed English and Welsh law and introduced the Voyeurism Act, making upskirting a specific sexual offence. Two countries have followed suit. In 2020, she worked as a campaign lead for Nyome Nicholas-Williams, changing Instagram's global breast-squeezing policy.